97/03

GAYLORD MG

°/03

everybody was kung fu fighting

everybody was kung fu fighting

AFRO-ASIAN CONNECTIONS AND THE MYTH OF CULTURAL PURITY

VIJAY PRASHAD

Beacon Press
Boston

Beacon Press
25 Beacon Street
Boston, Massachusetts 02108-2892
www.beacon.org

Beacon Press books
are published under the auspices of
the Unitarian Universalist Association of Congregations.

Printed in the United States of America

05 04 03 02 01   7 6 5 4 3 2 1

This book is printed on acid-free paper that meets the uncoated paper
ANSI/NISO specifications for permanence as revised in 1992.

Composition by Wilsted & Taylor Publishing Services

Library of Congress Cataloging-in-Publication Data
Prashad, Vijay.
      Everybody was Kung Fu fighting : Afro-Asian connections and the myth of cultural purity /
Vijay Prashad.
         p.   cm.
      Includes bibliographical references and index.
      ISBN 0-8070-5010-5 (hardcover : alk. paper)
      1. African Americans—Relations with Asian Americans.   2. African Americans—
Social conditions.   3. African Americans—Race identity.   4. Asian Americans—
Social conditions.   5. Asian Americans—Race identity.   6. Racism—United
States.   7. Race—Social aspects—United States.   8. United States—Race relations.
9. United States—Ethnic relations.   I. Title.
E185.615 .P73   2001
305.8′00973—dc21   2001001771

Contents

Illustrations

The Forethought: Raw Skin

If the snake sheds his skin before a new skin is ready, naked he will be in the world, prey to the forces of chaos. Without his skin, he will be dismantled, lose coherence and die. Have you, my little serpents, a new skin?[1]

My sense of being an Indian in the world is mediated through the struggles of South Africans for liberation. So much are they a part of me that when Chris Hani, head of the South African Communist Party and a major figure in the ANC, was assassinated in 1994, I was brought to tears. As a teenager, I remember joining my classmates in emotional discussions about the battles against apartheid. We talked about Gandhi's time in that far-off land and of the relationship between India and Africa. We sang, *"Amar raho, Nelson Mandela"* ("Be eternal, Nelson Mandela").

When I came to the United States, I fell into this tradition, first in the antiapartheid movement of the early 1980s and then with El Salvador solidarity work. I and many of my immigrant friends put our shoulders to the wheel of these struggles, to join the diverse world of the U.S. Left. Names like Sanjay Anand, Anna Lopez, Noel Rodriquez, Karen May, Sid Lemelle, and so many others complicated our identification with the main fights of the day. Those of us who came from other nations found our America in the heart of the global fights for justice. This tendency to work across the lines that divide us continues in the fabric of the social justice movements in the United States, whether through the concept of "allies" in the queer liberation movement or else in cross-ethnic formations such as Asians for Mumia and the Center for Third World Organizing.[2]

But all people of color do not feel that their struggle is a shared one. Some of my South Asian brethren, for example, feel that we should take care of our own and not worry about the woes of others, that we should earn as much money as possible, slide under the radar of racism, and care only about the prospects of our own children. To many of us from India, this is an uncomfortable bargain, but nonetheless it is one that is not unfamiliar in our times among all people.[3]

White supremacy reigns, as it did then, and blackness is reviled. Who can begrudge the desire among people to seek fellowship in their new society, to throw themselves into the cultural worlds of the place in which they live?

Since blackness is reviled in the United States, why would an immigrant, of whatever skin color, want to associate with those who are racially oppressed, particularly when the transit into the United States promises the dream of gold and glory? The immigrant seeks a form of vertical assimilation, to climb from the lowest, darkest echelon on the stepladder of tyranny into the bright whiteness. In U.S. history the Irish, Italians, Jews, and—in small steps with some hesitations on the part of white America—Asians and Latinos have all tried to barter their varied cultural worlds for the privileges of whiteness.

Yet all people who enter the United States do not strive to be accepted by the terms set by white supremacy. Some actively disregard them, finding them impossible to meet. Instead, they seek recognition, solidarity, and safety by embracing others also oppressed by white supremacy in something of a horizontal assimilation.[4] Consider the rebel Africans, who fled the slave plantations in the Americas and took refuge among the Amerindians to create communities such as the Seminoles'; the South Asian workers who jumped ship in eighteenth-century Salem, Massachusetts, to enter the black community; Frederick Douglass's defense of Chinese "coolie" laborers in the nineteenth century; the interactions of the Black Panther Party with the Red Guard and the Brown Berets in the mid-twentieth century; and finally the multiethnic working-class gathering in the new century.

When people actively or tacitly refuse the terms of vertical integration they are derisively dismissed as either unassimilable or exclusionary. We hear "Why do the black kids sit together in the cafeteria," instead of "Why do our institutions routinely uphold the privileges of whiteness?" There is little space in popular discourse for an examination of what goes on outside the realm of white America among people of color.

I have chosen to discuss the peoples who claim the heritage of the continents of Asia and Africa, not only because they are important to me, but because they have long been pitted against each other as the model versus the undesirable. I hope by looking at how these two cultural worlds are imbricated in complex and varied ways through five centuries and around the globe that I can help us rethink race, culture, and the organization of our society. This book is, if you will, a search for a new skin.

We begin our journey in the Indian Ocean region, with the destruction of the economic and cultural traffic that defined the premodern world. The birth of Atlantic racism superseded and (through fascism) transformed earlier xenophobic ideas into the cruelty of biological hierarchy. White supremacy emerged in the throes of capitalism's planetary birth to justify the expropriation of people off their lands and the exploitation of people for their labor. Of course, the discussion of the birth of racism begs the question of its demise: What is a useful antiracist ideological framework? The conservative theory of the color blind and the racialist theory of the indigenous, in their own way, smuggle in biological ideas of race to denigrate the creativity of diverse humans. The best liberal response to the color blind and to racialism comes from those who refuse to believe in the biological weight given to skin. This position, the liberalism of the skin, suggests that there are different skins, and we must learn to respect and tolerate one another.

Liberalism of the skin, which we generically know as multiculturalism, refuses to accept that biology is destiny, but it smuggles in culture to do much the same thing. Culture becomes the means for social and historical difference, how we differentiate ourselves, and adopt the habits of the past to create and delimit social groups. The familiar dichotomy between nature-nurture becomes the basis for distinction between the white supremacists and the liberals. Culture, unlike biology, should allow us to seek liberation from cruel and uncomfortable practices. But instead, culture wraps us in its suffocating embrace. If we follow liberalism of the skin, then we find ourselves heir to all the dilemmas of multiculturalism: Are cultures discrete and bounded? Do cultures have a history or are they static? Who defines the boundaries of culture or allows for change? Do cultures leak into each other? Can a person from one culture critique another culture? These are the questions that plague both social science and our everyday interactions. Those who subscribe to the liberalism of the skin want to be thought well of, to be good, and therefore, many are circumspect when it comes to the culture of another. The best intentions (of respect and tolerance) can often be annoying to those whose cultures are not in dominance: we feel that we are often zoological specimens.

To respect the fetish of culture assumes that one wants to enshrine it in the museum of humankind rather than find within it the potential for liberation or for change. We'd have to accept homophobia and sexism, class cruelty and racism, all in the service of being respectful to someone's perverse definition of a culture. For comfortable liberals a critique of multiculturalism is close to heresy, but for those of us who have to tussle both with the cruelty of white supremacy and with the melancholic torments of minoritarianism, the critique comes with ease. The orthodoxy of below bears less power than that from above, but it is unbearable nonetheless. We have already begun to grow our own patchwork, defiant skins.

These defiant skins come under the sign of the polycultural, a provisional concept grounded in antiracism rather than in diversity. Polyculturalism, unlike multiculturalism, assumes that people live coherent lives that are made up of a host of lineages—the task of the historian is not to carve out the lineages but to make sense of how people live culturally dynamic lives. Polyculturalism is a ferocious engagement with the political world of culture, a painful embrace of the skin and all its contradictions.

To show us what this polyculturalism means in practice, I offer three passages into the world of Afro-Asia: first into the Caribbean with descendants of formerly enslaved Africans and Asian coolies, then into the urban zones that house a working class rife with ethnic squabbles, and finally into the world of kung fu wherein nonwhite people dream of a revolution of bare fists against the heavily armed fortress of white supremacy.

As the title suggests, the mongrel Afro-Asian history recounted in *Everybody Was Kung Fu Fighting* does not require detached observation. It demands that we actively search for the grounds toward intervention by each of us into the cultural worlds that unite and divide us. I hope the history that follows offers the possibility of an enhanced solidarity, not only between Africans and Asians (who are the subjects here), but among all people (whose existence in the history should be written by you as you read through). This is a movement book, so move along . . .

Chapter 1

The Strange Career of Xenophobia

When Vasco da Gama guided his ships into the Indian Ocean in 1498 he saw himself as a great pioneer. Of course he was not the first to traverse the waters between the eastern coast of Africa, the coasts of India, and those of Malaysia, but the entry of a European into that cosmopolitan ocean did have world historical effects. More than three centuries later, one Indian historian called the intervening period the "Age of Vasco da Gama," a wry tribute to the *marinheiro*.[1] And *tribute* here has two meanings, both of which apply to da Gama—to do something as a mark of respect for someone, and to extract periodic payment for a sovereign. Da Gama's feat was one worthy of respect, not for him personally, but for all those brave European mariners and their African, Indian, and Arab navigators who helped them solve the riddle of the Doldrums. Until the late fifteenth century, logic dictated that the European sailor who attempted to make Asia by sea should try to hug the coast of western Africa, but the currents only pushed the ships back toward a Europe still thirsty for a sea route to India. Finally a few canny navigators just before da Gama decided to go with the flow of the waters. Like a sling-shot the Doldrums tossed their ships toward South America. The ships made their way south, circling toward the Cape of Good Hope, a maritime technique the Portuguese called the *volta do mar*.[2] From southeastern Africa, da Gama's troops plucked the wit of many years from Indian, African, and Arab navigators who steered the Portuguese galleons to their destination.[3]

To pay tribute to Vasco da Gama is also to recognize that his entry into the Indian Ocean radically altered the social relations that made life in and around those waters possible. The values of da Gama and the Portuguese he represented disagreed with those of the peoples of the Indian Ocean, and, distinguished as those values were by violence and avarice, the Europeans won. The victory of the Portuguese over the ocean radically transformed how the peoples of those waters saw each other. Before the arrival of the European ships, the Indian Ocean teemed with cultural complexity. Traders from across the region conducted commerce over goods of all manner (spices, fabrics, jewels) and spoke a host of languages to one another (Arabic, Swahili, Gujarati). The range of traded items was immense and it facilitated the generation of quite remarkable cultural forms from China in East Africa.[4] Certainly there are indications of trade in the Indian Ocean from the first millennium B.C.E. among the three riverine civilizations of the Nile, Mesopotamia, and the Indus (and out to the Romans, somewhat later).[5] By all accounts this traffic did not have the same kind of marked impact on the region as did the trade that developed from the eighth century onward. One might suggest that the Indian Ocean world was given shape by the creation of Baghdad as the capital of the Abbasid empire in 750 C.E., in the west, and by the joint Arab and Persian naval raid on Canton seven years later, in the east.[6] Careful scholars warn us against being overly romantic about the implications of the Indian Ocean world. Certainly cosmopolitanism seemed to be the norm of the waters, but this cordial, if tentative, acceptance did not itself exist without a keen sense of difference. When da Gama met the Samudri Raja (Sea King) in Calicut (in what is today the southwestern Indian state of Kerala), he was asked whether he wished to stay the night "with the Moors or with the Christians." Da Gama chose to garrison himself with his troops. It is clear that the Samudri Raja and his subjects already had an awareness of distinctions based on religion. But this differentiation was not equivalent to the Inquisition-driven Portuguese hostility to anything not obviously Catholic.

Two years after da Gama left the people of Calicut the valiant Pedro Alvarez Cabral stood before the Samudri Raja to demand that the sovereign expel all Muslims from his kingdom. This order was met, in cultural anthropologist and novelist Amitav Ghosh's words, "with a blank refusal; then as afterwards the Samudri steadfastly maintained that Calicut had always been open to everyone who wished to trade there—the Portuguese were welcome to as much pepper as they liked, so long as they bought it at cost price."[7] For millennia, traders from Europe could access the merchandise of the Indian Ocean rim from the coastline of Palestine, where Arabs brought goods overland from the Arabian Gulf and Red Sea. Silks, spices, precious stones and jewelry, porcelain and glassware, cotton textiles, and various kinds of grain filled the small ships and caravans sailing between Asia and Africa, as well as what would come to be known as Europe. And the people who accompanied these goods developed complex relations en route. Of the merchants we know a fair amount, mainly because they kept records or else wrote letters to each other.[8] But the realities of cosmopolitanism were not restricted to the merchant classes. Fisherfolk like the Paravas of the Madurai coast, the Orang Laut ("sea people") of the Strait of Malacca (and the Riau Archipelago), the Bugis of Makasar, the pearl fishers of Bahrain and Ceylon, and the trepang and trochus shell gatherers of the Lesser Sunda Islands shared and exchanged cultural forms across the landmasses and waters that bound them into relatively discrete communities.[9] Yet, by all accounts the Portuguese disregarded this culturally diverse world of the Indian Ocean. Assuredly they neglected the fluid (or fuzzy) idea of belonging that the Indian Ocean peoples adopted, one that recognized difference along multiple axes, but maintained ties among these groups.[10] The peoples of the Indian Ocean saw differences among communities, but there seems to have been little sense that a community generated its own cultural norms sui generis, and not in a complex interchange with other cultures.

Da Gama was not, however, the serpent who slithered with evil intent into the Indian Ocean Eden. The Indian Ocean world before and during the time of da Gama was knit by the contradiction between its cosmopolitanism and by its xenophobia, by its openness and closedness to the world. The closedness, the xenophobia, was not so different in kind from that imported by the Portuguese into the Indian Ocean. For example, the peoples of the ocean, like the Europeans, saw themselves as superior to those people who did not speak their languages and they called these unintelligible people barbarian. *Barbarian* derives from an ancient Greek word to indicate those who make "bar, bar" sounds, far too indistinct to be considered a language. For the Greeks, to be without a language was to be outside the ken of humanity. Aquinas, much later, wrote that "all those who do not know their own speech, the speech that they use between one another, may be called barbarians in relation to themselves."[11] That is, those who do not have a science of language, but who simply live within the common tongue (the *idioma vulgare*) are also rendered as absolute barbarians in premodern Europe.

In Asia, there seems to have been a well-developed discourse against barbarians in the earliest recorded texts. In southern Asia, one can read of the *mlechha* ("impure") one who does not conform to the Vedic sanctions of the migratory peoples who are known as the Aryans (or those who are Aryan-speaking).[12] Anyone who does not bow down before the cosmology of the Vedic texts is deemed by Aryan speakers to be lesser on a number of levels. They included the Greeks, the Huns, and the Shakas in this evaluation.[13] Historian Suvira Jaiswal, in a remarkable synthesis, has recently shown that the Dasas who fell before the armed might of the Aryan speakers had kin ties with their conquerors and they should not be seen as people entirely apart (at least during the period of the *Rgveda,* 1500–1000 B.C.E.). Furthermore, the word used to designate the Dasas may have come from the ancient Iranian *daha* ("man") and *dahyu* ("land" or "country"), which became Dasyu in the *Rgveda* to refer to "hostile Iranians, who were regarded as barbarians and outsiders." In the *Rgveda,* the earlier available text for the Aryan speakers, we read that the Dasyu are *anas,* meaning "without a mouth," which implies that "these people spoke an alien language (not necessarily non-Aryan) and were described contemptuously."[14] Sufficient evidence suggests that the Dasyus forged social relations with people who predated them to the subcontinent, a fact that the Aryan speakers used against them.

If southern Asia was prey to xenophobic ideas in ancient times, the rest of Asia was not immune. Michael Weiner's work on "race" in Japan shows us that until after the Meiji Restoration of 1868 (and in line with the discovery of race from the European lexicon) notions of difference drew upon homespun xenophobia. The Japanese of the Tokugawa period (1603–1867) called those whom they deemed to be culturally or politically inferior *yabanin* ("wild person" or person who lives outside the city), a category that included Christian missionaries and, for the elite, the peasants and workers.[15] The non-*yabanin* saw themselves as superior to others (ethnocentrism), but there is ambivalent evidence that they also hated foreigners (xenophobia). From China, we find that there was no absolute distinction made between people. Classical texts tell us that those who are not the same as the Chinese can be transformed into their ways (*yongxia-bianyi*) in two different fashions, either to become Chinese (*hanhua,* whether to speak as the Han or to adopt the culture of the Han) or to become transformed in general (*laihua,* to come and be transformed, with all the indications of being absorbed into Han territory).[16] From the ancient to the early modern world in Asia, we tend to find records of anxiety about cultural difference and, from that, of xenophobia. It would be inaccurate to reduce this ethnocentrism or xenophobia to racism, mainly because there was little sense that the difference was predicated on the body (biological determinism) and that those who are biologically inferior can be put to work in the service of their biological betters.

In Africa there was certainly fear and feelings of superiority in the face of difference. Perhaps the most well-known encounter took place in the mid-nineteenth century when the explorer David Livingston trod into a central African township. A child who saw him took "to his heels in agony of terror" and, his alarmed mother was so afraid that she, "at the first glimpse of the same fearful apparition," took to her tent. Perhaps she was afraid of his color-ation, for this was the meaning drawn by Livingston himself, but she could have equally been afraid of the entry of a stranger into the heart of her vil-lage. Four hundred years before this, the Venetian explorer Alvise da Cad-mosto reported that in what is today Senegal, people "touched my hands and limbs and rubbed me with their spittle to discover whether my whiteness was dye or flesh. Finding that it was flesh they were astounded."[17] In western Africa fair skin color was new, so it is hardly a surprise that the Senegalese expressed their curiosity and unfamiliarity with da Cadmosto. Difference and strangeness generate interest, whether it is eventually adjudged to be good or bad. The Ganda of the kingdoms of Uganda called those whom they did not know *munamawanga* or *munagwanga*, where *gwanga* referred to people of another place. The terms designated those who refused to become like the Ganda in diet, dress, language, and attitude. The Ganda called the food of the *munamawanga* "tasteless and liable to cause constipation" and they found their languages "difficult," "loud," and "ungraceful" (and could not fathom why the *munamawanga* would not learn their own Luganda). Despite an extensive calculus of difference, the Ganda did entertain the pos-sibility of integration, so that the Soga/Nyoro and the Toro did enter the Ganda clan system.[18] The Asante of western Africa called strangers *ohoho*, an Akan term that derives from *eho* ("one from over there").[19]

For the Swahili (whose name derives from *sawahil*, the Arabic word for "coast") of eastern Africa, frequent encounters on the littoral with those from afar did not discount the creation of notions of superiority. In premod-ern times the Swahili bore a fascination with things Persian, so some coastal rulers called themselves Shirazi, their calendar followed the Persian, many of the technical maritime terms came from Farsi, and until this day, the Per-sian new year, Nau Roz, is celebrated by the Swahili.[20] The coast was a place of great interest: in the 1500s, the Swahili took in Bengali, Moorish, Portu-guese, and Malayali sailors from shipwrecked boats; in the late 1700s, expedi-tions into the coastal region found "a village of *bastaard* Christians" in which "the people were descended from whites, some too from slaves of mixed col-our, and the natives of the East Indies."[21] But, at the same time, the Swahili speakers saw themselves as civilized (*uungwana*, a word that now means "kindness") in comparison with those "uncultured" (*ushenzi* or *gumegume*) people who lived in the interior and with whom they traded.[22] The Swahili sense of discomfort with difference is not an insular reaction, because many Swahili also borrowed generously from other traditions that came from afar.

African and Asian peoples constituted notions of distinction based not on skin color but on cultural exchange. The evidence we have from the rim of the Indian Ocean shows us that the peoples developed forms of ignorant ethnocentrism and xenophobia. To feel superior to someone is not necessarily to hate that person, and it certainly does not ordain that one can then capture, treat as fundamentally inhuman, and utilize that person principally for labor. Modern notions of "race" and modern, capitalist racist institutions render most of the fluidity of cultural difference moot. From da Gama's arrival onward, traditions of xenophobia in the Indian Ocean world were transformed into the hidebound theories of race that emerge from Europe's experiments with the enslavement of human beings for profit, most notably in the Atlantic slave trade. With the invention of race and the advent of racism, the Afro-Asian world would alter dramatically.

The Cosmos of the Indian Ocean

In July 1405, Zheng He (Cheng Ho), the famous eunuch admiral of the Ming dynasty (1368–1644), set sail from southern China on the first of his many voyages.[23] Over twenty-eight thousand sailors in three hundred junks, and a host of *bao chuan* ("treasure ships") left Nanjing with the intention, perhaps, of reintroducing the Indian Ocean ports to the wealth of China (neglected as they had been for a time by the early Ming aversion to commerce). Until 1433, the ships of Zheng He touched most of the ports of southeast and south Asia (including Palembang, Malacca, Java, Atjeh, and Calicut), as well, perhaps, of many ports at the northern and eastern rim of the Indian Ocean zone.[24] Zheng He was not the solitary pioneer, but one of many people who facilitated the eventual Chinese expeditions that lasted for almost three decades. As early as 863 C.E., Duan Chengshi offered a Chinese audience the first speculative knowledge of Africa, or what he called Boboli (thought to be Berbera in Somalia), based on voyages of which we now know little.[25] About half a century later, the Arab trader al-Mas'udi underscored the importance of the commerce in elephant tusks from Zanzibar (Zanj) to India and China, a trade that included rhinoceros horns, pearls, aromatics, and incense, in exchange for Chinese gold, silver, copper, silk, and porcelain.[26]

The curiosity of the Chinese elite for Africa's goods is perhaps best rendered in the story of the giraffe. In 1414 Ming records show that the voyages returned with a giraffe from Bengal as a gift for the throne. (Because the animal is not native to Bengal, it must have come from elsewhere.) The following year ambassadors from the African country of Melinda came to China also bearing a giraffe, leading the sinologist J. J. L. Duyvendak to suppose that the ruler of Bengal, Saifuddin, simply passed on a gift from Africa and intimated to his friends from there that the Chinese appreciated these animals. Shortly thereafter, on the fifth voyage of Zheng He (1417–18), the Chinese went to Melinda in search of this giraffe, and thereby made land on the eastern coast of Africa. What led them to travel there? Duyvendak offers a very intriguing hypothesis: in a Somali tongue the word for giraffe is *girin*, which is close to the Chinese word *qilin*, that "fabulous animal" known as the unicorn.[27] The emperor received the animal from this last voyage with honors, and the members of the Imperial Academy (the Han-lin) painted its portrait and documented its physique.[28] The curiosity was not just for the animal or exclusive to the Chinese. When Zheng He made land in the northern rim of the Indian Ocean zone, news of the arrival of the Chinese junks traveled from the amir of Mecca and the controller of Jedda to the Mamluk sultan of Egypt. Zheng He requested the right to dock in Jedda because of social disturbances in the Yemen. The sultan assented immediately, curious about the reports of these distant travelers, and "asked his officials to treat the visitors with honour."[29]

The mutual fascination between the Chinese and many of the peoples of Africa led to more than trade. Down the coast from Jedda, off the shore of today's Kenya, the historian Louise Levathes reports that "there are fishermen with fairer skin than other Swahilis. They are known as 'Bajuni.'"[30] The word *Bajuni* is not kin to Swahili, but it is linked to the word *baju*, which is used by the Chinese in Southeast Asia to refer to the long-robe, or *pao*. With evidence such as this, Levathes shows us that the Bajuni perhaps descend from the union of the Chinese and the Swahili. Indeed, al-Mas'udi describes the friendship between the Chinese and the Swahili with the word *'ishra*, one that denotes both camaraderie and intimacy. If the Bajuni's place in Africa can be dated to the early modern period, the people of Madagascar (speakers of Malagasy) can be traced to intermarriages between local inhabitants and emigrants from Indonesia who came to eastern Africa early in the first millennium C.E. Evidence suggests that these immigrants brought Asian yams, bananas, taro, sugarcane, the chicken, and, perhaps, the xylophone to this part of Africa.[31]

If the Bajuni and the Malagasy speakers reflect the intimacy of the relationship between the continents, the Swahili language of the coast of eastern Africa is a far more sweeping reminder, for it was born principally of the Bantu language family but with extensive vocabulary and rhythm from Arabic and Gujarati.[32] The clever languages of this world, also the results of many interchanges, can also be gleaned on the other side of the Indian Ocean, in the morphology and vocabulary of such coastal tongues as Sri Lankan Moorish Arabic as well as in the many languages of the western coast of India, from the Kolis' several dialects to Sanskrit-based Konkani.[33] These languages included words from the Arabs, but also from the African sailors and traders who settled in various enclaves of India, such as Janjira Island (south of today's Mumbai) and in Hyderabad. For example, since the captains of the African and Arab vessels bore the title Sidi (from *Sayyid,* or in the lineage of the prophet Muhammad), the African settlers on the Indian mainland came to be called Siddis (or *habshis,* from *Al-Habsh* the Arabic name for Abyssinia). Today in Janjira and in Habshiguda in Hyderabad the descendants of the immigrants consider themselves to be Siddis, but have little direct memory of being African.[34] Over the years diligent scholars have recorded the presence of peoples of Africa in the annals of Indian history, people such as Jalal-ud-din Yaqut (consort to Raziya Sultana), the remarkable Malik Ambar, and Sheikh Sayyid al-Habshi Sultani of Ahmadnagar (the famous mosque in the city is named for Sheikh Sayyid). The sixteenth century in southern Asia, indeed, is filled with tales of the Habshi sultans, many of whom played crucial roles during Emperor Akbar's conquest of Gujarat or else themselves ruled over Bengal (in eastern India).[35]

Migration of African peoples, unfortunately, has come to be associated firmly with the enslavement of human beings. The Atlantic brutalities from the fifteenth to the nineteenth century marked all Africans as chattel slaves, despite the rich history of Africa outside modern slavery and notwithstanding the complex relationship of Indian Ocean peoples with "slavery." Scholarly work on the Zheng He expedition reveals that for some time the Chinese nobility acquired the services of a few Africans, this alongside the services of enslaved peoples from across the Asian periphery (from Korea to Malaysia). In the 700s, one reads in Chinese texts of the "devil slaves" (*gui-nu*), "black servants" (*hei-xiao-si*), and "barbarian servants" (*fan-xiao-si* or *fan-nu*). While there is evidence of Africans among the enslaved population, most of the slaves seem to have been Malay and Chinese. The word *black,* for instance, should not be taken to mean those from Africa (or to be read entirely based on racist notions that follow from Atlantic racism).[36] Ma Huan, from Zheng He's expedition, described people from the perimeter of the Indian Ocean who did not match up to his standards of civilization in a vocabulary that agrees with that of the terms used above. Of the people of Bengal, he wrote that "all the people are black [or brown pear color, as one translation puts it], with but an occasional white person." Of Meccans, we hear that the people "are stalwart and fine looking and their limbs and faces are of a very dark purple color." Finally, he says of the inhabitants of the is-land that is now Sri Lanka, "they have naked bodies, all without a stitch of clothing, like the bodies of brute beasts." He calls Sri Lanka the "country of the naked people" (or "naked body country") and the people are said to live in caves.[37] I tend to believe that this is a descriptive text written by an elite man who saw people whom he did not regard as social equals. There is little hint that he uses terms like *black* in anything more than a descriptive sense, and his comparison of the people of Ceylon to "brute beasts" should not be read as a denigration of their humanity, but as a comment on their cultural mores as compared to the Imperial Court.[38]

Black need not refer to skin color alone, for it was often used to indicate other signs: the Tang differentiated between the Bai Man ("white man") and the Wu Man ("black man") based on the different color sheepskins they wore, while the Sulawesi Bugi's ancient *La Galigo* myth used the idea of "darkness" to indicate the distant unknown, the land of Zanj (Zanzibar) which they called Jengki.[39] The reduction of *black* to skin does great damage to the widespread use of colors as signs for a multitude of things. Nor should we be misled by reports of slavery in the Indian Ocean.

In China, as in most of the world, prisoners of war became the property of their captors and could be kept as the captors so desired. The Chinese, like the Arabs, Indians, Africans, and Europeans, enslaved their own, to enjoy the free labor slavery provided. Despite the evidence of enslavement, it is clear, however, that the premodern mode of production was not *based* on slave labor (as was the Atlantic economy in a later age) nor was the sort of slavery practiced based upon the dehumanization of one particular people. The slaveholder, by all indications, endowed the slave with humanity at the same time as the slave was rendered unfree. At its most benign, premodern slavery was a form of apprenticeship in which merchants and traders bought a slave, who was loyal to them, learnt their trade, entered their lineage group, and then was able to obtain manumission. Indeed, as Amitav Ghosh establishes in *In an Antique Land*, "Slavery was often used as a means of creating fictive ties of kinship between people who were otherwise unrelated."[40] Finally, slavery was also a way by which military leaders constituted their armies and drew in loyal battalions whose "slave" status seems to have been fairly nominal (the slave dynasty in Egypt, 1260–1517, and that in the Delhi Sultanate, 1206–90, are evidence of this).[41] One has to pay heed to the distinctions between domestic servitude and plantation slavery, of the relationships forged between masters and slaves in the Indian Ocean as opposed to the chattel relationship in the Caribbean, in the U.S. South, and in Zanzibar from a later period.

So although there was a trade in humans in the premodern Indian Ocean perimeter, it was not a trade that necessarily dehumanized a biologically or even regionally delimited set of people, however brutal the treatment meted out to them. A text from 1178 tells us that "the people of Chan-Ch'eng [the central Vietnamese kingdom of Champa] buy male and female slaves; and the ships carry human beings as cargo."[42] Some of these people may have been Korean, others Malay, and a few Africans. The bulk of enslaved people in China came from the landmass itself, just as those in India enslaved others on the subcontinent (sometimes offering caste justifications for it). Among the Arabs, whom Bernard Lewis takes to task for the extent of slavery, there is evidence that they enslaved anybody, but mainly those who spoke a language other than Arabic and who did not submit to Islam. In the Ottoman Empire we hear that the prized slaves came from among the Georgians and the Circassians of the Caucasus region, but they also came from among the Persians. When the Russians annexed the Crimea in 1783 this region was closed to the Ottomans, who then turned to Africa for the supply of unfree labor.[43]

From the late seventh century, Arab Muslims called their co-believers *mawali*, which means "freedmen," a term that refers to their entry into Islam via capture, enslavement, and then, after conversion, manumission. Faced with the divisions between Arab Muslims and the *mawali*, the founder of the Maliki school of jurisprudence, Malik ibn Anas (1323) wrote that "all the people of Islam are equal [*akfa*] to one another, in accordance with God's revelations."[44] This is not to say that there was no discomfort among the Arabs for those whom they considered non-Arab, since from as early as the intellectual corpus of Jahiz of Basra (776–869) we have evidence of a debate over the intelligence of the people of Zanj (those of the east coast of Africa). Jahiz asks why there is a prejudice against the Zanj, and surmises that this might be because the only Zanj known to the Arabs are the poor who are the only ones enslaved. What, he asks, would the Arabs think of the Indians if they met only those who had no notion of Indian science, philosophy and art?[45] In India, meanwhile, it is hard to pin down the geographical background of the enslaved people, since, as historian Graham Irwin notes, "one of the sad things one has to note about Asian history is that, where there was prejudice, the racial origin of a person will be mentioned. But where there was no prejudice, the ethnic origin of individuals may not be mentioned at all."[46] Indian records do not note the ancestry of the slaves, which suggests that there was none of the kind of virulent racism like that of the Atlantic trade, although there was probably some form of prejudice, certainly xenophobia. Slavery existed in the ancient world, but "the identification of blackness with slavery did not develop," Frank Snowden conclusively notes in *Before Color Prejudice*. "No single ethnic group was associated with slave status or with the descendents of slaves."[47]

Nevertheless, one should pay heed to the caveat from Joseph Harris who affirms in *Africans and Their History* that while the Indian Ocean trade in human bodies "did not even begin to approach the volume of the Atlantic slave trade [more than 10 million were transported], it was nonetheless a brutal enterprise, with skeletons of Africans strewn across the Sahara."[48] The example of Zanzibar, in the fine work of Abdul Sheriff, shows us how things changed dramatically with the advent of capitalist relations of production. Until the nineteenth century, the use of slaves for mass production was minimal on the periphery of the Indian Ocean. When the British began to prohibit the transatlantic trade in slaves in the mid-1800s, just as demand for certain items like cloves rose, merchants in Zanzibar harnessed slave labor power to produce such commodities for the world market.[49] Slavery in the Indian Ocean world, therefore, grew under the flag of the colonial powers.

Before we go forward on the question of race, it is pressing that we pursue further the problem of skin color as a template for difference. In ancient India, Sanskrit texts inform us that differentiation was on the basis of *varna*, the familiar fourfold classification of Brahmin, Kshatriya, Vaishya, and Sudra. Suvira Jaiswal argues that "the process of hierarchical gradation within each *varna* cannot be explained simply in terms of ethnic accretions, even though such expansion has been continuous in Indian history. It was largely due to the unequal accessibility of political and economic power that hierarchical status distinctions crystallized."[50] From textual and archaeological evidence, Jaiswal demonstrates that the differentiation of caste in southern Asia finds its origins in the ecology of Vedic cattle keepers and that state formation and patriarchy are the crucial pieces of the story, not any anachronistic notion of race. British colonial officials took the term *varna* and sought to find in it links to their own ideas of race based on phenotype (and skin color).[51] Therefore, they argued that *varna*, in Sanskrit, means color so that the caste system, for them, was a race-based hierarchy of skin colors. Considerable research, however, shows us that *varna* may refer to something akin to feudal colors or standards, and not to the coloration or pigmentation of the skin. Words such as *suklatva* ("whiteness") refer not to pigment but to classes of things.[52]

In China we see a similar development. In the third century B.C.E., Chinese classics ascribed colors to the different tribes that they deemed to be barbarians, the red or black Dai, the white or black Man, and the black Lang. The Chinese classics understood that those who did not enjoy the fruits of civilization lived in recoupable banishment. There was, however, no sense that these people are in a race-based, and therefore permanent, hierarchy. The Chinese notion of cultural difference is captured in the idea of *yongxiabianyi*, "to use the Chinese [Xia] ways to transform those who are different [the Yi people, in this phrase]": assimilation, or the end to the hierarchy, is possible. Historian Frank Dikötter rightly argues that the coloration of people in the Chinese texts was "symbolic. They indicated either the dominant tint of the minorities' clothes or the five directions of the compass: white for the West, black for the North, red for the East, blue-green for the South. Yellow represented the centre."[53]

In ancient Europe, too, the association with skin color did not make for a decisive difference. "The ancients did not fall into the error of biological racism; black skin color was not a sign of inferiority [or it was only a *contingent* sign of inferiority]; Greeks and Romans did not establish color as an obstacle to integration in society; and ancient society was one that 'for all its faults and failures never made color the basis for judging a man.'"[54] Furthermore, as in Asia, the Europeans associated the color black with certain phenomena (such as the underworld in Greek and Roman cosmology), but this association had "nothing to do with skin color," and it was perhaps only much later that this association was harnessed to antiblack racism.[55]

In Europe, as in certain circles within Asia, skin color developed aesthetic qualities, so that some people wrote well of fair, as opposed to dark, skin. Ancient texts recorded variable notions of beauty and asked that each standard be accorded its own validity. It was not odd, therefore, that Philodemus, Theocritus, Virgil, Ovid, and Martial had paeans to those with dark skin.[56] Ancient Chinese texts often use white jade as a metaphor for beauty, both for men and women. At the court of the Western Jin dynasty (265–316 C.E.), Dikötter tells us that "male nobles even used powder to whiten their faces."[57] In India too there is a tendency among certain groups to admire fair skin more than dark skin (although duskiness is often eroticized), but, as I argued earlier, to reduce an unhealthy obsession with skin color to the idea of "race" does not enable us to grasp the historical dynamics of skin color on the subcontinent.[58] Even when the Chinese were made to suffer a European pretense, they did not ascribe any ontological meaning to color difference. Most Chinese intellectuals during the Opium War (1839–42) deployed notions of skin color equally to denigrate their vanquishers. English troops were called "white devils/ghosts" or *baigui*—those whose skin was thought to be white due to daily baths of cold water and the consumption of milk. Indian troops in the British army were known as "black devils/ghosts" or *heigui*. While each group was distinguished by its skin color, both were condemned as devils or ghosts. People across space and time used color as a symbol for community or for the cardinal points, or else ascribed beauty to various colors, but this use of color itself cannot be taken to mean that they held fixed cultural meanings for each color. White was not always good, and black not always bad, and certainly when these colors are used, they are not always metaphors for the pigment of the skin.

Atlantic Racism

Vasco da Gama and his compatriots should not be considered the pioneers of a racial mythology, for they too came from a cultural world that was as yet untrammeled by the burdens of "race." In the early 1500s, Europeans differentiated one another and themselves from others on the basis of axes such as religion and language, and mainly the former. As the Portuguese galleons ruthlessly wiped other ships off the Indian Ocean, Martin Luther hammered his theses for the reformation of Christianity to the Wittenberg church (1517). Religious wars wracked Europe from this date (when the French Francis I began his onslaught on the Hapsburg Charles V) until at least the Treaty of Westphalia at the close of the Thirty Years' War (1648). Despite the growth of the Ottoman Empire under Süleyman I, the European powers remained engrossed in their doctrinal battles, exemplified by the quixotic struggles of Phillip II (who recovered parts of the Netherlands, but who lost the Spanish Armada in his attempt to take England in 1588). The Ottomans, in turn, did take Belgrade and make inroads into continental Europe, but they failed to clear the Portuguese navies from both the Arabian Gulf and the Indian Ocean.[59]

The Indian Ocean world fell victim to the voracious appetites of European mercantilism and to the values and techniques of warfare the merchant warriors devised. The Arab chroniclers of Hadramaut (Yemen) closely followed the activities of the Iberian ships in the Indian Ocean during the early years of the 1500s. "The vessels of the Franks appeared at sea en route for

India, Hurmuz and those parts. They took about seven vessels, killing those on board and making some prisoner. This was their first action. May God curse them."[60] Along the coastline, the wrath of the Portuguese entered the folklore of the people. Such was Swahili sentiment:

> *Enda Manoel, ututukiziye,* Go away Manoel, you have made us hate you,
> *Enda, na sulubu uyititiziye.* Go, and carry your cross with you.[61]

The Swahili damned Manoel, the epitome of the conquistador with his cross and sword.

Vasco da Gama's armed entry into the Indian Ocean did indeed import values quite opposed to those of the ocean's cosmos. Until 1498 the goods of the Indian Ocean came into Europe via the Levant, a region whose dominance over the trade was tangled by the Christian-Muslim wars over Jerusalem and the "Holy Lands." Even if the Crusades (1099–1291) failed for the Europeans, the links they fashioned had enduring cultural (the *Quran* was translated into a European language in 1143) and economic (because of increased demand for Asian goods) effects.[62] The transit from the Arabs to Europe was conducted mainly by Genovese and Venetian merchants whose access to the Indian Ocean was blocked by a strong Mamluk state, among others.[63] One might be tempted to say that the relatively peaceful trade of the Indian Ocean world was kept so by the armed might of the Arab states at the Palestinian littoral as well as by the brutality on the landmass of Asia, whether on the scale of the Mongols or of the local rulers. (The Mongols, of course, also facilitated relatively peaceful trade, and this was created by their ruthless suppression of revolt.) Certainly there is evidence of sea battles (the 1490s skirmish between the Gujarat sultan's navy and that of the Iranian notable Bahadur Khan Gilani), of cannons on Zheng He's fleet, and of piracy on the trade Routes (for example, the Bugis of Sulawesi, from whose legend we get the fearsome "Bugi Man" of our childhood).[64] Nevertheless, as Sanjay Subrahmanyam, the modern biographer of Vasco da Gama, concludes,

> what was fundamentally new about the Portuguese in the Indian Ocean was thus not the *fact* that they used force on water: it was the degree of expertise with which they did so, the fact that they did so over such large maritime spaces, separated moreover by such a distance from anything that could be thought of as their home territory, and the relatively systematic effort they brought to bear in this sphere.[65]

Ruthlessness was not unknown to premodern empires, but they mainly constructed their hegemonic power across the landmass. The uniqueness of the Portuguese, and right at their heels the English and the Dutch, brought their fierceness to the waters; the new mode of transport allowed them much greater geographical reach than the empires of the land. The naval cannons and the papal canons put paid to the careful codes of the Indian Ocean world.

While the European powers spilled the blood of their hated heretics in Europe, other forces gathered to create the conditions for the invention of the idea of race. Two sixteenth-century developments indicate the beginnings of raciology: the Iberian Inquisition and the slave trade. The Inquisition in the Iberian Peninsula tore tens of thousands of people of the Jewish and Muslim faiths from their homes and lands. Those who converted to Catholicism (the *conversos*) had to undertake a test for their purity of blood (*limpieza de sangre*) to prove their distance from Judaism and Islam. Until the Inquisition, to be a heretic was a matter of intellect, emotion, or even possession, but the Grand Inquisitor changed all this with the burden of blood condemning certain people to the gibbet. As Audrey Smedley explains in *Race in North America,* the test of blood was related to the "genealogical context of families." It was not, Smedley notes, "a belief that Jewishness actually resides in the blood. It reflected the jural dimensions of structured kinship rather than the fact of biological connection, the significance of 'pater' rather than 'genitor.'"[66]

The ferocity of raciology was born not only from the Inquisition, but also from events in Ireland, England's first colony. There Elizabeth I's armies razed the lands of those whom they regarded as heathens, wicked, barbarous, and uncivil. These folk were many of the indentured servants sent to the colonies, and it was these people who would not, until much later, be able to lay claim to "whiteness."[67] From the late 1620s to the 1650s, the slavers bought Irish people on their ships as part of their transatlantic trade in human bodies. By the late 1600s, the enslavement of those with fair skin was stopped and the Europeans traded solely in those with dark skin.[68]

The Inquisition and the Irish slave trade offered intimations of what was to follow, of the growth of an age when something called white supremacy began to have an inordinate role in the creation of the world.[69] Most research shows that European plantation owners and farmers in the Americas suffered from a labor supply and control problem: apart from insufficient and rebellious Amerindians, the European rulers tried to extract as much surplus from poor, bonded Europeans (notably the Irish) and Africans. Theodore Allen and Jacqueline Jones have compiled evidence of class solidarity between African and European laborers, and the absence of a class alliance between Europeans against Africans, and on this basis Allen argues that "'the white race,' and thus a system of racial oppression, did not exist and could not have existed in the seventeenth century tobacco colonies."[70] Only in the late seventeenth century or thereabouts, when the problem of social control was disrupted by such multiethnic uprisings as Bacon's Rebellion of 1676 for the widest democracy, was a theory of racial supremacy constructed, and on that basis did supremacists fight to erect a system of racial oppression.[71] Between 1660 and 1720, colonies such as Virginia went on the rampage to disenfranchise enslaved Africans: statutes and regulations stipulated servitude of Africans for life, revoked their right to bear arms and own property, made illegal what is called interracial marriage (miscegenation) or fornication, and finally, in 1723, ended the right to the ballot enjoyed by Africans.[72] "By the end of the seventeenth century," historian Winthrop Jordan concludes, "dark complexion had become an independent rationale for slavery."[73]

American slavers are not alone, for others joined them to provide the decisive context for the fabrication of the idea of race: the English East India Company (founded in 1600), the Dutch East India Company or the VOC (founded in 1602), and the French East India Company (founded in 1664) were the first joint-stock companies and crucial instruments for the development of northwest European imperialism. The subjugation of southern Asia, Indonesia, and most of Africa would be instigated and sustained by these three financial institutions whose reliance on slave labor contributed significantly to the development of "racial science." Shortly after the conquest of Goa by the Dutch, Jan Pieterszoon Coen, governor-general of the Dutch East Indies (1617–29) declared that

> may not a man in Europe do what he likes with his cattle? Even so does the master do with his men, for everywhere, these with all that belong to them are as much the property of the master, as are brute beasts in the Netherlands. The law of the land is the will of the King and he is King who is strongest.[74]

There are echoes here of Hobbes and Locke, and certainly of the notion that conquered humans can be the property of those who are deemed "human."

Frank Snowden, therefore, is quite correct in his assessment that antiblack notions perhaps would not have gained credence "in the modern world in the absence of such phenomenon as Negro slavery and colonialism."[75] Indeed, most scholars agree that the idea of race can be traced to the late 1600s and the conventional marker is François Bernier's *Nouvelle division de la terre par les différents espèces ou races qui'l habitent* (1684).[76] Bernier, a French traveler, spent more than a decade (1656–68) in India and western Asia, about which he wrote a famous travel book. His travelogue was one of many such, a panoply of books about places that Europe did not know before in any detail and about which, thanks to Magellan's circumnavigation of the globe in 1519–22 and the printing press, the European public was to know more than it could process. Bernier's account of his travels provided considerable knowledge to his contemporaries, but it also allowed them to live with the certain knowledge that their own society was the very best thing possible. Comparing Mughal India and Ottoman Turkey with the France of Louis XIV, Bernier wrote that "take away the right to private property in land, and you introduce, as an infallible consequence, tyranny, slavery, injustice, beggary and barbarism."[77] Upon his return to Europe and after the success of his travel book, Bernier wrote *Nouvelle division* which was one of the first of many such compendiums on race. Bernier divided humanity into four or five *"espèces ou races,"* with lines of demarcation based on physical traits (hair, stature, nose, and lips), geography, and, significantly, skin color.[78] Bernier's work was followed, in the eighteenth century, by that of the Swedish scientist Carolus Linneaus (who transformed the method of raciology with his scientific classification schemes) and of the German naturalist Johann Friedrich Blumenbach (who devised the field of physical anthropology and who provided the early linkage of African man with ape). This scholarship was the first to classify humanity into groups or races based on biological principles. Xenophobia was classified and institutionalized and the idea of race was born.

With the birth of race came a new genesis tale for Europe. In 1786, the English Sanskritist Sir William Jones announced that Sanskrit, Greek, Latin, Gothic, Celtic, and Old Persian shared a common ancestral language. Jones had been at work on a project to recover what European linguists of his day felt was the lost language of Noah and Adam when he stumbled upon common elements in these ancient, and diverse, languages.[79] In 1813 English linguists called the language Indo-European, and a decade later German linguists named it Indo-Germanic. By 1861 the language was known as Aryan, largely under the influence of the German Sanskritist F. Max Müller, who taught comparative philology at Oxford. The benign discovery of unities among languages gradually transmuted, against Max Müller's wishes,[80] into the claim that if certain languages had the same ancestor, then the peoples that spoke them must also be somehow related. Among European romantics India was appealing as a place of mystery, so the discovery of a link between the two cultural worlds was not met with disdain. Goethe, in 1791, proclaimed that "when I mention *Shakuntala*, everything was said," or that ancient Indian books bore within them the mysteries of the universe. Napoléon took a copy of some of the *Vedas* to Egypt (1798) and Friedrich von Schlegel, so central to "race theory," chanted that "everything, yes, everything without exception has its origin in India."[81]

Everything, that is, except the Jews. In the principalities of Germany, the context for the reception of the Aryan Myth was anti-Semitism. Jewish emancipation occurred between 1789 and 1815 across the European continent, a freedom that provoked a debate among German intellectuals on the "Jewish Question." "As Jews aspired to become citizens like everyone else," Leon Poliakov noted in his book *The Aryan Myth*, "Christian society, especially in Germany, trusted them even less, as usually happens when slaves are freed."[82] Many European scholars sought a way to detach the common Palestinian heritage of Jews and Christians. The idea of the Aryan was valuable for this, since it meant that the proto-Christians came from an ancestor other than the progenitor of the Jews.

The "Indo-European race," the myth went, emerged in the region of the Caucasus Mountains (hence Caucasian).[83] The Indians moved to hot lands, turned dark and slothful, and formed despotic societies (this around 3000 B.C.E.). In 1894, a Frenchman Terrien de Lacouperie even argued that the Chinese "race" came from the Caucasians, via the Bak Sings (a people from Elam/Babylon, with connections with the Sumero-Akkadians)—an argument well publicized in China via translation.[84] The Europeans, in turn, went to cooler climates, remained fair and energetic, and formed democratic societies. The theory, in this way, was able to distinguish between the contemporary colonized and the colonizer, as well as to sift the greatness of ancient Asia (whose worth came from the pristine Caucasian migrants) from the fallen contemporary Asians.[85]

The Brahmin response to the Aryan myth is an ample indication of the impact of European raciology among certain sections in southern Asia: in the early 1800s, the idea that the Europeans and Indians, then a colonized group, were of a common "race" was greeted with glee by some such as the Bengali notable Keshub Chander Sen, who exclaimed that English colonialism was "a reunion of parted cousins, the descendants of two different families of the ancient Aryan race."[86] Just as Sen tried to find a way to deal with English domination over his beloved Bengal, the Japanese writer Kanzuki Sato in 1889 was torn between the need to assert the Japanese people against the U.S. intruders and to come to terms with the fact of U.S. military dominance. If Sen took pride in a connection with the mythical Aryan migrations, so too did Sato, who intoned that "our ancestors passed through Mesopotamia, Arabia, Egypt, and India. Descendants of the Caucasoids, they traveled across the ocean and immigrated to our land."[87]

Elite subjects under the heel of imperial arrogance seek out ways to assert their own independence, without an assault at imperial racism. The Indian nationalist leader B. C. Pal, otherwise fairly liberal for his time, informed his readers in 1901 that the Aryan mind has a "pre-eminently metaphysical cast"—with the Greek descendants able to realize the parts in the whole (to give them democracy, ethics, and an aesthetics of harmony), while the Hindu descendants could see only the whole in the parts, "as an ever present reality" (hence, pantheism, lack of democracy and justice). Pal was ready to put Indians (or merely Hindus) down before the Europeans, just so the Indians might be part of the club above the other "races"—"thus we find among the Aryan races a type of social organisation which is essentially civic, while among the Semitic races we find what is practically military."[88] Two years later, while in jail for his revolutionary nationalist activities, the nationalist leader Bal Gangadhar Tilak repeated the Aryan tale, with the fabulous story of the Arctic home of the Aryans. As if to reply to the charge of Indian degeneration in his colonized present, Tilak wrote that the "vitality and superiority of the Aryan races, as disclosed by their conquest [of India], by extermination or assimilation, of the non-Aryan races with whom they came in contact . . . is intelligible only on the assumption of a high degree of civilisation in their original Arctic home."[89] Despite their nationalist sentiments, the bulk of Brahmin intellectuals retained hold of the racist Aryan theory, a fact that the Dalit leader Dr. B. R. Ambedkar rightly ascribed to the Brahmin's fantasy of their historical subjugation of the non-Aryans, those who are currently among the Dalit communities.[90] In the 1950s the Senegalese Afrocentric scholar Cheikh Anta Diop developed an inverse reaction to the Aryan Myth. Diop divided the world into the two races of Aryan and Dravidian, wherein the former was associated with northern Africa and the latter with both southern Africa and among the Dalits of India.[91] The Diop reversal takes for granted the fantasy myth of Aryanism, a posture that gives legitimacy to race ideas (I shall go over this at length in the next chapter). The Brahmin accommodation to, and the Diopian reversal of, the Aryan Myth shows us how those outside the camp of whiteness nourished the categories of raciology, and, more specifically, of white supremacy. Atlantic racism, then, is not the special inheritance and legacy of those who deem themselves to be "white."

Fascism in Many Colors

Fascism (in the European and U.S. core) and colonialism (in the Asian and African periphery) exemplify the highest stage of racist statecraft. The nineteenth-century European states took charge of vast areas of Asia and Africa at the same time as these states turned against liberal currents within their own societies. In the 1840s the English Parliament ruthlessly suppressed the Chartists just as their imperial representatives crushed the 1857 rebellion across the Indian subcontinent.[92] The "race-state" arose in the mid-1800s as European states constructed themselves in opposition to their colonies, the nether region that provided labor and raw materials. The fascist state of the 1920s and 1930s was the high point of the race state: the imperial core took its place atop a racist system of political domination and economic exploitation, not just against those in the distant colonies, but also against domestic difference (and its own workers, many of whom made a compact with the state in a racist and class collaborationist bargain). Just as some mainly highly skilled workers within the core acceded to the racist logic, so too did some peripheral elements find merit in the racist science of imperialism. Racism was born in the crucible of imperialism, but it is not the sole property of those who see themselves as white; others, people of color, adopted the idea of race, erroneously wed it to earlier ethnocentric or xenophobic traditions, and wielded it against politically weaker social forces or else those who they deemed to be foreigners.

Phrases such as "black fascism," "Israeli fascism" or "Hindu fascism" do not fall from my mouth with ease. People who have suffered and survived a historical genocide at the hands of white supremacy, Nazism, or imperialism hardly seem to be likely candidates for a fascistic movement. One tends to expect that those who have been at the wrong end of a jackboot would offer empathy for the wretched, and be first among the forces of liberation. But, recent scholarship has argued that one can indeed speak of a fascism in many colors, of a "black fascism," of an "Israeli fascism," and of a "Hindu fascism." Although sociologist Paul Gilroy goes too far in equating the fascism of the core with that of the periphery, he does offer a useful way to evaluate the fascistic tendencies among certain people of color.[93] While all fascisms are not identical, there is something Gilroy calls the unanimist principle that unites most fascisms, whereby the "people" are one, division is not integral to social relations, and the members of a nation are interchangeable and disposable. Furthermore, the unanimist principle perverts the idea of democracy into a racial hierarchy of the population in which those who sit atop

the totem are seen as chosen by God or destiny.[94] Israeli Prime Minister
Golda Meir's 1969 statement that there are no Palestinians in Israel, Idi
Amin's 1972 expulsion of Asians from Uganda ("Uganda is not an Indian colony"), and the Indian Hindu Right's anti-Muslim campaign of the 1990s (exemplified by the slogan Go to Pakistan or the Graveyard) are some examples
of unanimism.[95] If we set aside the problem of the "fascist minimum" (Is
there a minimum definition for a generic fascism?), we can perhaps agree
with the postulate that this "unanimism" is fascistic in that it does not seem
to allow for the mess of democracy and the strains of equality.[96] Specifically
for our purposes, fascism or a movement with fascistic tendencies has at its
core hierarchy, racism, and militarism.

The labor of diligent scholarship has produced work that shows us the
personal and institutional links between the fascisms of the core (Italian Fascism, German Nazism, and all the other European and U.S. radical intoler-
ances) and at the periphery (in Japan, China, and India). In the early 1930s,
leading Japanese intellectuals such as Masamichi Royama, Shintaro Ryu, and
Kiyoshi Miki drew upon the ideas of Italian Fascists such as Minister of Justice Alfredo Rocco, the writings of Nietzsche and Heidegger, and the Nazi
assault to extend its territory (*Lebensraum*).[97] Just as these Japanese scholars transformed the works of European fascists to suit their social reality,
in western India a set of Indian activists and scholars drew upon such
nineteenth-century German thinkers as Johann Kaspar Bluntschli, from
contemporary Nazis such as Hitler, and from the experience of Italian fascism. While B. S. Moonje visited Italy to see the Ballila and Il Duce, M. S.
Golwalkar and V. D. Savarkar praised Hitler and drew from him for their
Theory of the Nation (and its Race Spirit, its *Völksgeist*).[98] These are examples
of personal connection between revolutionary nationalists (some fascists)
of various stripes, but it is insufficient to assume that personal contact is
proof of fascism itself. What is of considerable interest is that the various
fascistic movements across the globe came up with similar solutions to an
international crisis of capitalism in the 1930s, whether in regions of the second rank (Italy, Germany, Japan), in semi-colonies (China, much of the
Southern Cone, and South Africa) or from intellectuals in colonized regions
(India being the best example).[99] In the 1930s, the Indian maverick Communist M. N. Roy argued that Sun Yat-sen's ideas and his practices in Republican China cast "the ominous shadow of Fascism," and a study of his ideas
shows that it is a "related ideological species" to Italian Fascism.[100] Beyond
what I have stressed are fascistic tendencies, it seems unlikely that one could
sustain that these Asian movements are fascist. The Asian economies did not
experience the type of crisis suffered by central and southern Europe, princi-

pally because they did not enjoy the moment of imperialist growth of a previous era (from the Berlin Conference of 1884 till World War I): the European fascist scapegoat was military collapse, foreign powers, or the internal economic enemy (the figure of the Jewish trader). Furthermore, although Asian peoples lumbered under the yoke of a foreign power, the response to this overlordship was not generically posed in a racial form. That is, the argument that Asia could be liberated only by the renaissance of the Asian race (*Völkgeist*) was not a popular ideology, even in Japan which would otherwise pose the best example of a type of fascist regime. Given this lack of popularity for a racial or volkish nationalism during this era, the fascist movements that developed did not build up a mass character, an essential determinant.[101]

To say that there was no mass popularity for volkish or racial nationalism is not to say that Asia was immune from raciology. The development of raciology in Asia came principally in the context of a nationalist sentiment that grew under the shadow of European imperialism. Asian popular movements and intellectuals attempted to construct their own national stories in response to their colonizer's condescension and in an effort to unite peoples whose destiny was seen as a reason for Asia's failure to withstand the onslaught of Europe. By the late nineteenth century, three hundred years into the development of the concept of race, this would be countered by an attempt to forge national identities and communities, rather than local ones. A central figure for the construction of Asian notions of cultural nationhood was the English philosopher and father of sociobiology, Herbert Spencer. Greatly influenced by Darwin's 1859 *On the Origin of Species,* Spencer devised the theory that in human evolution the fittest survived and transmitted evolved traits across generations, which was clearly enunciated in his late 1860s two-volume *Principles of Biology* and his 1876 first-volume *Principles of Sociology.* If the idea of the "survival of the fittest" was taken from Darwin, the belief in hereditary transmission of modified organisms was drawn from the by then largely discredited work of the eighteenth-century French naturalist Jean-Baptiste Lamarck. What attracted cultural nationalists among the colonized Asians was Spencer's idea of the "survival of the fittest" and of the hereditary coherence of a people (we should keep in mind, though, that this idea grew on the ground of earlier xenophobic ideas). Colonized people could recover their glory if they earned their freedom and asserted themselves against weaker foes. The 1884 Japanese translation of Spencer's evolutionary theory acted as a touchstone for the entry of Atlantic racism into Asia. In China, as well, it was Spencerian rhetoric that drew to the fore such newly racialized slogans as *yousheng-liebai,* "the superior win, the inferior lose."[102] "Against a background of widespread social change brought about by policies of industrialisation," Richard Siddle notes in *Race, Resistance and the Ainu of Japan,* "national and social conflict were increasingly presented in terms of the 'survival of the fittest' (*yusho reppai*) in the 'struggle for survival' (*seizon kyoso*) in the journals and newspapers that proliferated between 1890 and 1920."[103]

In southern Asia, Spencer did not have the popularity he enjoyed among Japanese and Chinese intellectuals, but the germ of his evolutionary and volkish nationalist ideas made a decisive impact upon the Hindu Right. V. D. Savarkar, the spokesperson of a Brahmanical Hindu supremacy, at once argued that a nation is the political expression of a race, "This tendency of people having these [religious, racial, cultural, linguistic or historical] affinities to form themselves into a group or into a Nation and not by the mere fact of being mapped together, has its rooted deep down in human or even animal nature," (1938)[104] and that the nation is forged by history and by culture, "Above all the Hindus are bound together by the dearest, most sacred and most enduring bonds of a common Fatherland and a common Holyland, and these two being identified with one and the same country our Bharatbhumi, our India, the National Oneness and homogeneity of the Hindus have been doubly sure," (1937).[105] These unanimist and Spencerian views exemplify the most well-developed racist ideas within the broad field of Asian nationalism, especially as these currents transformed the meaning of "nation." As the Left within the nationalist movements adopted the idea of "nation" to unite the peoples around social customs (languages, boundaries, histories), the Right sought to create bloodlines for national unity. In China, scholars on the Right drew upon the idea of *zu,* which would have meant family, clan, tribe, or lineage, to create a trans-clan solidarity of a Chinese people or "race" who claim a common ancestor (the Yellow Emperor). Writers such as Yatsuka Hozumi in Japan worked to transform the idea of *minzoku* from shared culture (or folk) to shared ancestry (with the Ainu, the Koreans, and the Chinese, as well as the Europeans, being seen increasingly as foreign and lower).[106]

The Spencerian-inspired nationalist idea of "survival of the fittest" required "lower races" that could be brutally colonized. Multicolored fascistic movements in Asia did not turn their ire against white supremacy, something that is perhaps of no great surprise today (when fascistic movements, such as the Hindu Right, are able to make concessions to U.S. imperialism with no great trouble).[107] The thrust of its racism fell against distant Africans, Jews (in mimicry of European fascism), and domestic "others" (whether the Muslims and Dalits in India, the Ainu and Koreans in Japan, or the Tajiks, Mongols, Tibetans, Koreans, Yi, Yao, and Daur of China).[108] Eugenics provides us with the sharpest example of racist intolerance, one that finds its roots in imperialist Great Britain, expansionist United States, and Nazi Germany.[109] In China, the idiosyncratic texts of Zhang Junjun (notably his 1935 "Reform of the Chinese Race") and the institutional work of Dartmouth and Columbia graduate Pan Guangdan worried about the dilution of Han blood by barbarian blood.[110] In India, M. S. Golwalkar wrote in support of the Nazi genocide (the "purging of the country of the semitic Races—the Jews"), since, "Race pride at its highest has been manifested here. Germany has shown how wellnigh impossible it is for Races and cultures, having differences going to the root, to be assimilated into one united whole, a good lesson for us in Hindustan to learn and profit by." Golwalkar's "foreign race" is not the English, but the Muslims—what he called, "the minorities problem."[111] Historian Zenji Suzuki argues that within the context of the "race problem" in the United States, eugenics scientists worried more about transference of human traits and miscegenation, while in Japan the interest of scientists was more on plant and animal hybrids.[112] While this may be true, Suzuki neglects figures such as Ishimoto Shizue, who is considered to be the Margaret Sanger of Japan and who, according to historian Elise Tipton, had social eugenics interests as Sanger had.[113] In India, both Sanger and Edith How-Martyn attempted to introduce birth control as a means to reduce population, an attempt fought off by Gandhi, who preferred abstinence, and by the All India Women's Conference, which was aware of the racism of birth control (lower "races" must be controlled) and preferred family planning as the option.[114] Multicolored fascism attempted to draw in eugenics ideas, but the fact that imperialist forces often used these very ideas against them was a decisive block to their adoption.

As the idea of shared ancestry entered Asian thought in an enumerated and highly elaborated form, notions of anti-blackness and anti-Semitism made their cognate entry too. One can glean the sorts of ongoing rearrangements of social categories in the 1860 Japanese mission to the United States, only seven years after Japan's humiliation at the hands of U.S. Commodore M. C. Perry and his gunboats. During their stay in the United States, delegate Kenzaburo Yanagawa wrote that "blacks are inferior as human beings and extremely stupid." Historian W. G. Beasley, who studied the mission in detail, notes that such comments on social issues "have the air of received wisdom, derived from statements by their hosts."[115] En route to Japan, the mission stopped in Angola. The Africans, one official felt, resembled Buddhist images, and he came to the conclusion that "the natives of India and Africa both belong to one and the same tribe, of whom the Buddha must have been a chieftain." The official made it clear that it was quite absurd for the Japanese to have worshipped such primitives. Historian Marius Jansen, after quoting that official, comments that "the new structure of relative national prestige is not yet built, but the old hierarchy of respect is clearly in process of dissolution."[116]

While racism had been part and parcel of burgeoning nationalist movements in the mid and late nineteenth century, by the 1930s racist thought did not flourish within the powerful currents of anticolonial nationalism that developed in Asia. Just as the Japanese invaded Manchuria in 1931, the director for Social Welfare Projects wrote in the Ainu newsletter,

> No discrimination between races (*jinshu*) is a worldwide [ideal] trend and few would deny this. But what is the situation in reality? Do not Orientals suffer discriminatory treatment by Europeans and Americans as a yellow race? We Japanese are always indignant about this. But Japanese citizens, who have these bitter experiences, within our own country treat people of the *buraku* who follow certain occupations as outcastes, despite no racial difference whatsoever.[117]

Masaaki Kita, another Japanese official involved with Ainu welfare, suggested that by intermarriage and by "fusing" (*yugo*), the Ainu and the "general public" (*ippanjin*) would become one in reality.[118]

The powerful tow of secularism and of the Marxist nationality theory drew many Indian nationalists toward a composite theory of the multination called India. Indian nationalist Jawaharlal Nehru's popular classic *The Discovery of India* (1946) adopted the strong version of a collage culture with his refusal to embrace the idea that Aryan has a racial significance and with his rendition of Indian culture as vibrant due to its complexity: "It is not some secret doctrine or esoteric knowledge that has kept India vital and going through these long ages, but a tender humanity, a varied and tolerant culture, and a deep understanding of life and its mysterious ways."[119] In China, Lin Yutang in 1935 wrote along the racialist grain that "one observes a new bloom of culture after each introduction of new blood," and that "blood infusion" was a positive development for any people.[120] In 1944, Chiang Kaishek (Jiang Jieshi) noted that the five "peoples" of Zhangshan (Mongolians, Manchus, Tibetans, Muslim Turks, and the Han) are differentiated "due to regional and religious factors, and not to race or blood."[121] Chapter 5 will develop the genealogy of secular anti-imperialism at some length so I won't go into it in any detail here. Suffice it to say that the Spencerian brand of nationalism was not alone, and that it did not wholly represent the Asian view of race and of imperialism.

White supremacists did not take kindly to the idea that certain people of color might share the heritage of those whom they deemed to be white. At the end of the 1800s, U.S. writers agreed that the Aryans were the oldest relatives of the "cultured Greek, law-making and organizing Roman, the blonde Norwegian, dark-eyed Spaniard, the mercurial Frenchman, the plodding and persevering German, the hardy-purposed and energetic Anglo-Saxon, the enterprising and practical Anglo-American."[122] By the modern age, the distant relatives of the Aryans (people such as the Indians) had degenerated by indolence into decadence and "effeminacy." Theodore Roosevelt wrote of the "pathetic humor" evinced by English writers who linked the biological destinies of the "Anglo-Saxon" to the "Asiatic." The "Anglo-Saxon," for Roosevelt, combined strains of German, Irish, and Norse, a stock of "mainly Teutonic, largely Celtic, with Scandinavian admixture." Of the Aryan Myth, Roosevelt noted, quite correctly as it happens, but for the wrong reasons, that "Aryan is a linguistic and not a biological term," and that it is "*very* doubtful that an Aryan race existed."[123] With the 1857 *Dred Scott* ruling behind him, and with the 1896 *Plessy* ruling to come, it goes without saying that polygenesis, or separate creations for the so-called races, made absolute sense to the likes of Roosevelt. In light of this, the desire to prove kinship among "Aryans" was a liberal, though antiblack, gesture.

In the 1920s, Adolf Hitler tacitly supported the Japanese imperial designs against the Russians—what he called "Austrian Slavdom"—and he wrote in favor of what he considered to be Japan's quest against the "millennial Jewish empire" (Japan actually opposed European, not *Jewish*, capital interests).[124] But Hitler simultaneously called for an end to economic development in Japan because he felt it was foreign to Japanese "culture"; economic growth was something to be reserved for the Aryans.[125] Certain Indian nationalists sought out the Germans for assistance against the British Empire. When they appealed to Hitler, he called them "inflated Orientals" and "Asiatic jugglers," and decided that "I, as a man of Germanic blood, would, in spite of everything, rather see India under English rule than under any other."[126] While Hitler felt some affinity for ancient Aryan culture, from whom he borrowed the architecture of his Aryan race, especially the Swastika, present-day Asians were only fit subjects for colonization:

Germanization can only be applied to *soil* and never to *people*. For what was generally understood under this word was only the forced outward acceptance of the German language. But it is a scarcely conceivable fallacy of thought to believe that a *Negro* or a Chinese, let us say, will turn into a German because he learns German . . . Nationality or race does not happen to lie in language, but in the blood.[127]

Despite Hitler's unequivocal revulsion for people of color, multicolored fascists continued to speak in his name. The most colorful figure in this is Lawrence Dennis (1893–1977), born of an African American mother and a white father in Georgia, and little known now as one of the leading fascist intellectuals in the United States during the 1930s and 1940s.[128] Passing as a white man, Dennis studied at Phillips Exeter and Harvard, worked for the U.S. Foreign Service and various finance concerns. During the Depression of the 1930s, Dennis adopted the fascist argument about the instability of liberal capitalism notably in his 1932 book *Is Capitalism Doomed?* and then in his 1936 *The Coming American Fascism.*[129] In *Is Capitalism Doomed?* Dennis argues that "for the creation of its necessary markets, capitalism, in the past, has had to rely on spiritual impulses derived from non-commercial sources, mainly from militant nationalism and the love of adventure." Therefore, while Dennis's goal was to create a system on behalf of the plutocrats, he recognized pragmatically that "the people must have a prophet and prophets have never come out of the world of profits."[130] Dennis was greatly enamored of Hitler's macho militarism, for it provided modern men with the ethics of adventure and not what he found to be the sterility of liberalism. "If a man suffers in war, he is a hero; if he suffers for his faith, he is a saint; if he suffers for capitalism, he is a sucker."[131] Hitler, Dennis argued, awoke the emotional and spiritual need to suffer for a cause and not just for a stagnant capitalism. Given his commitment to the fascist cause, Dennis downplayed the racism of the Nazi movement. For example, he claimed that "the Jews in Germany were the victims of too much democracy," because the need to garner mass support from the German people provoked Hitler to target the Jews.[132] Like other African Americans angry with the hypocrisy of European "liberalism," Dennis asked the U.S. establishment to show why German expansionism and racism was any different from U.S. expansionism and racism.[133] And like other African Americans, from the communists to fascists like himself, Dennis betrayed a soft spot for the Japanese and the Ethiopians.[134] Dennis's sentiments toward the Japanese and Ethiopians were not representative of U.S. fascism and conservatism, since the fascists were more inclined to follow the wisdom of Lothrop Stoddard that the revolutionary instincts of the colored peoples of the world must be stopped in their tracks.[135] Dennis, a black fascist, was not immune to the sentiments of Afro-Asian traffic that engulfed African America.

Time to Spit Fire!

In the early years of the twentieth century, raciology could not subsume the currents of anti-imperialist thought that swept Africa and Asia. After the Berlin Conference of 1884–85, at which Europe's leaders partitioned and scrambled for Africa, the British colluded with the Italians to gain access to the strategic Ethiopian highlands and ports—as did the sultan of Obbia, who took shelter with the Italians as he fought off a challenge from the sultan of Zanzibar.[136] At Adowa on February 29, 1896, however, the astute Ethiopian leader Ras Makonnen outsmarted General Baratieri's troops. This was the first major defeat of a modern European power at the hands of the dusky people of the world, and its memory travels across the generations. From Adowa we get the Rastafarian idea of "Ethiopia" as the font of freedom and autonomy. (Rastafarianism was named for Ras Tafari, Haile Selassie, emperor of Ethiopia.) Only after this battle did the intellectuals of the Black Atlantic revisit the biblical mention of Ethiopia, and see in it a presage of the rise of the kingdom of liberation. But Adowa's glory transcended those who claimed African descent, for Tao Menghe in distant China called the battle "the first thunderclap of the colored races."[137] In 1904, the Japanese army removed the shine off racist imperialism with their defeat of the Russians at Port Arthur. As the first Asian power to defeat a European army in a modern war, Japan raised its stature in the eyes of Asians (from Zhangshan, who said that "we regarded the Japanese victory as our victory," to Nehru, who wrote that "Japanese victories stirred up my enthusiasm") as well as Africans.[138] In 1935, when the Italians tried to take Ethiopia once again, George Padmore, a major intellectual figure of the Black Atlantic proudly wrote in the African American journal *The Crisis* "that the Ethiopians and the Japanese are the only two colonial nations which have ever defeated white powers at arms."[139] Ethiopia of the 1930s was as important to Afro-Asian solidarity as Spain was to the communism of Europe. The two symbols of Afro-Asian military antiracism, Japan and Ethiopia, came together to oust the Europeans, even if this new Maginot Line was to be forged in the vise of multicolored fascism.

In 1930, Ras Tafari was crowned as Haile Selassie, Lion of Judah, and across the Black Atlantic rang the biblical psalm 68: 31, "Princes shall come out of Egypt; Ethiopia shall soon stretch out her hands unto God." Before the kingdom could settle into a rhythm of development, the Italians began to undermine it from their forward base in Somalia. Selassie sent his foreign minister to Japan right after his coronation, putatively to felicitate Emperor Hirohito on his 1926 coronation. Envoy Blattengueta Herouy Wolde Selassie's real mission was to see Japanese modernity firsthand and to open channels for commercial exchanges. Ethiopia and Japan forged an Afro-Asian alliance against a racist imperialism, even as both had their own imperial ambitions. Upon his return to Ethiopia, the foreign minister wrote a book that praised Japan and offered it as a model for the nonwhite world. Indeed, the Ethiopian constitution of 1931 was modeled after the Japanese constitution from 1889.[140] In 1931 an Ethiopian trade commission traveled to Japan and by 1932 Japanese goods entered the horn of Africa "causing a great deal of adverse comments by the European traders."[141] "This is what the white man does not like," George Padmore noted. "A colored nation trading with another at their expense. This is intolerable!"[142] Writing for *The Crisis*, J. A. Rogers put the case eloquently:

> Japan is now the chief business competitor of the white nations in the Indian Ocean. Already she dominates the East African trade. Her cotton goods have crowded out European and American ones in the Abyssinian market. The white man's commercial day in the Indian Ocean is ended, unless he is willing to increase the purchasing power of the natives by giving them higher wages and a better price for their products, which he is not likely to do. Today the natives, who are very poor, even according to European standards, must buy, if at all, low-priced products such as those furnished by Japan, China and India. Already Japan has a concession of land in Abyssinia the size of New Jersey. Nippon aims at nothing less than control of the Indian Ocean. Further, the Ethiopians are more friendly to the Japanese than to the white man. Most Africans, black, yellow or brown, and even white, detest European whites and with cause. Is there an understanding between Japan and Ethiopia in case of an attack by Italy? We do not know. The European powers recently used their influence to prevent the marriage of an Abyssinian prince and a Japanese noblewoman.[143]

How do we understand this African American jubilation to events in Ethiopia and Japan? Historian Winston James has done an excellent job showing us how the class politics of Harlem in the early decades of the twentieth century were so thoroughly informed by both an antiracist and a racialist dimension.[144] Both the Universal Negro Improvement Association (UNIA) and the African Blood Brotherhood dealt with the pulls between a socialist vision and a racialist one, a vision of blood solidarity and one of working-class assertion, and in most cases, these movements simultaneously held together both tendencies. The relationship between Japanese radicals and the African American community also worked in the maw of this contradiction, on the one hand, torn toward a unity of the oppressed against imperialism, and on the other hand, driven to a "race war" along the terrain sketched out by white supremacists.[145] If we tend to think of W. E. B. Du Bois as the representative of the first strand and Marcus Garvey of the second, what do we make when both of them vigorously support the struggles of the Irish (and equate India, Egypt, and Ireland as the mainstays in the anti-imperialist battle)?[146] Certainly the tendency of Du Bois was to favor socialist anti-imperialism which was aware of the color line, while Garvey went more in the direction of the "race war," but both felt pressure from a similar contradiction. This dynamic was most clearly apparent in relation to Japan in the interwar years.

In 1918, Du Bois declined to support U.S. entry into the war against Japan and China, because he felt that such a battle would be "based on color prejudice." How could one support the United States against China, he wrote, which was at the time "the most ruthless exploiter of Chinese labor and a nation that passed and maintains the Chinese Exclusion Act."[147] The idea of Japan as the Ethiopia of Asia was alive and well in the African American community and there was widespread dissatisfaction with U.S. policy, so that Garvey too declared in 1918 that "we hope that Japan will succeed in impressing upon her white brothers at the Peace Conference [at Versailles] the essentiality of abolishing racial discrimination." Tugged by racialism (or pluralism), Garvey indicated that the war allowed Japan to become "the acknowledged leader of the yellow races," and since the "white races are already leading themselves, the Negro must now concentrate on his leadership."[148] From antiracist struggle, we divert to a racialist nationalism.

The immense feeling of solidarity among Asians and blacks in the streets of the United States was developed from both the fascists and the communists, from the Right and the Left. After 1941, Japan returned to the radar of the United States, and only then did some of the less grounded African American writers find a proliferation of Japanese radicals with some prestige within working-class black neighborhoods. In early 1942, the FBI arrested a Filipino man by the name of Policarpio Manasala who was also known in the literature as Doctor O. Takis and Mimo De Guzman, and is now known as Ashima Takis.[149] The government dug into its files, including the meticulous notes of Special Agent P-138 who gave them so much on Garvey, to create a picture of sustained connection between Japanese and African Americans. In 1932, Takis "showed up at the home of a Negro named Burt T. Cornish, an elevator operator in St. Louis who was active in fraternal affairs."[150] Takis, Cornish, and others formed the Pacific Movement of the Eastern World (PMEW) and came into contact with Robert O. Jordon (known by those who disliked him as the "Harlem Hitler"), a Garveyite from Jamaica, who came to Harlem in 1920. PMEW, according to Takis, used Japanese government funds to assist African American socioeconomic development. In Garvey's UNIA, Takis argued that "the Japanese are colored people, like you," and "the white governments do not give the negro any consideration." In 1935 when the Ethiopia war was in the offing, Jordan and Takis with Yasuichi Hikida formed the Ethiopia Pacific League (called by some "Tojo's Movement"), which would soon have a membership of five thousand. With hatred for Jim Crow in his eyes, Jordan could not see Japan's conquest of China as imperialism, and nor was he able to fully grasp the heinousness of Nazism. Far more important, for him and for others, was the hope of an alliance against white supremacy, and one grounded in an alliance of those who felt its brunt. This was not an unusual sentiment, for as the war against Japan became imminent, many African Americans, notably leaders of the NAACP, evinced an ambivalence toward the conflict, since they felt that this was a case of "today *them*, tomorrow *us*."[151] There was more buoyancy about the defense of the Spanish Republic, or the desire to fight the Italians in Ethiopia, than to battle the East Asians.[152] The sentiment for solidarity went both ways. While white officers encouraged the Japanese American troops in the 442d Regimental Combat Team to use "white facilities," the Nisei troops felt "uncomfortable with the double standard and sympathetic to the blacks." In some cases, German POWs enjoyed "white" status, while black and Nisei troops remained on the other side of the color line. "Among us," Mike Masaoka remembers, "discrimination became the subject of many intense discussions, out of which developed a deep new sense of social justice involving others as well as ourselves."[153] Deep solidarity was felt by the delegates (and a young Harry Haywood) at the 1936 National Negro Congress when secretary John P. Davis read Mao Ze-dong's message to the Congress and in support of Ethiopia against the Italian invasion. "This struggle must spur you on to strengthen your ranks in a united fighting front, guided by the program of the militant Negro leaders which today raises its voice for a determined struggle for freedom."[154]

Meanwhile, on the streets of Detroit, a Japanese radical Satohata Takahashi came into contact with Abdul Mohammed in the 1933 to form the Society for the Development of Our Own (SDOO).[155] Takahashi, like Takis, was linked to the Kokuryukai or the Black Dragon Society, which assisted the Japanese government in the 1910 invasion of Korea and the 1931 invasion of Manchuria. The SDOO also attracted about five thousand people (mainly African American, with some Filipinos and Indians), but its real influence came over the Allah Temple of Islam (ATI) (Elijah Muhammad's first foray into organized religion). Takahashi spoke at the ATI and he greatly influenced Elijah Muhammad, whose speeches began to take on a pro-Japan racialist cast—"the Japanese will slaughter the white man." Elijah Muhammad told his followers, as well, that the Mother Ship of the "Asiatic Black Man" was being made by the Japanese.[156] If Elijah Muhammad drew from Takahashi, the Japanese radical took from Garvey, whose self-determination ideology was derived wholesale by Takahashi: "Let us organize ourselves for one aim and one destiny under this organization. We must do this, because we are living in a critical time, a time for dark peoples to organize for one common cause."[157] Takahashi's group in Detroit was affected when the Muslims felt the wrath of the FBI, at which point Takahashi sent one of his young men to Harlem. That young man was Takis.

Takis walked the radical terrain created by the Communist Sen Katayama (1859–1933) within the African American Community. Katayama came to the United States in 1884 and rubbed shoulders with African Americans as a farm laborer, houseboy, cook, and later as a student in Tennessee.[158] A founding member of the U.S. Communist Party, Katayama was also given much respect within Garveyite circles. Special Agent P-138 met with Hudson Price, the associate editor of *Negro World*, in 1920, who told him that "there were two Japanese whom were very much in sympathy with Garvey's movement and he said that means a great deal to them as the Japs were smart people." One of those men was Katayama.[159] In the early 1920s, Katayama earned the respect of Claude McKay and Harry Haywood, U.S. representatives at the Fourth Communist International meetings in Moscow, when Katayama ensured that McKay speak at the open meeting.[160] Here is how Harry Haywood remembers the "Old Man":

> Sen Katayama, the veteran Japanese communist, was a special friend of the Black students in Moscow. He was born to a Japanese peasant family, was educated in the U.S. and became one of the founders of the Japanese Social Democratic Party in 1901. A member of the ECCI, he had spent several years in exile in the U.S. and was considered somewhat of an expert on the Afro-American question. Katayama was most interested in our studies and our views on the situation in the U.S., particularly as it concerned Blacks.

"Old Man" Katayama knew all about white folks, and we Black students regarded him as one of us. We often came to him with our problems and he always had a receptive ear. It was Katayama who told us of Lenin's earlier writings about U.S. Blacks and Lenin's views on the Black Belt. He died in Moscow in 1933 at the age of 74.[161]

Katayama's culturally complex biography points the way for a better analysis of the world of the PMEW and SDOO, for Old Man Katayama tapped into a well of solidarity that could either come out as a socialism well aware of racist domination or else as a racialism, but both at work on the same terrain of oppression. This perhaps explains why the U.S. Communist Party, founded by Katayama, would ask Takis to speak at a 1933 St. Louis rally.[162] These experiments in cultural complexity worked on a terrain suffused with racialist and nationalist ideas that twisted around each other like snakes around a vine: to ignore them or to start from elsewhere would not have been entirely possible. I'm not interested in a nostalgic look at *this kind* of culturally mingled practice. Rather, the historical moment provides a window on to the complex terrain of action created by the very diverse social world of what are falsely seen as zones inhabited by one or another "people."

Despite widespread recognition of Japanese expansionism in Asia,[163] then, Africans and African Americans differentiated between Japanese colonial ambition and that of Europeans. Du Bois put the case plainly: "Japan is regarded by all colored peoples as their logical leader, as the one non-white nation which has escaped forever the dominance and exploitation of the white world. No matter what Japan does or how she does it, excuse leaps to the lips of colored thinkers."[164] Expansionism in Asia was a fact, but Japan uses the "same methods" that white Europe has used, military power and commercial exploitation." The real difference, according to Du Bois, is this, that Japan's "program cannot be one based on race hate for the conquered, since racially these latter are one with the Japanese and are recognized as blood relatives. Their eventual assimilation, the accord of social equality to them, will present no real problem."[165] The admission of Japan as an ally, however fraught, came side by side with a militant and informed reaction from the African American masses. Not only did African Americans want to go to help defend Ethiopia, but also on May 18, 1936, several African American organizations led their members onto Harlem's streets in response to Italian atrocities in Addis Ababa, a testament to the depth of solidarity with the Ethiopians.[166]

In May 1934, the YMCA on West 135th Street in New York City held a meeting on the problem of Japanese expansionism. Dunje Omuru, a Japanese graduate student, claimed that Japan was "laying the foundation for the rest of the darker races to get similar respect." W. A. Domingo, the Jamaican president of the Inter-racial Forum, and H. Wong, a Chinese member of the Anti-Imperialist League, argued against Omuru, taking the view that "Japan was not interested in human welfare but only in markets to sell cheap goods and sources of raw materials." Wong raised a pertinent question at the end of his talk, "if Japan cannot deal squarely with the people in Korea and Manchuria, which are near to her, who are their blood brothers, how can we expect them to be any better friends to colored people?"[167] The contradictions of racism penetrated communities of color, many people of which made an attempt to slide under the radar of raciology whether through their association with Aryanism or through their attempt to put themselves forward as regional powers. Even as the Japanese government championed the "colored races," it was loath to being compared with Africans. In 1933, the Japanese government lodged a formal protest against Nazi racism ("the government and the people of Japan are highly indignant at Germany's holding us inferior"). "Even in the United States," the Japanese Foreign Office noted, "Japanese are not subjected to the same treatment as Negroes."[168] Wong and Domingo rightly critiqued the Japanese state for its complicity with racism, but simultaneously Omuru was right that Japan was a symbol for the "colored races," a symbol despite xenophobia, and without, as Du Bois noted, "race hate."[169]

The "race state" of Europe predates fascism, but it is in the fascist state that Europe brought the logic of racism to bear against its own population. Outside Europe the forces of national liberation began to make themselves felt, but on the terrain both of a nostalgic cosmopolitanism and a pragmatic racialism. Cultural complexity had a value, but most of the national liberationists saw it either as a benevolent relic of the past or else a pragmatic instrument well developed in the socialist tradition as internationalism. The idea of complex fellowship was largely absent. Beside the nostalgic cosmopolitanism (or socialist internationalism) sat a rather well-known racism, which made itself manifest in the Ethiopian and Japanese nationalist idea of culture. Resistance to racist imperialism came, then, both on the terrain of racism and in opposition to it.

In Vasco's Wake

Despite the defeat of Nazism, racist thought is by now sedimented in our social practice, five hundred years after Vasco da Gama took his turn around the Cape of Good Hope, a misnamed cape if there ever was one. Indeed, when 1998 rolled around there was some talk about a celebration of the event on the scale of the five hundredth anniversary of Columbus's feat, but neither the revelry nor the protests matched the fervor of 1992. The festivity around Columbus entered battles over the curriculum of the U.S. schools and over the way in which the United States chooses to remember its foundation in genocide. The irony was that Columbus never set foot in the United States, but his Caribbean sojourn continues, in most quarters, to provide the genesis for the history of this New World (far better to start one's history with discovery than with genocide, that is, if we set aside the millennia of history made by native peoples before Columbus's jaunt). All attention in the 1990s, then, was on Columbus, this not so much to do with the declined power of the Iberian Peninsula whose corroded imperial glory was less about capitalism than the highest stage of feudalism. The emphasis on Columbus had to do with the U.S. media and the hegemony of the U.S. state after the decline of the USSR.

Da Gama's commemoration was far less dramatic: an academic conference here and there, a few books on the man, and Expo-98 organized by the Portuguese government. The Indian government refused to participate in the events, and sporadic protests occurred across the coastline, from Goa to Kerala. Da Gama's biographer Sanjay Subrahmanyam quite correctly noted that the comparison between da Gama and Columbus "is historically more than a little problematic"; one cannot draw a straight line from da Gama and the eighteenth century to call him the forerunner of colonialism, and further, that da Gama "was probably opposed to the imperial ideology espoused by the Portuguese state in his own period."[170] All this is perhaps true, but nonetheless the entry of da Gama ushered in a dynamic whose fuel in time would be the virulent racism that forms the warp and weft of our social relations. Race is here to stay, it seems, with all its psychosocial and economic violence. Columbus and da Gama operate as metaphors for how our world entered modernity: by the genocide in the New World (Columbus) and by the end to the cosmopolitanism of the Old World (da Gama).

Salman Rushdie wrote the best elegy for the old cosmopolitan world in *The Moor's Last Sigh* (1995). Moraes Zogoiby, known as the Moor, is born of the da Gama–Zogoiby dynasty among the Jewish community of Cochin in the state of Kerala. The cultural world of the Indian Ocean lives on in the Moor's consciousness, and it is this historical memory, and its practices, that is under challenge from the fascistic politics of Raman Fielding (based on the reactionary Shiv Sena leader in western India, Bal Thackerey). At the novel's end, the Moor travels to Andalusia to visit his reprobate and reclusive father, Vasco Miranda.[171] As they climb the stairs of the father's home, Vasco tells his son the familiar joke about when the Lone Ranger and Tonto are surrounded by hostile Native Americans. "We're surrounded," says the Lone Ranger, and Tonto, ever the wit, replies, "What do you mean *we*, white man?" The Moor digests this joke and then offers us what is perhaps his analysis of the last sigh of cosmopolitanism in our world:

> In a way I had been in Indian country all my life, learning to read its signs, to follow its trails, rejoicing in its immensity, in its inexhaustible beauty, struggling for territory, sending up smoke signals, beating its drums, pushing out its frontiers, making my way through its dangers, hoping to find friends, fearing its cruelty, longing for its love. Not even an Indian was safe in Indian country; not if he was the wrong sort of Indian, anyway—wearing the wrong sort of head-dress, speaking the wrong language, dancing the wrong dances, worshipping the wrong gods, travelling in the wrong company. I wondered how considerate those warriors encircling the masked man with the silver bullets would have been toward his fellow-headed pal. In Indian country, there was no room for a man who didn't want to belong to a tribe, who dreamed of moving beyond; of peeling off his skin and revealing his secret identity—the secret, that is, of the identity of all men—of standing before the war-painted braves to unveil the flayed and naked unity of the flesh.[172]

The desire to go beyond skin does not necessarily mean to plunge oneself into the socially impossible world of individuality. We are social beings who make communities with an urgency, and it is a stern charge to make us take refuge in the lonely world of oneself. What Rushdie seems to imply and what this book takes as its central point is that human identity is constructed atop the "flayed and naked unity of the flesh" and that the cultures we produce are multifaceted and multivalent, that they borrow from as much as they tend to disagree with each other. Racism attempts to occlude our cosmopolitanism (of the songs in and out of our bones), and it often appropriates our mild forms of xenophobia into its own virulent project. Difference among peoples is something that we negotiate in our everyday interactions, asking questions and being better informed of our mutual realities. To transform difference into the body is an act of bad faith, a denial of our shared nakedness.

Chapter 2

The American Ideology

W. E. B. Du Bois proclaimed that the problem of the twentieth century would be the problem of the color line.[1] Indeed, looking back at a century of racist oppression, Du Bois could only have judged that the hundred years ahead would mirror its past, and that the main fights for progressive forces would be along the color line. In 1900 Pan-Africanist intellectuals gathered in London to "encourage a feeling of unity and to facilitate friendly intercourse among Africans in general; to promote and protect the interests of all subjects claiming African descent."[2] It was at this gathering that Du Bois first enunciated his dictum, in trepidation and with hope for the world to come.

Anticolonialism in the entire oppressed world threw down a severe challenge to colonial puissance, whether through countless acts of disorganized resistance or through the sporadic organizations of anticolonialism. The fights of the anticolonial and antiracist forces produced the social democratic agenda of the elite, whose concessions, whether of the Great Society or the Scandinavian variety, came in response to the challenges from below. Withdrawal of colonial rule in the 1940s and 1950s—India/Pakistan in 1947, Indonesia in 1948, and Ghana in 1957—was met with a shift in strategy from the captains of capitalism, who produced a phenomenon that the first president of Ghana, Kwame Nkrumah, was to quickly label "neocolonialism." "The essence of neocolonialism," wrote Nkrumah, "is that the State which is subject to it is, in theory, independent and has all the outward trappings of international sovereignty. In reality its economic system and thus its political policy is directed from outside," by which he meant by mainly U.S. and

European finance capital.[3] During the era of neocolonialism, the presence of the USSR allowed the nascent "Third World" to lobby between the powers for the means of development. As the USSR collapsed in the 1990s, neocolonialism was replaced by the theory of neoliberalism in which freedom came to mean liberty of the moneyed to act unburdened by notions of justice and democracy.[4] Neoliberalism threatens us with the reproach of equality, and forbids us to create organizational platforms based on our historical and current oppression. To fight against racism is twisted into a racist act, for to invoke race even in a progressive antiracist agenda is seen as divisive. The same may be said of other oppressions: Did feminism produce a high divorce rate, or didn't sexism set the terms for the failure of companionate marriages? Are people poor because of trade unions or because of the ravages of profit?

The problem of the twenty-first century, then, is the problem of the color blind. This problem is simple: it believes that to redress racism, we need to *not* consider race in social practice, notably in the sphere of governmental action. The state, we are told, must be *above* race. It must not actively discriminate against people on the basis of race in its actions. At the dawn of a new millennium, there is widespread satisfaction of the progress on the "race problem"; this is so to some extent, but the compass of attacks against blacks and Latinos remains routine. If we do not live by 1896's *Plessy v. Ferguson,* we continue to live by its principle axiom—that "race" is a formal and individual designation and not a historical and social one.[5] That is, we are led to believe that racism is a prejudicial behavior of one party against another rather than the coagulation of socioeconomic injustice against groups. If the state acts without prejudice (that is, if it acts equally), then that is proof of the end of racism. Unequal socioeconomic conditions of today, based as they are on racisms of the past and of the present, are thereby rendered untouchable by the state. Color-blind justice privatizes inequality and racism, and it removes itself from the project of redistributive and anti-racist justice. This is the genteel racism of our new millennium.

In this chapter I propose to settle accounts with the two major theoretical and political approaches to racism. The first is that of the color blind, for this is the dominant framework that stretches from neoconservatives to all manner of liberals, and frequently includes people of all colors, many of whom have "made it" (often at great odds, and with the immense effort of families and friends—an effort that is generally ignored when their success is touted). Cultural critic Michael Eric Dyson correctly notes Martin Luther King Jr.'s use of an argument "beyond race" in which he conceived of color

blindness as "a crushing blow to the pigmented morality of white chauvinists."[6] While today King's words ("content of their character" not "color of
their skin") are used against antiracists, in his own day King deployed a kind
of color-blind argument to pledge a black humanity, forged in slavery, survival, and struggle, to the reconstruction of society, not the maintenance of
extant social relations. Against King, color blindness is generally used in our
day as a way to argue that things must remain the same, for the structural
features of racism cannot be touched by the manner in which contemporary
color blindness operates.

If color blindness occludes the stuctures and practices of actually existing racism, a kind of primordialism puts too much stake in race. Despite
all indications that race is not a phenomenon that can be gleaned in the
bloodstream,[7] but that it is a social institution, those who advocate a primordialism see race both as people organized by the color of their skin and by
genetic predispositions. The most virulent practitioners of this line of argument are the militant and illiberal white supremacists, such as those who
congregate in the militia movement, the fascist brigades, the Ku Klux Klan,
and other such monstrous organizations. I limit my discussion of their position here mainly because the arguments are well made elsewhere.[8]

Beyond the color blind and the primordial is the problem of multiculturalism. It is currently the most compelling framework for a supposed social justice movement, but as literary critic Stanley Fish puts it so clearly,
there is no justifiable principle for multiculturalism.[9] "Boutique multiculturalists" who like the faddishness of difference cannot be taken seriously,
since they reduce different ways of life to superficial tokens that they can
harness as style, but refuse to engage with those parts of difference with
which they disagree. In short, they want the fun, but not the fundamentalism. "Strong multiculturalists" claim to tolerate difference, but, often only if
what differs is a kind of "reasonable" difference (thereby joining ranks with
cultural browsers). Fish argues that since few people in the world live in homogeneous zones, it behooves us all to be multiculturalists. The tolerance
we practice should be based on a kind of "inspired adhoccery" where we
make decisions on the fly and not based on any regulated principles.[10] I
admit there is something attractive about unregulated life, about existence
along the grain of the quotidian choices made by people. What is unclear
from Fish is whether there is any power for the regulation of the ethical
choices we make and the acts we commit in our everyday lives. I'm not keen
on a life governed by the anarchical production of morality by a free market.
My sense of "inspired adhoccery" is that a population galvanized by the

struggle for social justice willfully creates principles of and institutions for interaction and then mediates those principles through itself.

Multiculturalism is a principle for the regulation of social life from above, one that can only fitfully find itself in the sorts of struggles that produce the values of interaction from below. A close engagement with the concept of multiculturalism allows us to cultivate the category of the polycultural, one that not only encourages the inherent complexity of cultures, but that also stakes its claim to political, and delimited, claims rather than the pretense of universal, and nonembodied, values. But more on that later.

The Color Blind

The moral and political weight of the civil rights movement forced a recalcitrant U.S. government to offer some rights to disenfranchised sections of the population. There was little hope, in 1965, that the United States government would go beyond its own minimalist definition of "human rights" (as habeas corpus) given its refusal to endorse the socioeconomic side of the UN's Universal Declaration of Human Rights (1948). When Martin Luther King Jr. and others turned to the question of poverty (to launch the "poor people's movement"), they made a claim for a maximalist notion of "human rights"—not just the right to civil liberties, but also to a home, to a job, to education, and to dignity (articles 23–27 of the 1948 declaration). Instead of taking on this more comprehensive demand, the civil rights movement was offered a modest program for redressal: affirmative action and the franchise.[11] To deal with the theft of labor of people of certain "races" (in the form of chattel slavery, and also debt peonage in agriculture, industry, and service), the state proposed to make an effort to produce some measure of equality. The state was forced to act on behalf of those for whom it had rarely acted; it had to abjure its formal or ceremonial sense of distance from the inequalities of society. Of course, the state is never neutral, since it either absents itself when the powerful exercise their might or else it acts for them, often seeming to be nothing more than a chamber of commerce. When the Constitution enshrined the right to private property, it made inviolable the basis of social inequality and, in fact, became the protector of the propertied classes. Affirmative action, as an unobtrusive gesture, was the compromise afforded by the propertied to end social unrest.

A generation before affirmative action was institutionalized, the United States proposed to rebuild Europe (the Marshall Plan) and Japan (the occupation from 1946–53) after World War II, yet there was to be no such provision of funds to African and Asian states who crept out of the harrow of colonialism. The International Monetary Fund (IMF) and the World Bank did not provide funds to this new "Third World" with the same generosity of spirit as the Marshall Plan had (the reconstruction of Japan was perhaps due to guilt for Hiroshima and Nagasaki).[12] The U.S. attitude to Africa, for instance, was marked, on the one hand, by the 1961 assassination of the first premier of the Democratic Republic of the Congo, Patrice Lumumba, and, on the other hand, by the use of new leader Mobuto Sese Seko for U.S. corporate ends. From 1961 to 1977, for example, U.S. firms invested $1 billion in the excavation of raw materials as well as $500 million in commercial bank loans toward the creation of infrastructure to facilitate export. Lest one think that this money was for charitable purposes (a kind of international "affirmative action"), the U.S. firms expropriated $2.9 billion between 1965 and 1975.[13]

If African Americans did not receive a domestic program of reparations for the injustices of history, as well as for the production of a democratic citizenry, Africa itself (and much of Asia and Latin America) was to be further exploited. The denial of the socioeconomic rights of the formerly colonized peoples was couched in various arguments about the Third World's excessive population (neo-Malthusianism), its retrogressive cultures and lack of democracy (neo-Weberianism), and its unfortunate comparative disadvantage in economic terms (neoclassical economics). These are the cognates of the claim that reparations for African Americans are "handouts" or "charity" rather than the overdue bill for centuries of unpaid labor. While domestic affirmative action and international aid became the mild forms of redress offered by the U.S. government, it was not a concession that came easily. Nathan Glazer and Daniel Patrick Moynihan used their scholarly credentials and political access to question the policy from its inception. "Nothing was more dramatic than the rise of this practice [of quotas] on the part of the American government in the 1960s, *at the very moment it was being declared abhorrent and illegal.*"[14] The message here was that if a concept is by fiat made illegal, then it disappears: there is no need to act against it, just ignore its impact on history. "The nation is by government action increasingly divided into racial and ethnic categories with different origins," Glazer argued. "New lines of conflict are created by government action. New resentments are created; new turf is to be protected; new angers arise; and one sees them on both sides of the line."[15] Rather than seeing these conflicts as the legacy of de jure racism, neo-conservatives like Glazer and Moynihan produced a discourse of de facto racism that blamed the state for inequities just as it tried to mend, perhaps quixotically, racist socioeconomic relations. Within this line of thought, affirmative action, rather than racism, was to bear the burden of social dysfunction. Thomas Sowell provided an early example of a logic that has become all too familiar now: those who are assisted by affirmative action are stigmatized by it.[16] Racism did not stigmatize people; affirmative action did.

If affirmative action and other state social redressal policies came under fire from the neoconservatives, they drew upon race itself to buttress their arsenal.[17] "Let me be blunt," Daniel Moynihan wrote in 1968, "if ethnic quotas are to be imposed on American universities and similarly quasi-public institutions, it is the Jew who will be almost driven out."[18] The role played by the figure of the Jew in the 1960s was to be farcically adopted by the Asian American from the 1980s onward. And we heard it spectacularly from Ronald Reagan, who called Asians "our exemplars of hope and inspiration" (the compliment was returned by an Asian, Dinesh D'Souza, who extolled the rise of Reagan from an "ordinary man" into an "extraordinary leader").[19] The "Jew" and the "Asian American" provide a singularly useful way to attack the problem of equity. Phrased in terms of "overrepresentation" and "merit," these minorities, it is argued by some, would be hurt by social engineering since they are (1) already overrepresented in the professions and (2) they would face quotas that would impinge on their métier. During a Heritage Foundation event on affirmative action in the 1980s, Representative Dana Rohrabacker (Rep-CA) had the bad taste to say that he used Asians as "a vehicle to show that America has made a mistake on affirmative action."[20] Asians are used in this instance, then, as a weapon against the most modest form of redistribution devised by the state.

In the international arena, the proponents of neoliberal economic policies use the sometime success of the so-called East Asian tigers to undermine the African, Latin American, and other Asian states' claims to reassess the terms of trade and debt policies (much of this enunciated in the now defunct UN Commission on Trade and Development under the guidance of the Argentine economist Raúl Prebisch). A global amnesia forgets that the success of the "tigers" was short-lived, produced in relatively small states (South Korea, Taiwan, Hong Kong, Singapore), and created not so much by deregulation and the "free market," but by strong state redistribution of land and of price controls.[21] Despite this well-documented history, there is a tendency to assess the "tragedy of Africa" through the lens of helplessness (at worst) and charity (at best), especially when compared to the "miracles of East Asia." The parallels with the domestic "model minority" stereotype are clear.

In his *Foreign Affairs* essay "Social Capital and the Global Economy," for example, State Department social theorist Francis Fukuyama offers Asian Americans and Asia as models of civic values. He berates African Americans whose problems he believes are created by "single-parent families" and weak "larger social groups" and Africa for its deficiency of "voluntary associations outside kinship."[22] These are standard and inaccurate tropes both of Africa and of African Americans.

Fukuyama's view is not unusual, for the popular press tells us that Asian Americans succeed "essentially without the benefit of affirmative action."[23] Most of us are familiar with the idea of the "model minority," and indeed there are several strong denunciations of the myth. What is not so clear is the means by which this stereotype is used not just to uplift Asians, but pointedly to demean blacks and Latinos.[24] "The black leadership has dominated the discussion [on civil rights]," Ed Koch noted a few years ago. "The Asian Americans, because all they ask for is to be treated equally, have not played a part in the discussion."[25] The implication is that blacks want special treatment and believe themselves to be entitled to something more than other Americans. This special and unfair treatment does not go without a victim, we are told; Jerry Reynolds of the Center for Equal Opportunity argues that "any time racial preferences are used, there's a victim. And in California, the victim often has an Asian face."[26] Stephen Nakashima, the Asian community's Ward Connerly, argued along this grain that "discrimination in any form inflicts unjust injury upon its victims; the injury is no less because the person who, or the institution which, inflicts it purports to act with good intention."[27] The argument was made most spectacularly, if rather wantingly, by Bob Dole during his run for the presidency. On March 23, 1996, Dole gave a speech at the Little Saigon Shopping Mall in Orange County to a mainly Republican Vietnamese audience. "We ought to do away with preferences," he said in his noncommittal style. "It ought to be based on merit. This is America and it ought to be based on merit."[28] Following up on the lines of Dole and others, we then heard from Susan Au Allen (head of the Pan-Asian American Chamber of Commerce, whose most famous act was to help scuttle the nomination of Bill Lam Lee to the Clinton justice department). In a profile of her she claimed that

> We are not asking for privileges. We don't ask ourselves what this or that bit of civil rights legislation will do for us. All we want is the chance to work hard for our families, keep more of what we earn, and not have our children kept out of good schools when their grades and test scores show they should get in.[29]

Essentially the argument is that Asians are good citizens and hardworking; they do not need state assistance. Blacks need state assistance; they must be bad citizens and lazy. This is the chain of reason for the color blind.

There are many reasons why the argument of the color blind appeals to some Asians.[30] Beyond the idiosyncrasies of national origins, there are class reasons for making common cause with the Right: the "leaders" of the community come from professional and merchant fractions of the elite and not from the working-class segment. Therefore, while most Asian Americans powerful enough to have their voices heard supported the end of affirmative action in California, 61 percent of Asians voted to save it.[31] For Asians who enter the United States under the good graces of the 1965 Immigration Act, few have a sufficient grasp of the civil rights struggle and its legacy. We have eaten the fruits of the struggle, of the educational systems set in place in our socialized societies (India, China, Vietnam, and Japan), and of the scrupulous screening of the Immigration and Naturalization Service (INS). The process of *state-selection* endows us with arrogance about "merit" and ability without any historical acknowledgment of the forces that produced us. "Asian Americans are inconvenienced, perhaps, but not hurt," Emil Guillermo puts it nicely. "If anything Asian Americans should be proud that the system works, and that we more often than not can compete on merit. We shouldn't be dragged into the racially charged political debate as 'victimized overachievers.'"[32]

In order to combat the idea of the color-blind state policy, itself a divisive instrument cloaked as unifying one, it's important to offer an account of the affirmative privilege obscured by the current arguments. Asian Americans are in the spotlight in the battle over state-funded public schools. The mission of public education is to alleviate gross inequities by the production of skills in the general population. The Asian American is used as an instrument to show how these schools discriminate against Asian Americans in favor of blacks and Latinos, that Asian American merit is squandered on behalf of the process of equity. In private schools, however, where Asian Americans are discriminated against in favor of whites, there is no talk of the Asian American. In fact, there is silence on the problem of affirmative privilege and the disregard to merit when it comes to children of alumni (or legacy admissions) and other such markers of privilege. If the merit argument is to have any credence, then we should take it all the way and raze the edifice of privilege. Instead, the Asian American is used to tear down public institutions, while the discrimination of the private sector keeps affirmative privilege intact. This is part of the overall attempt to dismantle state institutions and shift state funds from mass education to private education (vouchers, and so forth).

Consistent struggle has raised the problem of discrimination on to the U.S. agenda. In the 1980s, for example, the problem of quotas in private schools did make a brief appearance. At Harvard University, for instance, Asian Americans applicants had to get forty points more on the SATs than white applicants got. Of those Asians who applied to Harvard, the college accepted 13.3 percent; of white applicants, the college welcomed 17 percent.[33] Some of this is because of the legacy system, by which 20 percent of Harvard's incoming class are children of alumni. Legacy, a system set up in the 1920s to stem Jewish admissions into Ivy League colleges, allows colleges to affirm privilege and to maintain the status quo. In 1992, Harvard admitted more legacy students than black, Chicano, Native American, and Puerto Rican students combined.[34] When the United States Court of Appeals for the Fifth Circuit upheld *Hopwood v. State of Texas* in 1996 to end affirmative action in Texas, Representative Lon Burham put forward a quixotic bill in the Texas legislature to outlaw legacy admissions. "There has been racially and class-based discrimination that benefits upper-income white kids," he said. "It doesn't take a lot of imagination to figure out this is what the schools are doing."[35] If racism secured certain preferences for whites in the past, then these unjustly acquired benefits are preserved into the present through such programs as legacy admissions (and then held in trust as these children secure admission for their children, regardless of merit).[36]

Education is only one avenue to gauge affirmative privilege. J. Morgan Kousser's comprehensive book shows us how the arena of voting rights is also encumbered by privileges of the past.[37] The theft of the 2000 elections in Florida confirms Kousser's analysis, and should give us pause on the question of a just franchise. George Lipsitz's summary on the "possessive investment in whiteness" traces how housing discrimination (and the creation of equity), transportation subsidies, corporate welfare, and other such parts of the system of affirmative privilege act against people of color.[38] When the U.S. House Progressive Caucus put forward HR 1278: Corporate Welfare Reduction Act in 1995, it called for the elimination of $800 billion in tax subsidies to corporations.[39] "At a time when the poor, the children, the elderly and veterans are being asked to make sacrifices to help balance the federal budget," Representative Bernie Sanders (Ind-Vermont) argued, "those who are most able to be self-sufficient should be the first in line. Americans can no longer afford to provide tens of billions of dollars in wealthfare to aug-ment the quite adequate resources of corporations and wealthy individuals." The bill failed.

The rollback of social services within the United States is the domestic variant of "neoliberalism," the recomposition of capital to the interests of large transnational firms and to those elites who live their lives by the logic of the Dow Jones. There is little discussion of the expropriation of immense values during the period of direct colonial rule nor is there any concern for the sustained impoverishment of most of the world through the policy of indebtedness. The collapse of so many national economies is not the result of an inevitable process now known as globalization. Rather, it is partially caused by a project that seeks to maintain certain regions of the world as producers of less-valorized goods and services while others retain control over advanced technology and financial markets.[40] Public institutions that seek to redress inequality are to be downsized in favor of private institutions committed to the extraction of profit. The logical chain runs from the attack on public education in the United States to the provision of agricultural sub-sidies in India. However, the attack on the "public" is not consistent, since the U.S. and German governments remain pledged to the provision of do-mestic agrarian subsidies, just as they fight to end the same subsidies in the Third World. If there is no policy consistency, there is a remarkable coher-ence of interest—what enables the dollar and euro to maintain their fiscal prominence seems to become "international" policy; the rupee and the bhat are irrelevant.[41] Color blindness as an international ideology neglects, in bad faith, the *production* of inequality in our world by the manipulation of the finance markets to benefit those who already have wealth. After all, it is an axiom that those with wealth want to, at least, maintain, at best, enlarge, their holdings: given this conservative approach to the world's assets it should be apparent why those with a large hold on the pie commit them-selves to the political philosophy of the color blind. We are perhaps further from King's "content of their character" message than we suspect.

Afro-Dalits of the Earth, Unite!

We are even further from that message when we walk the terrain of primor-dialism. In 1993, the conservative thinker Joel Kotkin published *Tribes: How Race, Religion, and Identity Determine Success in the New Global Economy,* a well-received book in which, Kotkin argued, certain "tribes" drew upon their "vocation of uniqueness" to "shape the economic destiny of mankind."[42] There is something perverse about Kotkin's use of the word *tribe*, which generally refers to social formations held together by primordial ties (a racist concept deployed by a colonial anthropology to manage and control dissident populations).[43] Kotkin chose five "global tribes" to exemplify dynamic social groups: Jewish financiers, British imperialists, Japanese corporate executives, Chinese investors, and Indian traders. Despite his own attempt to downplay primordialism—"the global tribe has grown as much through intimate contact with other civilizations as through any intrinsic cultural superiority"—Kotkin's book was reviewed as a manifesto for the value of ethnic primordialness, at least for certain privileged communities.[44] That there was no discussion of Africa in the book bespeaks Kotkin's perversity, because a series of events around the release of *Tribes* enabled the U.S.-European media and politicians to revisit the trope of an inherently *tribal* Africa: the crisis first in Somalia (1992–93), then in Rwanda and Burundi (1994).[45] The idea of "tribal conflicts" and "ethnic antagonisms" returned to public discourse with a vengeance in the context not only of the trials in Africa, but also to explain the collapse of social life in the former USSR and Eastern Europe. The war in the Balkans and in Chechnya could be seen only through the lens of enduring, even "ancient" divisions, not in terms of political currents that shape the world today. The discourse of primordialism could find only one way to manage divisions: to bomb or blackmail people into submission so that they will accept states partitioned along tribal lines. This is the "new military humanism" of our epoch, to make ethnicity the basis of state management.[46]

In Kosovo, international agencies like the United Nations participated actively in the manufacture of borders along the lines of ethnicity. Before Kosovo, the UN was active in the retrieval of a spurious anthropological notion of "indigeous people," one deployed no doubt to deal with the ravages of bourgeois state power, but nonetheless one that tends to treat certain people as an ahistorical fetish.[47] In the early 1980s the UN set up a Working Group on Indigenous Populations that defined the indigenous in the following way:

> Indigenous communities, peoples and nations are those which having a historical continuity with pre-invasion and pre-colonial societies that developed on their territories, consider themselves distinct from other societies now prevailing in those territories or parts of them. They form at present non-dominant sectors of society and are determined to preserve,

develop and transmit to future generations their ancestral territories, and their ethnic identity, as the basis of their continued existence as peoples, in accordance with their own cultural patterns, social institutions and legal systems.[48]

There is little that recommends this definition. It is too general and it leaves too much unsaid. When does "invasion" begin and what does it mean to have "historical continuity"? Much of the interest in "invasion" refers to the American *conquista*. The idea of a foreign entity entering and then claiming a territory is not applicable everywhere. And one wonders when the "indigenous" peoples become dominant do they cease to be "indigenous" (the word *present* in the last sentence is also befuddling)? In the 1980s, the World Bank–IMF got behind the idea of the indigenous populations, they created a development agenda around the concept of the indigenous, and in 1993, the United Nations celebrated the Year of the Indigenous People. The UN–IMF notion of the indigenous people treats them in the same romantic vein as the Noble Savage, without the capacity to make their own decisions in the contradictions of the modern world. Oppressed peoples who live off land that is increasingly being swept up in the onrush of agrobusiness and extractive industries face a multifaceted challenge, not one that can be grasped within the one-dimensional idea of the indigenous. This kind of institutionalized idealization has a long history in Europe and the United States. French anthropologist Claude Lévi-Strauss is prosaic on this in his interview with Didier Eribon: "I'm not interested in people as much as beliefs, customs and institutions. So I defend the small populations who wish to remain faithful to their traditional way of life, away from the conflicts that are dividing the modern world."[49] Where Lévi-Strauss is able to see this isolation, ensconced as he is in the comfort of the Left Bank, defeats me; his friends from Brazil such as the Guarani-Kaiowá, a people from the state of Mato Grosso do Sul, suffer and struggle against capitalist agriculture, a reality that they cannot isolate themselves from in a fanciful way. The romance of the "indigenous" treats them as if they are trapped in the local while the rest of the world (us) is seen as footloose in the global.[50] If intellectuals once saw the working class as the liberation of humanity, many now turned opportunistically to the "indigenous people," and several began to write histories with the "indigenous" as its subject.[51]

In the maw of the "indigenous" appears the Afro-Dalit thesis. *Dalits* (literally, "broken-people" or the oppressed) are those Indian people who Hindu supremacy once called "untouchables" (*achut*) and who now call themselves Dalits to underscore the social relations of their oppression. In response to the degradation of the ecological landscape of the world by capitalism, several Afrocentric and Dalitcentric scholars argue that an originary (or indigenous) Afro-Dalit people must come together and throw off the yoke of Aryan-Caucasian domination. For them the specificity of capital's power is neglected in favor of a reversal of the white supremacist fantasy. In April 1999, noted Afrocentric scholar Runoko Rashidi traveled to India as a guide to a group of African Americans who wished to see "India Through African Eyes." At the Trivandrum (Kerala) airport, shouts of "Free Mumia Abu-Jamal" greeted the tourists and at a program at Bhubaneswar (Orissa), the Indian moderator read from Claude McKay's *If We Must Die,* revealing gestures of a longstanding Afro-Asian solidarity.[52] The year before, Rashidi told an Indian audience that he travels to India "to help establish a bond between the Black people of America and the Dalits, the Black Untouchables of India," a tie that "will never be broken." Rashidi's use of the translated term *Black Untouchables of India* refers to a book, published in 1979 in India and reprinted in 1995 by Clarity Press in Atlanta, *Dalit: The Black Untouchables of India.* The author of this book, V. T. Rajshekar was one of Rashidi's hosts during the 1999 trip and is the editor of *Dalit Voice,* whose pages have welcomed African American scholars for at least a decade. On December 5, 1999, Rajshekhar's Bharatiya Dalit Sahitya Akademy (Indian Dalit Literary Academy) bestowed upon Rashidi the Dr. Ambedkar International Award.[53] "Dalits were the original inhabitants of India and resemble Africans in physical features," Rajshekar wrote in his book. "It is said that India and Africa was one land mass until separated by the ocean. So both the Africans and the Indian Untouchables and tribals had common ancestors."[54] The search for a primordial unity toward social struggle against racism is not, as we've seen, at all uncommon these days.

Rajshekar and Rashidi are part of a scholarly tradition that breaks the narrow confines of area studies to seek connections among peoples who fall outside the continental divides that otherwise dominate the academy, seeking to find links between places and peoples who are separated in the world by flimsy boundaries, but whose destinies are parceled by intricate mazes and corridors of disciplines and departments. Afrocentric and Dalitcentric scholars, many of whom rise from unprivileged social locations, enliven a tradition of autodidactic scholarship that has ceased to be as socially important as it once was, but whose reach is by no means small. For one, many of these scholars cultivate readership through the new media, often with their own journals, magazines, printing presses, and the Internet. And, both the Afrocentric and the Dalitcentric traditions illuminate the ambiguity of nationalism, as they are at once a narrow involuted approach to social groups, and, importantly, "a utopian narrative–a rallying cry, an expression of desire . . . an articulation explaining what is good and beautiful, as style," what historian Wilson Moses names, for example, "Afrotopia."[55] Without a doubt there is much to criticize in the virulent and offensive work of scholars like Leonard Jeffries. However, there is much within Molefi K. Asante's 1987 manifesto *The Afrocentric Idea,* notably the desire to seek out a philosophical account of African history that is not bound entirely by the ethnocentric and Eurotropic paradigm of so much historical work.[56]

At base, Afrocentric and Dalitcentric scholars make a biological claim that Africans and Dalits are one people, that Dalits indeed are Africans who emigrated to India in ancient times. Recorded Indian history begins with the Harappan civilization (dated 3000 B.C.E.) which was a set of highly developed cities in the Indus valley in what is today's Pakistani and Indian Punjab and Kashmir. "The founders of the Harappan civilization," Rashidi writes, "were Black. This is verifiable through the available physical evidence, including skeletal remains, eyewitness accounts preserved in the Rig-Veda."[57] The Harappan cities disappeared from the historical record thousands of years ago, and they were only serendipitously rediscovered in 1922 when the British tried to drive a railway through northwestern Punjab. The cities of Harappa, therefore, do not have an unbroken tie with the present and the script of the time remains undeciphered (there are, also, no "eyewitness accounts"). Only a few clues facilitate a reconstruction of Harappan life, and all attempts to do so fall short of the kind of decisive claims made by Rashidi and others.

Harappa, since its discovery, has become the hub of all kinds of political claims: Dalit activists in the 1920s argued that Harappa was evidence of a Dalit civilization, that the Aryans (the word they used to delineate their caste oppressors) were as foreign as the British, and that both the British and the Aryans must forthwith depart—if not in person, then certainly they must relinquish their hold over wealth.[58] In recent years, Hindu fundamentalists and their U.S. allies have argued that Harappa is the home of an ancient Aryan efflorescence (and, consequently, that the only foreigners in India are Muslims).[59] As well, there are some white supremacist scholars who want to claim Harappa for the patrimony of Greek civilization, since, they hold that all that is worthwhile in world history must have descended from the white race. Afrocentrists and Aryanists share an obsession to harvest the world's cultural wealth into their own camps. Afrocentrist historians, such as Wayne Chandler and C. A. Winters, undo their own scholarly judgment when they

claim that not only were the first inhabitants of India black, but that all origi-
nality in Indian theory and practice, such as Jainism, Buddhism, and Patan-
jali's yoga, came instead from Ethiopia.[60] Each of these approaches is as limited as the other, for none of them recognizes the very small evidential base
available from Harappa (since its script is as yet undeciphered and there is
only so much that one can read from the bones), nor do they distinguish
between cultural connection and cultural origins, whatever that means.[61]

What is astonishing is the extent to which Afrocentric and Dalitcentric
scholars rely upon outdated scientific notions of race. Both sets of scholars
are joined in their determination to assert that the peoples of ancient India
were black. By black, they refer to epidermal and cranial terms set by European ethnologists (Chandler refers to the Harappans as "Negritos" and Rashidi weighs in with "Africoid Dravidians").[62] If Dravidians or Dalits (a slip-
page that is not historically tenable, since the former refers to a linguistic
group and the latter to a sociopolitical entity) are black, Rashidi argues that
the Aryans are white, and that the Aryans invaded the Dravidian-African
civilization creating the caste system "with a cold-blooded racist logic with
Whites on the top, mixed races in the middle and the mass of conquered
Blacks at the bottom."[63] Rashidi, and many scholars of his ilk, know that they
are in bad faith when they rely so strongly on epidermal determinism to sustain their argument. During his 1999 trip, Rashidi reported that "in Orissa
I saw and photographed the blackest human beings I've ever seen. In fact, it
was my impression that the blackest people were here most highly esteemed
and considered better than the others who were not so dark!" The enthusiasm for epidermal determinism occurs despite Rajshekhar's early warning
that "in India, it is no longer easy to distinguish a touchable from an Untouchable, especially for foreigners (unlike in the U.S. where the difference
between skin colors is more pronounced)."[64] Whether it was ever possible
to tell caste by skin color is a question for debate, but certainly to make such
judgments now is rather impossible. Indeed, in an interview with me in 1999,
Rashidi conceded that "I feel bad about it. I think I oversimplified the situation of Dalits to make it palatable to a [U.S.] Black constituency. I gave the
impression that Dalits are Black people." Nevertheless, he argued that "I
think large sections of Dalits would be seen as Black people if they lived anywhere else."[65]

What Rashidi's sentiment about "being seen as Black" refers to is not
the science of race but to racism: in most cases those who appear dark are
seen as black despite their skin color, and in antiracist movements until the
1980s black was used as a decidedly political color, illustrated by Stokely Car-

michael's remark that Fidel Castro was "one of the blackest men in America."[66] Black once meant those within Europe and the United States whose labor was valued, but whose lives were disregarded by a buoyant racism. During the long night of Thatcherism, black would be reduced to refer to those whom a racist science once called "Negroes" rather than referring as it also had to those who hailed from the Indian subcontinent (and those who *come from* Africa, such as many Asians in the UK who came from Kenya and Uganda as well). *Black* is now not so much a term of solidarity with those subjugated by imperialism as a term to unite those of "African ancestry" (and, perhaps, those who claim aboriginality or indigenousness).[67] When the Kenyan and Ugandan governments decided to expel their citizens of Asian (mainly Indian) descent in the late 1960s and early 1970s, they assumed that such people were "foreign" (even though many came from families that had made eastern Africa their home for generations[68]). The Ugandans went one step further, expelling Kenyan workers whom they saw as equally foreign. No one noticed their plight, however, because "they were few in number and [they] came from a neighbouring African country" and they "were solely working-class."[69]

Idi Amin saw the Asians and the Kenyans alike as nationalist threats. But when we look back at the tragedy of Amin's Uganda, we see only the Asian refugees, since the racialized lens refused to focus on ostensibly black African Kenyans who had to cross the border to lands some of them had never seen before. During the expulsions, a meeting was held at Makerere University in Kampala, one of the most renowned colleges in eastern Africa. Several students argued against the expulsion with the statement that "exploitation bears no particular colour." Echoing Stokely Carmichael on Castro, they noted that many "African" businessmen might quite easily be labeled as "black Asians."[70] For these young students the captains of capitalism did not belong to their community even if they tried to make common cause on the basis of race. The students turned color on its head and named their political allies black for the duration of the fight. Black, for them, was a political color.[71]

For political purposes, it is valuable for elites to deploy racial terms, since these offer easy terrains for mobilization, and they do not challenge the status quo in any substantial way. Frantz Fanon cannily called this use of race "vulgar tribalism" (the urge for an imitative bourgeoisie to dominate its own nationality), which Randall Robinson of TransAfrica recently renamed the "Vernon Jordan Disease."[72] This is the framework from which to understand Louis Farrakhan's historical meeting with Republican executives at Boca Raton, Florida, in 1997, and the Dalit-led Bahujan Samaj Party's temporary alliance with the formation of Hindu Supremacy, the Bharatiya Janata Party in 1995.[73] Despite these political ties with what would seem to be the opposition, Afro-Dalit scholars continue to call for a black (Harappan-Dalit-African) alliance against international Aryans.[74] The simplified world of U.S. racism (black-white) is used to create a political theory for a global movement, even when such a dichotomy yields few progressive benefits within the United States. (Can a wide enough coalition be built on its basis, and do the organizations of separatism have a political vision that enables something larger than the creation of pockets of influence?) It is perhaps at this point that one can understand the defensive approach toward authenticity, for there is a current within progressive antiracists that fights for resources on that ground rather than in terms of demographic representation or of moral redress. But authenticity as a claim is a trap that it is all the better to avoid.[75]

Darkness of skin provided the basis for Atlantic servitude and colonialism, but it does not itself provide any indication of political solidarity. There are many people dark of skin whose ancestors worked to promote slavery and who remain complicitious with the bondage of multinational capitalism. To celebrate skin color (Black is Beautiful) is one thing; to make political and historical claims on the basis of skin color is another. In the 1940s the Dalit leader B. R. Ambedkar argued against the claim of primordialism and urged Dalits to seek political communion in opposition to "the legal system of pains and penalties to which they have been subjected."[76] At a social level, poet and activist Pauli Murray recounted the experiences of many African Americans who hoped that the badge of color would be sufficient to forge relationships in Africa, but explained that in the end "the poignant reality is that a dark skin does not automatically qualify one to fit into the African environment." Murray had in mind the rigors of life in the oppressed parts of the world, which are far from easy for those reared in the U.S. middle class, but she also stressed the common cultural codes and practices that draw all Americans, regardless of color, to "discover their kinship, feel outsiders together."[77] To disregard the many fissures along the lines of race and to misread the cultural forms that intertwine people despite Jim Crow and its legacy is to revert to a racist idea of culture and of social being.

David Chioni Moore, in a fine analysis of Langston Hughes's trip to Soviet Central Asia, notes that Hughes developed an "afro-planetary vision." This vision seeks linkage "based not on biology but on 'experience,' experience that is not internal but rather contrapuntal, and that does not *result* from an a priori colored skin but that rather *causes* color 'consciousness.'"[78] Can we put Hughes's vision at the center of our work and take up the challenge to think about the *experience* of race in a dialectical fashion rather than in the one-dimensional way of both the color blind (*ignore race*) and the Afro-Dalit (*race as biology*) theory? The historical record allows us to reconsider the relationship between African Americans and Dalits outside raciology, in terms of the *experience* of struggle against forms of chattel slavery and debt peonage.[79] Faced with the rising of the Dalits in the Punjab, an American missionary wrote that the landowners "dread the loss of their own power and influence over [the Dalit landless workers], they have very much the same feeling as that which one may suppose animated the slave holder in America at the prospect of the liberation of the negro."[80] A few years after this obscure report, the oppressed caste leader Jyotibai Phule dedicated his 1873 treatise *Gulamgiri* ["Slavery"] to the "good people of the United States. As a token of admiration for their sublime disinterested and self-sacrificing devotion. In the course of Negro slavery; and with an earnest desire that my countrymen may take their noble example as their guide in the emancipation of their Sudra Brethren from the trammels of Brahmin thralldom."[81]

Within the United States, the documented connections between Dalits and African Americans are not available until the early twentieth century. In 1934, Du Bois's *The Crisis* ran an extract from Gandhi's autobiography where the Indlian leader wrote about being refused a haircut by a white South African barber. Gandhi did not get self-righteous about the refusal, but he took a lesson from white supremacy for the treatment of Dalits by Brahmanic supremacy.

> There was every chance of the [white] barber losing his custom if he cut
> black men's hair. We do not allow our barbers to serve our untouchable
> brethren. I got the reward of it in South Africa, not once, but many a time,
> and the conviction that it is the punishment for our own sins has saved me
> from being angry.[82]

Gandhi's subtle, and often ambigious, critique of white and Brahmin supremacy led to some difficulties in the African American press. When he was challenged on some statements on intermarriage, Gandhi sent an exclusive letter to the Baltimore *Afro-American* which ran under the headline, "GANDHI HITS U.S. BAR." Striking out against caste and untouchability, Gandhi pointedly said that the "prohibition of marriage between colored people and white people I hold to be a negation of civilization."[83] Gandhi's message was not unusual, for the commentary of solidarity had flowed between India and African America since the late 1910s. A friend of Du Bois and Marcus Garvey as well as resident in the United States during his time of exile for "terror-ism," Lajpat Rai wrote extensively about Jim Crow in his *Unhappy India* (1928) to counter the discussion of untouchability in Katherine Mayo's im-perialist *Mother India* (1928). Lajpat Rai knew the terrain of U.S. racism well and argued that the United States had a "severer form of untouchability than in India," since "even today the untouchables of India are neither lynched nor treated so brutally as the Negroes in the United States are."[84] Despite Lajpat Rai's unnecessary denial of all violence against Dalits in India, the provocative statements drew a slew of commentary in the African Ameri-can press. The conservative African American columnist George Schuyler pointed out, for example, that "the social and economic position of [African Americans] are somewhat similar and in some respects identical" to those of the Dalits.[85]

In 1935, Dr. Howard Thurman wrote that as an African American, he could "enter directly into informal understanding of the psychological cli-mate" of the Dalits and that African Americans and Dalits "do not differ in principle and in inner pain."[86] When Martin Luther King Jr. went to India in 1959, he investigated the exploitation of Dalits, as well as the means taken by the Indian Republic to ameliorate the effects of *Suvarna,* or Brahmin supremacy.

> We were surprised and delighted to see that India has made greater prog-ress in the fight against caste untouchability than we have made here in our country against race segregation. Both nations have federal laws against discrimination (acknowledging, of course, that the decision of our Supreme Court is the law of our land). But after this has been said, we must recognize that there are great differences between what India has done and what we have done on a problem that is very similar. The leaders of India have placed their moral power behind their law. From the Prime Minister down to the village councilmen, everybody declares publicly that untouchability is wrong. But in the United States some of our highest officials decline to render a moral judgment on segregation and some from the South publicly boast of their determination to maintain segregation. This would be unthinkable in India.[87]

While King clearly exaggerates, he draws upon the commonality of condi-tion to seek a solidarity of ideology.

There are many among the scholars of the Afro-Dalit encounter who also wish to seek parallels and not illusionary bloodlines. Dr. Y. N. Kly, senior member of the African American nongovernmental organization Interna-tional Human Rights for American Minorities, notes that "when we consider the nature of the suffering endured by the Dalits, it is the African American parallel of enslavement, apartheid and forced assimilation that comes to mind." Furthermore, when African Americans read of the Dalit situation, it "may help to demystify the system of minority-majority relations enforced by the Anglo-American ruling class upon the African American minority," and it may help undo the "notion of the uniqueness of the African American problem."[88] In short, the comparison of an oppressed Indian to an oppressed American offers a decisive thrust at American notions of exceptionalism, and hope for a new solidarity. It is these ideas of political unity and cultural interconnection that bring us to the concept of the polycultural.

Polyculturalism

> *With your liberal minds, you patronise our culture*
> *Scanning the surface like vultures*
> *With your tourist mentality, we're still the natives*
> *You're multicultural, but we're anti-racist.*
> *We ain't ethnic, exotic or eclectic.*[89]

In 1690, the English East India Company founded the city of Calcutta atop three villages on the banks of the Hugli River. In a few decades, the city became the heart of the English trade in the region, and from the mid-1700s the English adopted it as their capital of India. Being a commercial hub, this colonial city drew in a population that does homage to the cosmopolitan Indian Ocean world: all manner of Bengali speakers flocked from the countryside and provincial towns to the city, as did those who spoke the various languages that would be called Hindustani (workers from along the lazy bend of the Ganges all the way to its entry into the plains from the Himalayas). In addition, Calcutta was host to a Jewish community (whose first resident in August 1798 was the Aleppo-born and Baghdad-raised Shalom ben Aharon den Obadiah Ha-Kohen), to an Armenian community (whose first wooden chapel was erected in 1707 in Old China Bazar Street, named for the Bengal-China trade), to a Chinese community (whose pioneer Yong Atchew came to the city in 1780), to a Parsi or Zoroastrian community (forged by the arrival of Dadabhoy Behramji Banaji from Surat in 1767), and finally a wide variety of Europeans (including those born of the congress of Europeans and Indians, whose descendants are now called Anglo-Indian).[90]

In Calcutta's early years, the English lived alongside the other communities, but by 1742 they reinforced the palisades around their primary settlement and retreated. Captain Alexander Hamilton recorded that the "White Town," their racist citadel, rose "like about a baronial castle in medieval times."[91] The English attempted to erect a bifurcated city, like those of the Atlantic world. And yet Calcutta retained within it the contradictory and complex tenor of the Indian Ocean world. "Black Town" composed as it was of so many immigrants and cultural traditions reflected the heterogeneity of social life. And in fact there is some evidence that people of "Black Town" saw their lot as a shared one built as much around class as the construction of race. From the proverbs of the day, we get such gems as *Companir latgiri, parey dhaney poddari* ("Usurping the wealth of others, the Company's servants have become aristocrats"), which tell us something of the pretensions of that commercial section of "Black Town" that were able to buy some dignity from the East India Company.[92]

Two centuries later when the consistent struggle by the organized and disorganized Indian national movement removed the English from India, the new national government had to manage or nurse the wealth of social and cultural difference. Bitter riots between social groups in 1946–47 disturbed the Indian people's jubilant entry into freedom. In the aftermath of the riots and the formation of the Indian republic, the leaders devised a formula to manage social difference, "unity in diversity." In 1948, the victorious Indonesia people, faced with a similar welter of difference, chose the same recipe, *Bhinneka Tunggal Ika* ("unity in diversity").

These states implicitly recognized the contradictions of social identity foisted upon the democratic nation-state, which on the one hand proclaimed the horizontal equality of its citizens and yet realized that each abstract individual was also the ensemble of extant social relations (based on a variety of social fractures). Karl Marx in an early essay entitled "On the Jewish Question" argues that the democratic state does not deal with, or emancipate itself from, religion (and, consequentially other social identities), but instead it stands apart from the mess of civil society and cultivates its own narrow domain of the universal.

> Far from abolishing these real distinctions [of civil society, such as poverty, religious differentiation, race, and so forth], the State only exists on the presupposition of their existence; it feels itself to be a *political state* and asserts its *universality* only in opposition to these elements of its being.[93]

Since the state deems the differences within civil society as "nonpolitical distinctions," it is able to arrogate for itself the role of being above those very distinctions. The formal democratic state can then manage difference with such strategies as "unity in diversity," or, much later, in the United

States, as multiculturalism. The state does not emancipate people from distinctions (or undermine the power embedded in certain social locations), but it emancipates itself from them. In addition, the state draws on cultural traditions that form part of the terrain of those distinctions among its peoples. After all, the cultural form of the German state under critique by Marx came from, among others, a Christian heritage and the "so-called Christian State has a political attitude to religion and a religious attitude to politics."[94] The overall cultural framework of the state privileges certain social elites whose location is not disrupted by the management strategies such as "unity in diversity," given as it is to protect the cultural heritage of each social group (all of which are treated equally despite the fact of a socio-economic hierarchy of distinction). What, then, begins as part of an anticolonial project devolves into the state logic of management of difference.

From its birth as a republic, the United States adopted a slightly different strategy to manage difference. The state's motto is *e pluribus unum* (out of many, one). Its general attitude toward difference has been that it must be melted and remolded into the identity of the mythic universal American, one who is forged in the smithy of certain constitutional values and a product of the vast geographical spaces open to settlement by sturdy pioneers. In the ports, and later on Ellis Island, the state's managers expected that all "Old World" social identities perforce must be confiscated so that the immigrants could then and still today reinvent themselves as Americans. This story belies the massacre of the Amerindians, whose stolen lands became the wide-open spaces of the yeomen and pioneer women, as well of those enslaved Africans, who by the eighteenth century found their bodies reduced to a fraction of humanity. Yet the icon of the assimilable immigrant persists, held up as a model for all residents—new, old, or enslaved—and to all peoples of the world who are to marvel at this unique experiment in social relations. The fact, however, is that the United States is not exceptional in any regard, because people have always been on the move, emigrating and immigrating in search of better circumstances. The world is made up of people, ideas, flora and fauna that have traveled remarkable distances. The history of the countries in South America mirrors that of the United States, since they too comprised European colonies whose new residents massacred most of the earlier populations, fought wars of national independence against Europe (José San Martín and Simon Bolívar stand in for George Washington), and have since created various means to manage their cultural and political differences.[95]

The former USSR and the People's Republic of China (PRC), as well as most socialist and social-democratic states, adopted the Marxist theory of nationalities to produce tangible ways to both create platforms for unity (a federation) and institutions to protect less powerful nationalities from those that are more integrated into federal power. India's theory of "unity in diversity," for example, allowed for the establishment of linguistic states. Such measures meant Bengali speakers could continue to develop their cultural heritage without being swamped by the power of a state wedded to Hindi and English (although this framework to deal with difference itself does not protect cultural forms, for it requires vigilant social movements and the disruption of social institutions). Finally, there are many states, such as Switzerland, that ideologically claim to be homogeneous (a assertion belied by a casual glance at their history) in order to create a racist barrier against immigration. The United States, then, is hardly an exception in terms of diversity and its theory of multiculturalism is not unusual in a world that produces similar resolutions to cultural matters.

Slavery codes and later Jim Crow legislation allowed the United States to delay its engagement with the problem of social diversity. The institutions of slavery and of segregation meant that people of color remained outside the ken of white "society," and entered only as labor or as spectacle. The civil rights movement destroyed the negative peace of Jim Crow America and forced the state to come to terms with its segregated society. In the aftermath of the civil rights movement, students of color fought against the assumption that American culture can be entirely grasped by a study of Europeanized high cultural artifacts. For many there was an active discomfort with the notion that U.S. history was the tale of various presidents and their coterie. As colonial structures fell around the world such demands came to the fore in the famous student rebellions from Mexico City to Paris, from Berkeley to Lahore, all in 1968.[96] In that year students in San Francisco went on strike and demanded a new look at what was called culture in the United States. This wide-ranging directive led to the formation of the first ethnic studies program at San Francisco State College, which today includes the programs of black studies, La Raza studies, American Indian studies and Asian American studies.[97] Notwithstanding that ethnic studies is today still quite marginal, the program was to be the irritant in the side of a complacent academy and a society pledged to avoid the challenges of historical difference for the shibboleths of assimilation. The opening afforded by the U.S. state's slow acceptance of diversity allowed immigrants and oppressed peoples to not only hold on to cultural elements from their homeland (and bred into their bones) but to express and even exaggerate those cultural traits hitherto denigrated as being inferior. This desire to confront the cultural injury of white supremacy with the salve of a plural heritage is the very best of multi-culturalism.

Critics of this cultural nationalism in the United States very early saw the failure of its strategy as well as its links to a state-centered management of difference. Linda Harrison, a member of the Black Panther Party in east Oakland, noted in 1969 that "the power structure, after the mandatory struggle, condones and even welcomes the new-found pride which it uses to sell every product under the sun. It worships and condones anything that is harmless and presents no challenge to the existing order. Even its top representatives welcome it and turn it into 'Black Capitalism' and related phenomenon." The idea of "Black Capitalism" evokes, for Harrison, the figure of a consumer buying *black* goods at overcharged prices, "on the way to and from the shopping and spending they are still observing the oppression and exploitation of their people—in different clothes."[98] Indeed, U.S. capital, under pressure from the oil shock of 1967–73, of the militant rank-and-file worker struggle, and of a crisis of overproduction, sought to open up markets hitherto ignored, particularly among consumers of color.[99] When the U.S. post office created its Zone Improvement Plan and introduced the zip code in 1963, advertisers and other firms had a way to identify and utilize segregated space to target social groups and to cultivate tastes.[100] Blacks, Asians, Amerindians, Latinos, and others came to find capital interested in *them* (or at least a small fraction of those among them with disposable income), as African American consumers, Asian consumers, Amerindian consumers, Latino consumers, as "image tribes."[101]

Always alert to the prospects of profit before anything else, major capitalist firms developed a strategy in the late 1960s to bend the Group of 77 nations from their attempts to garner cartels over oil, bauxite, tin, and other raw materials (as well as agricultural commodities): the African Development Bank, the Inter-American Development Bank, and the Asian Development Bank, all were created in Filipino sociologist Walden Bello's studied words, to guarantee "northern hegemony by allocating influence according to the size of capital subscriptions, not membership." So, the United States, with its junior partner western Europe, was able to leverage control over the economies of the Third World (that in the 1950s had attempted to create the Special United Nations Fund for Development [SUNFED], an alternative, social-democratic development agency).[102] Multicultural development proffered loans to capital-starved nations with the provision that they then hire U.S. and European firms to do the tasks once done by domestic firms, via import-substitution schemes.[103] Here we see the operation of multicul-

turalism as a business strategy on a global scale. Angela Davis is right, therefore, to argue that multiculturalism "can easily become a way to guarantee
that these differences and diversities are retained superficially while becoming homogenized and harmonized politically, especially along the axes of
class, gender, and sexuality."[104] The calculated Republican convention of
2000 and the cabinet of George W. Bush offer a window into multicultural
reaction, where the diversity of faces is used as a cover for an essentially racist
project. The party of Lincoln (Continentals), as critic Michael Eric Dyson
put it, places blacks in symbolic positions and "that symbolism will more
than likely be used to cover policies that harm the overwhelming majority
of black Americans."[105] Multicultural imperialism offers an allowance for so-
called local cultures to remain intact as long as the cultural forms are those
that facilitate consumerism. Just as the state's discourse of democracy and
citizenship fails to grasp its implication in extant social differentiation (as
pointed out by Marx), so too does the multinational corporation's discourse
on consumerism fail to grasp its role in the affirmation of "persisting, unequal power relations" which it represents (via the idea of an abstract consumer) as "equal differences."[106]

In its crudest rendition then, multiculturalism adopts an idea of culture
wherein culture is bounded into authentic zones with pure histories that
need to be accorded a grudging dignity by policies of diversity. In his work
The Ticklish Subject, critic Slavoj Zizek calls this attitude "racism with a distance," since the benevolent multiculturalist treats the concept of culture as
a homogeneous and ahistorical thing that can be appreciated, but that remains far outside the enclosed ambit of one's own cultural box.[107] To retain
this distance and this sense of a self-enclosed culture is to pretend that our
histories are not already overlapping, that the borders of our cultures are not
porous. This "racism with a distance" forgets our mulatto history, the long
waves of linkage that tie people together in ways we tend to forget. Can we,
for example, think of "Indian" food (that imputed essence of the Indian subcontinent) without the tomato, that first fruit harvested by the Mayans, and
a base for most curries? Are not the Maya, then, part of contemporary "Indian" culture? Is this desire for cultural discreteness part of the bourgeois
nationalist and diasporic nostalgia for authenticity? Literary critic R. Radhakrishnan asks if the search for authenticity is

> a spontaneous self-affirming act, or if authenticity is nothing but a para-
> noid reaction to the "naturalness" of dominant groups. Why should
> "black" be authentic when "white" is hardly ever seen as a color, let alone
> pressured to demonstrate its authenticity.[108]

Is the desire for authenticity a mangled response to the triumphantalism of a corporate and racist culture thinly disguised as American culture? While all cultural forms are under pressure from capitalism, those "of color" feel a special lack of worth, given the national, and racist, origins of the capitalist core. Certainly, those "of color" who sense a loss of culture to the onrush of capitalism create means to hold on to that culture (as an artifact) while little is done to challenge the basis of the sense of cultural erosion. What, Radhakrishnan questions, is the loss felt by those who are not "of color" to the problem of "culture" in this latest phase of capitalism? "White culture" also changes, but, of course, the equation of power means that whiteness is neither under scrutiny nor is it seen to be threatened by such cultural *invasions* except by a strand of avid cultural chauvinists.[109] Multicultural imperialism is challenged by two principle foes: those bourgeois nationalist, well-meaning anthropologists, primordialists, *indigenistas,* and fundamentalists who claim to represent people of color and stand against the loss of culture; and those unreconstructed cultural racists who fear that their "European" cultural hegemony will be displaced (the polite ones among them take strategic refuge in the idea of the color blind). Often these two groups engage in what postcolonial critic Gayatri Spivak calls an "ignorant clash," mainly because they are both on the same side of the argument. Both believe that culture is a thing that requires protection from history and adaptation, and both tend to worry about certain phenomenal social forms (such as dress, language, diet) rather than about the general corporate reconstitution of social norms in which our individual autonomy is inhibited by the choices made for us by corporate institutions.[110]

After decades of debate over the problem of authenticity, it is by now clear that to posit an authentic core for culture creates serious sociopolitical problems. In a recent exchange, political scientist Susan Moller Okin and her interlocutors debated whether or not "multiculturalism [is] bad for women." One camp was of the view that "minority groups—immigrants as well as indigenous people" (in other words, those "of color")—demand "group rights" that undermine democratic principles, while the other camp argues that to champion those very principles at the expense of cultural autonomy is much the same as the colonization of the mind.[111] The figure of woman is rightly central to this debate because a hidebound, and unselfconscious, multiculturalism can fall prey to a notion of cultural difference (even cultural relativism, in its strong sense) that legitimates gender oppression. Where the debate fails is that, once again, it is lodged at the level of the law (the state's emissary) and focused on how to *manage* the problem of diversity rather than how to undermine the structures that engender the illusion of absolute difference and then the zoological maintenance of culture out of fear of survival (for primordialists and *indigenistas*) or out of fear of contamination (for racist cultural chauvinists). Here we have two problems, one over whether multiculturalism should be seen and practiced as the management of diversity, and the second over whether the idea of culture requires the notion of authenticity.

The idea of difference management (diversity) seems to have largely usurped those agencies that deal with multiculturalism. In my estimation, multiculturalism emerged as the liberal doctrine to undercut the radicalism of antiracism.[112] Instead of antiracism, we are now fed with a diet of cultural pluralism and ethnic diversity. The history of oppression and the fact of exploitation are shunted aside in favor of a celebration of difference and the experience of individuals who can narrate their ethnicity for the consumption of others. That the U.S. state adopted the liberal patina of multiculturalism to fend off an important challenge from the progressive and democratic forces is not reason enough to discount the power of cultural plurality, for multiculturalism opened the space for struggle against the conceit of cultural homogeneity (at the same time as the logic of diversity management quickly tried to close that space off, since it claimed to solve the problem by mutual respect rather than by the struggle to dismantle privilege). "A Multiculturalism that does not acknowledge the political character of culture will not, I am sure," argues Angela Davis, "lead toward the dismantling of racist, sexist, homophobic, economically exploitative institutions."[113] The difference between antiracism and diversity management, then, is that the former is militantly against frozen privilege and the latter is in favor of the status quo.

Do the cultures in multiculturalism need to be granted an authentic core, one that is inviolable and chaste? There is little sense that, under the cover of authentic culture, there lies a long history of dissent, some of it on the fault lines of gender against certain cultural norms that work in the interest of some sections of society (whether men, or else of the elite).[114] Furthermore, most of those who indulge in this debate assume that liberalism or democracy is a finished project, that what threatens it are those "of color" who "are too frequently imagined as the abject 'subjects' of their cultures of origin huddled in the gazebo of group rights, preserving the orthodoxy of their distinctive cultures in the midst of the great storm of Western progress."[115] The limitations and failures of liberalism do not enter the agenda so that the champion of liberalism stands outside the process as the colonial critic of misbegotten cultures. If we uncouple authenticity from culture, we might see the multiple coeval engagements between "liberalism" and that which is seen to require its ministrations, for the history of the colonial encounter shows us how the two begot each other.[116] The notion of the "hybrid" was deployed to work against authenticity, and despite the best efforts of its theorists, it has come to indicate the fusion of two previously formed cultural traditions.[117] Authenticity may be a useful strategic way to frame fights to gain resources, but the trap of authenticity is set against the antiracist struggle. For culture to have an authentic core undermines our ability to articulate the intertwined cultural histories and struggles that will provide the sort of political will necessary for demands upon resources (rather than pleas for them on authenticity grounds alone).

Disenfranchised by white supremacy, many people of color lean on narrow nationalist frameworks to make claims upon the state. The most obvious strategy is to ask for resources based on authenticity ("we need to be represented by our own, or else we need money for our community"). The demand is unimpeachable, principally because it calls for a redress of past history. When the 2000 U.S. census allowed people to tick one or more boxes for race, the NAACP and other civil rights organizations took umbrage. Hilary Shelton of the NAACP noted, "Census statistics are used for the allocation of programmatic dollars—everything from education and health care to transportation" and that the tabulation of race numbers allows for civil rights groups to "most fully and consistently enforce our existing civil rights laws."[118] Without the numbers of people of color it is hard to argue against job discrimination or other such acts of affirmative disenfranchisement. On college campuses, progressive faculty adopt the language of authenticity to argue for more faculty of color and for a further diversification of the curriculum. The Asian American students need Asian American faculty members and Asian American studies. Race is used here in light of historically considered categories that have been the basis of racism in the past, and therefore that have functioned to exclude certain people from political, economic, and social power. To gain redress, race has to be quite central, since it was on the basis of race that disenfranchisement took place.

The strategy of redress, however, is limited by its entrapment in the framework of bourgeois law. A person (or institution) has to prove that another person (or institution) has done substantial harm to himself or herself for the case to be taken seriously both before the court of law and bourgeois public opinion. Harm to a community in the past provokes the problem of remedy: Who should pay for which crimes, and who must collect the redemption? Angry white students sometimes say that they are tired of the implication that they are culpable for the acts of their ancestors or of their race. The onus is placed on those who have been historically oppressed to settle the problem of a remedy, and the experience of Jewish survivors of the Holocaust and of interned Japanese Americans shows us that the standard for redress is posed rather high (an apparently insurmountable problem for the reparations claim of descendants of enslaved Africans). To counter the injudiciously high standards, many of us turn to questions of cultural authenticity and of demography to make our case. On college campuses, for instance, we ask for representation based on our numbers and on the need to have cultural presence of certain groups based on these numbers. The limits of multiculturalism—notably the assumption that culture is definable and discrete—badger this strategy. The call for amends on the multiculturalist platform leads, in many cases, to a Hobbesian war of one against all among the oppressed: the divide-and-rule strategy comes to pass. Besides, demographically insignificant groups, such as Amerindians, do not have access to this political strategy, and furthermore, the appeal often transforms the student into a customer who makes a market-based demand that is quite opposed to the moral struggle for social justice. The cry for cultural authenticity is a defensive gesture against a recalcitrant, white supremacist set of institutions: we must recognize it for what it is and seek more creative ways to transform the structures from whom we seem to be simply asking for some spoils.

This brings me, finally, to the idea of the polycultural.[119] In an article for *ColorLines Magazine* in 1999, historian and cultural critic Robin Kelley dismissed the idea of the purity of our bloodlines, finding the world of cultural purity and authenticity equally unpleasant too. Kelley argued that "so-called 'mixed-race' children are not the only ones with a claim to multiple heritages. All of us, and I mean ALL of us, are the inheritors of European, African, Native American, and even Asian pasts, even if we can't exactly trace our bloodlines to all of these continents."[120] Rejecting the posture of a "racism with a distance," Kelley argued that our various cultures "have never been easily identifiable, secure in their boundaries, or clear to all people who live in or outside our skin. We were multi-ethnic and polycultural from the get-go." The theory of the polycultural does not mean that we reinvent humanism without ethnicity, but that we acknowledge that our notion of cultural community should not be built inside the high walls of parochialism and ethno-nationalism. The framework of polyculturalism uncouples the notions of origins and authenticity from that of culture. Culture is a process (that may sometimes be seen as an object) with no identifiable origin. There-fore, no cultural actor can, in good faith, claim proprietary interest in what is claimed to be his or her authentic culture. "All the culture to be had is culture in the making," notes anthropologist Gerd Baumann. "All cultural differences are acts of differentiation, and all cultural identities are acts of cultural identification."[121]

Kelley's idea of polyculturalism draws from the idea of polyrhythms—many different rhythms operating together to produce a *whole* song, rather than different drummers doing their own thing. People and cultures, from the outset, then, are seen to be at the confluence of multiple heritages and "living cultures, not dead ones . . . [that] live in and through us every-day, with almost no self-consciousness about hierarchy or meaning." Even though people form what appear to be relatively discrete groups (South Asians, African Americans, Latino Americans), most of us live with the knowledge that the boundaries of our communities are fairly porous and that we do not think of all those within our "group" as of a cohesive piece. We forge group solidarity even, or especially, when we are thrown together by imputed solidarities. Furthermore, multiculturalism tends toward a static view of history, with cultures already forged and with people enjoined to respect and tolerate each cultural world. Polyculturalism, on the other hand, offers a dynamic view of history, mainly because it argues for cul-tural complexity.

The history of Garveyism is, in fact, illustrative of polyculturalism. The Garvey movement has been the largest mobilizer of black people in the world. Despite the fact that the *Universal* Negro Improvement Association restricted membership to those who claimed African descent, Garvey was close to the Indian nationalist exile Lajpat Rai (who again also courted Booker T. Washington), and he hired as the editor of *Negro World* the Indian writer Hucheshwar G. Mugdal. The *Negro World*, under Mugdal, opened it-self to the international struggles against white supremacy. In early 1922, the paper published a letter from an Indian man, Ganesh Rao:

> I am one of those millions that are being oppressed by the imperialistic
> English government. My interest, my responsibility, my duty, has thus
> impelled me to study the tragic tales of other oppressed peoples, e.g. the
> Negro, and his future. From my humble study so far I have confidently felt
> that the UNIA is doing the real work for the uplift of the Negro, and the U
> stands for, in word as in action—Universal . . . India is in her birth-throes;
> she soon shall be free. Ethiopia, self conscious, is working for her indepen-

dent and unhindered progress. Peace shall not dawn on this world until
Asia and Africa and their ancient peoples are free and enjoy all human
rights. Oppressed people of the world unite. Lose no time![122]

Mugdal simply continued an internationalist strain long evident in Garvey's
biography. In New York Garvey took the counsel of the Indian liberal Haridas T. Muzumdar and his strong anticolonial rhetoric attracted a young
Ho Chi Minh to his Harlem meetings.[123] This interchange, at a late stage, is
a continuation of the history of interaction between Africans and Asians
across the Indian Ocean. There can be no history of Gujarati peoples, as we
saw in the previous chapter, without consideration of Zanzibar, Tanzania,
Ethiopia, and Muscat. A polyculturalist sees the world constituted by the
interchange of cultural forms, while multiculturalism (in most incarna-
tions) sees the world as already constituted by different (and discrete) cultures that we can place into categories and study with respect (and thereby
retain 1950s relativism and pluralism in a new guise). What would history
look like from a polycultural perspective? Well, rather than see Hong Kong
business exclusively as a hybrid of an ancient Confucianism and a modern
capitalism, as in the work of Tu Wei-Ming, we might take heed of the Jesuit
role in the making of early modern "Confucianism," as in the fine work of
Lionel Jensen.[124] Rather than evince surprise at English education in India,
we might recognize, along with Gauri Viswanathan and Kumkum Sangari,
that "English" as a discipline emerges in the East India Company colony of
lower Bengal.[125] Rather than treat Indian students at Yale as aliens, we might
consider that the university received seed money from Elihu Yale, onetime
governor of Madras, whose wealth came from the expropriated labor of Indian peasants.[126]

These examples are not random, for they enable us to indulge in one of
the traits of the polycultural approach—to snub the pretensions of Europe
and the United States, which arrogates certain parts of world knowledge to
itself, thereby placing its ideas at the top of a cultural hierarchy leaving the
rest of us to fend off both the legacy of colonial knowledge and violence with
our meager economic and cultural resources. Several historians of Europe
these days recognize the interlocking heritage of the Eurasian landmass, as
well as the substantial links between Africa and Europe.[127] The interchange
between the continents produced what is today so cavalierly called "Western
rationality," "Western science," and "Western liberalism": this erases the influence of those Arab and Jewish scholars who extended Aristotle's insights,
those Indian wizards who made mathematics possible with their discovery

of the zero, those Iroquois whose experiments with federalism helped frame some of the concepts for the U.S. Constitution.[128] Instead of laying claim to the complex heritage of these modern phenomena, chauvinists of color argue for such traditions as "Hindu Economics" and "Islamic Science," as well as cede the terrain of democracy to Europe.[129] Polyculturalism refuses to allow the "West" to arrogate these combined and uneven developments of so many sociocultural formations, since it scrupulously investigates the connections that dynamically generate them.

The polyculturalist outlook says to the proponents of the color blind that their position is in a bad faith, since it acts to perpetuate the racist status quo. To the primordialists it says that to deny internal differentiation and intermixture of cultural forms may allow it to leverage power over those whom it treats as part of its group, but it does not provide an adequate agenda to dismantle the status quo kept in place by the color blind. Instead, the posture of authenticity occludes its privilege. Antiracists sometimes argue that authenticity is one of the few avenues to make claims on institutions. Polyculturalism offers some solace but implicit within it is the understanding that this defensiveness is a trap that is able only to garner crumbs from the racist table—and these days few of them. Should the antiracists accept the idea of authenticity to build a black studies or Asian American studies department (staffed respectively by blacks and Asian Americans) or should we make wide claims on the resources of the entire educational ensemble, to train people of color to be mathematicians, geographers, philosophers, historians of France?[130] In 1969, David Hilliard, speaking to the students at San Francisco State College, enunciated the Black Panther Party position against "an autonomous Black studies program that excludes other individuals." Hilliard understood the need to claim resources, but he was wary of the claim for it being made on the grounds of exclusions and of a hidebound notion of cultural autonomy. He said,

> We recognize nationalism because we know that our struggle is one of national salvation. But this doesn't hinder our struggle, to make alliance with other people that's moving in a common direction, but rather it strengthens our struggle. Because it gives us more energy, it gives us a more powerful force to move and to withstand the repression that's being meted out against us.[131]

Within this framework, concern for the obliteration of cultural forms is met not by an encirclement of the false cultural wagons, but by the generous embrace of all the energy that is ready for a genuine antiracist struggle. Hilliard did not argue against cultural nationalism simply on the expedient ground that the black liberation struggle required allies for demographic strength. On the contrary, talk of "energy" seemed to indicate that the entry of all manner of antiracists would qualitatively strengthen the movement, give it a kind of dynamism. Difference may yet be valued, for, as legal scholar Leti Volpp holds, to retain an idea of cultural difference (notably of forms of social life) is not the same as to abdicate the right to adjudicate between different practices in struggle.[132]

A broad antiracist platform would not (like liberal multiculturalism) invest itself in the management of difference, but it would (like a socialist polyculturalism) struggle to dismantle and redistribute unequal resources and racist structures. Furthermore, polyculturalism, as a political philosophy, does not see difference "as evidence of some cognitive confusion or as a moral anomaly" (as liberal multiculturalism is wont to do), but it sees those features of difference with which it disagrees as "the expression of a morality you despise, that is, as what *your* enemy (not the universal enemy) says."[133] The advantage of this reaction is that it explores the politics of various positions which are then measured on the basis of the ethico-political agenda forged in struggle (not as some universal, ahistorical verities). For example, the liberal chauvinist may argue that immigrants should assimilate into the U.S. core culture, taking for granted that there is such a thing as a core in the first place. The word *assimilate* is used as a universal value, so that few of us can reply that we don't want to assimilate, we want to remain separate ("Then why did you come here?" is the response). If we reframe the problem not as assimilation but as conformity, we have a political leg to stand upon ("my being here is already assimilation, but I refuse to conform to some of your mores").[134]

The answer to American ideology, then, comes against a language of "skin," but not in a color-blind fashion. Polyculturalism does not posit an undifferentiated "human" who is inherently equal as the ground for its critique of the world, one that says something like "we are all human after all," but seems to offer only the smallest palliatives against racist structures. Instead it concentrates on the project of creating our humanity. "Human" is an "unfinished product," one divided by social forces that must be overcome for "human" to be made manifest.[135] In the nineteenth century near Delhi, Akbar Illahabadi intoned that we are born people, but with great difficulty we become human (*aadmi tha, bari muskil se insan hua*). A polycultural humanism, for this tradition, is a "practical index" that sets in motion the processes that might in time produce a *humanity* that is indeed in some way equal.[136]

Chapter 3

Coolie Purana

I've often thought of my city, Hartford, Connecticut, as a tropical township where it snows. The bulk of the population comes from the islands (Puerto Rico, Trinidad, and Jamaica), Guyana, and the U.S. South. The predominantly working-class population from the English-speaking Caribbean has set up its own institutions, a West Indian club, a West Indian parade, endless shops that sell patties and curry goat, and, lest we forget, cricket clubs. For many U.S. blacks, the people from the islands dominate the cultural scene, mainly because they have access to financial and institutional resources that are not readily available to those who came from the Carolinas, Georgia, and Florida.

Among the teenagers dance hall music is as popular as hip-hop and "Jamaican *bidis*," or hand-rolled cigarettes bought at Jamaican, Indian, or Puerto Rican *bodegas,* are the rage—especially for underage smokers. Though *bidis* are made in southern Asia, they're considered Jamaican in Hartford. And with little awareness of its South Asian provenance, many young African Americans and Afro-Caribbean youths throw down the word *thug*, which is "to cover up" in Hindustani, but came to mean "deceiver" in the nineteenth century when the British colonial officials identified certain brigands as *thuggees.* Hartford isn't an anomaly with regard to this type of cultural exchange in the United States or elsewhere. For instance, the Asian working class in New York City sport a style that is mainly hip-hop, the cultural mode that emerges from the African American community. For middle-class Asians especially, hip-hop is *used* as a way to be urban and to be Asian *American.*[1] The English band Culture in the Mix calls its music "Afro-

Sangeet" (*sangeet,* "music") to signal its constitutive nature. Really, the examples are endless, and when I hear words like *thug* and *bidi,* when I hear cars drive by playing the Indo-Caribbean dance hall singer Supercat, I think about the polycultural nature of the working class, not syncretic (two discrete entities melding with a consciousness of difference), but forged together from the beginning through the byways of Jamaica, the streets of Hartford, the avenues of New York, the dole queues of London, and beyond. Polyculturalism exists most vividly among the poor and working class, among people who are forced to live among one another and who ultimately work together toward freedom. And it was a shared bitter servitude that would bring enormous numbers of Asian and African people together around the world.

The World the Coolies Made

Massive rebellions of enslaved peoples in the Americas (Haiti, 1792; Barbados, 1816; Guyana, 1823; Jamaica, 1831–32), a decline in the market share of the slave plantation profits, as well as a rise in antislavery agitation in the metropole, brought a gradual end to chattel slavery in the nineteenth century. While in the United States it took a civil war to achieve slave emancipation, in the British Empire emancipation took place relatively peacefully in 1834 (a full three decades earlier than in the United States).[2] Despite the end of chattel slavery, the immense manual labor–driven production system erected by the British still required a sustained supply of workers. The slave system had never produced an adequate means to reproduce labor, and after emancipation many of the newly freed workers did not want to come back to work on the plantations. In Australia the planters turned to convict labor, in South Africa to "apprentices" (captive children) and "Prize Negroes" (freed slaves), and in the Caribbean they tried first to hire free Africans from other islands (so that, for example, freed slaves from St. Kitts came to work in Trinidad), then free African Americans en route to Africa, West African emigrants, European labor on indenture contracts, and then Portuguese speakers from Madeira, Cape Verde, and the Azores. But finally Australia, South Africa, and the Caribbean (as well as South America) turned to the labor markets of British India and China from where thousands of emigrants left to do "coolie work" (formerly "nigger work") on the plantations of early capitalism.

Coolie is a word that produces, among Indian and Chinese people, the same gut response as does *nigger* among blacks. It has no established etymology; some place it from the Tamil *kuli* ("hire"), others find it in use in sixteenth-century Portugal as *Koli*, after the name of a Gujarati community, still others notice that it sounds like the Chinese *ku-li* ("bitter labor") or like the Fijian *kuli* meaning "dog." One way or the other to be called a coolie is to be denigrated, and to be considered at best as a laborer with no other social markers or desires. The word *coolie* operates, then, like the nineteenth-century English word for factory worker, *hand* (where the entire ensemble of human flesh and consciousness is reduced to the one thing that is needed to run the mills of industrial capitalism).[3]

But a "coolie" is not quite the same as a "hand," because the former word applies more to those vilified by white supremacy as lesser beings, while the latter word is generally used for white labor. In 1914 a member of the Ghadar ("Revolt") Party of mainly Punjabi agricultural workers in California offered his comrades the following poem to underscore the special import of the word *coolie:*

> We are faced with innumerable miseries.
> We are called coolies and thieves.
> Wherever we go, we are treated like dogs.
> Why is no person kind to us?[4]

The word *coolie* entered the European lexicon in the context of imperialism to index a person of inferior status who simply labors for hire. Whereas the European laborer, by the nineteenth century, was seen as a juridical citizen who could formally bargain for his (sometimes, her) rights as a seller of labor power, the coolie was seen as racially suited for various forms of hard labor in tropical conditions. Colonial anthropologists and planters argued that the constitution of the coolie allowed him or her to better handle the heat and humidity. While the Europeans, we are told, had a sense of judgment, the coolie was easily inflamed by the passions of the sunshine and of unreason. Europeans who moved from the trades and the fields to the factories had to sell their labor as a commodity, where each hour of work time earned them a set (sometimes negotiated) wage. The labor of Asians, like that of Africans and Amerindians, however, was not commodified in an identical fashion. Instead it was "animalized," and the productive efforts of the workers were treated by white supremacy as the rote part of their ill-fated primitive existence.[5]

When the first Chinese and Indian workers came on the plantations, the stench of slavery was not far gone from the work process or from the slaves' residential quarters. These "coolie slaves" said of their lives that they were "bound" (and when freed, they were known as *khula,* or "opened from bondage").[6] In the nineteenth century, commercial pressures forced peasants off the land in both India and China. Historian Thomas Metcalf estimates that in northern India, the catchment area for many of the indentured workers, "notices of eviction were being issued at the rate of 60,000 annually [in the 1870s], with the object not of clearing the land but of forcing the tenant to submit to an enhanced rent."[7] Meanwhile in China the upheaval of the Taiping Rebellion (1850–64), and other assorted acts of defiance, tore through the innards of the Ch'ing regime. The effects of "gunboat diplomacy" of the European traders who encircled China had a marked impact on the agrarian life in the interior, from which millions of people escaped to Southeast Asia and to the Americas.[8] In the Caribbean and southern Africa, the Indians and Chinese came under a rigid legal instrument that provided, according to historian Walton Look-Lai, a

> curious legal anomaly—a civil contract enforceable mainly with criminal sanctions, historically a hybrid creature of the nineteenth century plantation need to replace Black labor with some alternative form of bound labor, not as extreme as chattel slavery, but certainly not free in the increasingly accepted metropolitan liberal sense of the term.[9]

In North America, whether in Canada or the United States, even if the Asian immigrated voluntarily, the work regime was such that, as the *San Francisco Chronicle* put it in 1879, "when the coolie arrives he is as rigidly under the control of the contractor who brought him as ever an African slave was under his master in South Carolina or Louisiana."[10] Often tricked into indenture, the Asian did not know the language of the new country, was consigned to a plantation for at least five years (with reindenture common), lived in conditions akin to slavery, worked not only for a wage, but under the threat of severe punitive sanctions and indebtedness, and was not allowed free movement out of the plantation (as in the Caribbean) or of the province (as in southern Africa). Confinement, racist violence, and the demands of production erased most of the liberal claims of capitalism.

"Nothing will induce a Negro to weed a field" was the belief among the colonial planters in the Caribbean.[11] Indeed by the time the bulk of the Asians got to the plantations, many of those of African heritage had parlayed their cultural skills, particularly knowledge of English, for better jobs. They wanted nothing more to do with the harsh life that had been the fate of their families for generations. Fieldwork became "coolie work." Sankar, an indentured worker, complained that "de kirwal [African] driver e know to read, he ha de book but he cyan write an e taking all de wuk in de estate."[12] The Wood report in 1922 noted that the literacy rate of the East Indians (that is, those who came from India) was very low and that "the East Indians—the backbone of the agricultural industry in both Colonies—are the 'underdogs' politically when compared to the negroes, owning to the superior educational advantages of the latter," and the next year, the governor of Trinidad noted that the East Indian was "not so suitable for this type of work [civil service] as the West Indian."[13]

The historical entry of the Asians after the African workers earned their freedom created a major bridge between these two peoples. The latter did not work under the direct control of the planters any longer and their cultural capital enabled them to produce a substantial middle-class, urban-based leadership. Such structural differences did not seem enough to the planters and the colonial state, which created fabulous strategies to segregate the workers and to pit them against each other. Spatial segregation should not be underemphasized. In Trinidad, for example, the African peasantry resided in the north part of the island, while the Indians lived and worked in the south and the center. Sankar commenting on the distances that engulfed Trinidad said that "we eh interfering wid dem [Africans]. We living for weself. We talking about weself, we singing, playing drum an eating, sleeping, eating together, we indian self, we eh meddle wid dem."[14] We Indian self, we Chinese self, we African self, we selves who work as "hands," as "coolies" and as "niggers." We who retreat into our private spaces to escape the racist "public" dominated by white supremacy. And the slave or coolie had precious little private life. The chiefs of capitalism considered the working-class body to be without intelligence or emotion and generally irrelevant in the long term, since working bodies could be imported from the warrens where they bred (in China, Africa, or elsewhere). On slave plantations, the African woman became a sign of sexual laxity since her progeny (by rape or otherwise) was the property of the slave owner, whereas the African man was a sign of sexual danger, since he was seen as a threat to white men's claim to the ownership of white women's bodies.[15] Being at the front lines of plantation capitalism, African women came to be regarded as "breeders" whose duties included the reproduction of children. Conditions were equally heinous for the small number of female indentured workers. Eighty-five percent of the Chinese women in San Francisco in 1860 did sex work as debt slaves to their contractors, servicing white and Chinese laborers.[16] Limiting the number of women and the types of social interaction allowed the state to exert political control over the emotional lives of their workers. Despite these barbaric circumstances, however, the coolies made novel arrangements for love and sex, such as with same-sex partners, or else across the color line, whether Punjabis with Chicanos, Africans with Indians, Chinese with Africans.[17] Attempts to dehumanize and desexualize the coolie could not undermine the capacity of workers to constitute joy out of the most shabby materials.

Structurally, the entry of the indentured workers served to depress the wages of the newly freed Africans from western Canada to southern Africa.[18] By 1849, the Caribbean planters worried about the lack of discipline of the "pampered Creole Labourer born and bred on the estate," as they valued the "stranger, the quiet willing coolie," and from 1876 to 1895, the Natal (South Africa) government hired Indian coolies for low wages, but also because they made it known that the Africans could not be relied upon.[19] U.S. capitalists felt the same way, as the *Vicksburg Times* put it in 1869, that "emancipation has spoilt the negro and carried him away from the fields of agriculture. Our prosperity depends upon the recovery of lost ground, and we therefore say let the Coolies come."[20] "Undoubtedly," intoned one Southern U.S. politician, "the underlying motive for this effort to bring in Chinese laborers was to punish the negro for having abandoned the control of his old master, and to regulate the conditions of his employment and the scale of wages to be paid him."[21]

With the growth of mechanization of industrial work and of Taylorism of field labor through the length of the nineteenth century, the capitalists attempted to renegotiate what counted as "skill," a sure way to cut down the power of craft unions.[22] The employment of the immigrant-indentured became a perfect way to both reduce costs of a relatively de-skilled production process and to undermine the nascent unions (so as to derail the attendant growth of a radical political consciousness). The Chinese Exclusion League emerged in this context in the United States not so much to prevent Chinese immigration (for the Chinese in 1880 constituted only .002 percent of the population), but to encourage the idea that the United States was a white republic in which "people of color" might work but not thrive. Indeed, in 1905, Samuel Gompers of the American Federation of Labor told a white audience that "the caucasians are not going to let their standard of living be destroyed by negroes, Chinamen, Japs, or any others."[23] White labor, represented by Gompers, offered its skin, its manhood, and its civilizational claims as the opportunity costs against the low wages of the feminized workers of color. Rather than attack capital for its ruthless assault on the dignity of all people, Gompers and organized white labor blamed both African and Asian Americans for destroying the capital-labor relationship. "Absolute servility (civility is not enough) is expected from those who take the place of 'John' [the former slave] or 'Togo' [the Asian coolie] and it will take many years to obliterate these traces of inferiority and re-establish the proper relations of the employer and the employed."[24]

From organized white labor we get the rather pathetic plea in favor of a manly workforce instead of a feminized one. But from the planters and the captains of industry we get a marked preference for low-wage labor, anyone who can be compelled on pain of destruction to work for as little as possible, and to be powerless at the worksite. Indenture was one obvious strategy to ensure cheap labor. But the U.S. South did not do away with all its mechanisms to control the formerly enslaved workforce. In 1868 General Sherman's Field Order No. 15 promised some means toward the creation of a free life for the African American population, but this was to be revoked in the compromise of 1876. W. E. B. Du Bois, in his majesterial *Black Reconstruction in America, 1860–1880,* demonstrated how this "counter revolution of property put into the South a laboring class without political power."[25] Racism was the cost to be borne by society so that capital could enjoy the fruits of unbridled profit.

When machinery was introduced on a large scale, plantation owners and governments used it to further stratify their workforce. The white managers in the United States used the entry of machines to cast off ex-slaves and hire the Chinese immigrants who, the managers from Massachusetts to California claimed, had the "higher standard of intelligence" required to run the machines.[26] In British Guyana, the white government followed suit and reported in 1871 that the "Chinese laborer possesses greater intelligence than either the Indian or the Negro, and is much quicker at learning to manage machinery than either of them."[27] Such stereotypes developed at the official level and had a very real effect—as they continue to do—on people's lives. Colonial planters exerted power on the shop floor or field through the divide-and-rule strategy. The overseers divided the tasks on the plantations, for example, for racial- and gender-based work groups, with some groups given easier jobs than others were given. Faced with complaints, the overseers and the plantation owners responded with racist stereotypes to confirm their choices. These stereotypes, however, changed when the occasion demanded it. If the East Indians protested their conditions, the planters called them excitable, but when they worked, they were called docile. When childlike, the African was said to be safe, but when he became a *savage,* the colonial writers underscored, he became dangerous.[28] Even though the Africans produced most of the food for the city of Georgetown in British Guyana, they were seen as lazy (with a "rude and stubborn independence"). Rather than find capitalist social relations culpable for the impoverishment of the Africans, the managers blamed the Africans for their lack of thrift. When the Indians saved, the managers blamed them for the reduction of economic activity on the island.[29] The racialized landscape of the plantation composed the language of race that was being written as science within Europe at this time. Indeed, from John Locke in the seventeenth century onward, famous writers who owned substantial economic interests in the colonial plantations of the Americas developed the theory of racial hierarchy. The plantation logic and physical anthropology constituted each other.

These stereotypes were also translated into folklore. Stories of "Sammy" (from the word *Swami*, "the generic Indian coolie") and "Quashie" (from the word *Kwesi*, "the generic African freed worker") became part of British Guyana's folklore. In the folk tales of plantation racism (regaled as often by the workers themselves), Quashie chides Sammy for being prone and willing to accept poor work conditions; Sammy responds, "Yes, you rascal neegah man: me come from India dis forty-six year: supposing me and me matty no come dis side fo' work, you rascal neegah been a starve one time." As Walter Rodney notes in *A History of the Guyanese Working People, 1881–1905*, neither of them captures the problems of each, since "Quashie" mistook the intentions of those who came on indenture, and "Sammy" could hardly have known the capacity of the African workers to re-create the landscape to match their desires.[30] In this way the stereotypes of labor immigration turn, gradually, into the social relations of mutual contempt. Later the slow growth of a petty bourgeoisie who might have offered some leadership would only exacerbate the troubled situation: in southern Africa this class was to come in the main through the "passenger" Indians, who paid their own way to become merchants; in the United States this class came from the students and exiled politicians, like Har Dayal and Taraknath Das. But the fissures did not entirely squelch the feelings of solidarity among people who lived cheek by jowl in the nether end of the imperialist chain. "Dat negro, dat call kaffir, just like me, only black, only dem black like hell," so says Fazal, an ex-indentured laborer.[31] But "just like me" nonetheless.

It would be a mistake to assume that former slaves and coolies alike did not struggle against their condition. However, to overcome a system that we've seen was so determined to keep them apart often required more than these nascent movements could bear. In 1842 and 1848, African workers in British Guyana went out on strike against a 25 percent reduction in wages, but in both cases the Indian and Portuguese workers failed to join them. The

Portuguese had only started to arrive in Guyana in 1835 and the Indians in 1838, so that they had not been on the land long enough to learn to trust the Africans or to feel that such struggles had long-term benefits for them.

Nevertheless, the failure of solidarity endured in the memory of Africans for decades thereafter and it, significantly, also led to the withdrawal of many Africans from syndicalist action for two generations.[32] In the United States, five thousand Chinese workers, frustrated by the harsh conditions of labor as they built the Central Pacific rail lines, took to the streets in 1867 with the slogan Eight Hours a Day Good for White Men, All the Same Good for Chinamen. Their managers considered importing ten thousand African Americans to replace the strikers, but they decided instead to use armed force to get the Chinese back on the line.[33] In 1857 the Creole press in the Caribbean noted that indentureship is "the enemy, instead of the auxiliary, of freedom."[34] The *problem* may certainly have been indenture, but the emergent African middle class saw the problem, in concrete terms, as *the indentured themselves.* In 1866 Chinese workers on a Trinidadian plantation went out on strike, but Afro-Trinidadian policemen shut them down. Between 1869 and 1872 Indian workers in Guyana went on an enormous and impressive struggle for small grievances to major demands for economic and sexual dignity (against the exploitation of Indian women by managers and overseers).[35] They did not earn the support of the Creole press and other Afro-Guyanese workers. Given this propitious circumstance, the British reported in 1871 that "there will never be much danger of seditious disturbances among East Indian immigrants on estates as long as large numbers of Negroes continue to be employed with them."[36]

The divide-and-rule strategy for social control is not conspiratorial, since it works frequently in the open in the ways in which a society is structured to pit people against one another. Not every leader was unaware that this animosity served only white imperialism. The African American abolitionist Frederick Douglass rose in the defense of the Chinese laborers only four years after Emancipation. "I want a home here not only for the negro, the mulatto and the Latin races," he told a crowd in Boston in 1869, "but I want the Asiatic to find a home here in the United States, and feel at home here, both for his sake and for ours." Douglass noted that "contact with these yellow children of the Celestial Empire would convince us that the points of human difference, great as they, upon first sight, seem, are as nothing compared with the points of human agreement. Such contact would remove mountains of prejudice."[37] When the Chinese Exclusion Act of 1882 came on to the floor of the U.S. Senate, one lone voice held out in dissent, the African

American senator from Mississippi, Blanche K. Bruce.[38] But these early voices are few and far between, and their social effects lie almost entirely in the language of solidarity they have left for us rather than its practice. And yet true moments of alliance if not large-scale movements did occur.

The Devil's Workshop

The world of working-class polyculturalism is best illustrated by the festival tradition of Hosay. In 680 c.e., the grandson of Muhammad (Prophet of Islam), Hussain, died at the battle of Karbala, a death mourned to this day by those who call themselves Sh'ia. When the East Indians first began to draw upon their cultural resources to claim the land on which they now lived, they found that their new neighbors did not seem averse to participation. Those Sh'ia who came from northern India imported the commemoration of the martydom of Hussain, a festival called Muharram in Asia, but called Hosay in the Caribbean (a name that comes from Hussain). Hosay in the early decades of the Caribbean plantation became an East Indian originated—but regionwide holiday for the workers when the planters perforce had to allow their bound coolies permission to leave the confines of the plantation for the day.[39] Like Carnival, Hosay became a festival with vibrant *taziyas* (in the Caribbean, *tajdah*) or handcrafted replicas of Hussain's tomb, often made by Portuguese shopkeepers, carried with aplomb by the polycultural workforce. Hosay was all about social interaction, whether among those on a plantation who strove to build the best *tadjah,* or across plantations to meet and greet people who came together on the ships, *jahajibhai* ("brothers of the ship"), or indeed athwart the color line, to consort with Africans, Amerindians, Chinese, and others. In 1884, a Guyanese planter recorded that the Hosay had "gradually degenerated into a Saturnalia in which Hindus, Mohammedans, and Negroes mingle promiscuously, and rum and ganjah add to the religious fervour of the processionists."[40] The procession would leave the plantation, join with those of other estates, march along a route that included the grog shops of the Portuguese and the Chinese, mock one another, and then end back at their respective plantations. The similarities with Carnival could not be mistaken, and a report from 1904 Guyana observed that at Hosay,

> a few young black men, who reminded me of the masqueraders, followed, their faces lit up with enthusiasm, and marching with a martial tread. The rear was brought up by about a hundred black women, contorting themselves in the eternal cake walk.[41]

Indeed, some features of Hosay were so popular that during Easter, African Christians built a black *tajdah*.[42] Of course, white planters and officials worried about the African participation in East Indian festivals and social life. In 1866, the *Berbice Gazette* noted that "we cannot afford to allow those of the inhabitants of the colony who are removed over so little from heathenism and savagery, to relapse."[43] One magistrate was furious with the "rowdyism" of the 1873 festivals in Guyana, and he excoriated the Africans for their participation in the Hosay. "Even if they celebrated the day upon which Mumbo-Jumbo performed some extraordinary feat, there might be some meaning in the absurdity."[44] What reason did they have, he suggested, to get involved with what he saw as a Sh'ia, and not a working-class, festival.

Hosay, like Canboulay or Carnival, was a space for the interaction of peoples many of whom could not otherwise gather together because of a colonial anxiety about unrest. Free transit was unknown in the plantation colonies, so any festival that broke the strictures on movement became popular with all those among the working population. If workers could not get together on an economic platform, they certainly did find solidarity during cultural gatherings. Each year sugarcane workers held actions against the plantations, but mainly these protests happened as isolated events on the estates. The protest of 1884 was to be very different because it coincided with the Hosay of that year. Since it was tied to the lunar calendar, historian Prabhu Prasad Mohapatra explains, the Hosay did not always come during the season when the sugarcane plantation workers typically went on strikes or conducted other labor actions.[45] From the formation of the sugarcane colonies up to the start of the nineteenth century, colonial cane sugar dominated the European palate, as workers came to rely upon this soft drug as the energy boost for their long days in the factories. "You believe perhaps, gentlemen, that the production of coffee and sugar is the natural destiny of the West Indies," said Marx in 1848. "Two centuries ago, nature, which does not trouble herself about commerce, had planted neither sugar-cane nor coffee trees there. And it may be that in less than half a century you will find there neither coffee nor sugar, for the East Indies, by means of cheaper production, have already successfully combated this alleged natural destiny of the West Indies."[46] The problem was not only India, but also the beetroot. When Napoléon took the Continent, European states enhanced their domestic beet production and created high tariffs to prevent being under the mercy of mainly English imperial cane sugar. The bounties on cane sugar harnessed the growth of the beet sugar industry, which by 1881–82 controlled almost exactly half the world trade in sugar (in 1840, beet sugar was only 4.35

percent of the trade).[47] This dramatic decline in the fortunes of cane sugar had a marked impact on the peoples of the Caribbean, whose destiny had been tied to this most succulent member of the grass family. The drop in sugar prices in the 1880s led to the amalgamation of some estates, to the restriction on cultivated acerage, to further mechanization, and to a reduction of labor costs. The latter occurred in two ways, either through a cut in wages or else by the release of wage laborers to the ranks of the independent farmers (groups of Indians combined resources to buy small plots of land on which they grew staples or, if the market appeared to be reasonable, cash crops).[48] Each year, in the autumn, Mohapatra demonstrates, the sugarcane plantation workforce conducted some labor action against this set of pressures, and in 1884, the Hosay fell during the strike season.

In 1884, the *Port-of-Spain Gazette* depicted the East Indian workers as a people "whose every thought and habit are antagonistic to our system of civilization" and they constituted "a permanent source of danger hanging over our heads."[49] Because of this, a petition for the Hosay from a driver named Sookoo and thirty-one petitioners was rejected by the colonial authorities. Regardless of this verdict, the polycultural workforce continued to erect *tadjahs* and prepare for the festival. The officials also prepared, with the HMS *Dido* at ready off San Fernando and with policemen given arms in Port-of-Spain, San Fernando, Couva, Princes Town, Chaguanas, St. Joseph, and Arouca. The manager of Sookoo's estate, W. Dopson, locked the gates, but a worker, Bal Gopaul Singh, broke them down. When Dopson warned the workers that they'd get shot, Singh offered the brave reply that "it is only powder they have got in their guns. They cannot shoot people like fowls."[50] When the East Indians normally came to town from their plantations to make a complaint, they came "carrying their cutlasses and other agricultural implements," both as a sign of strength and of their labor.[51] At Hosay too the workers brandished their implements, and in 1884 the presence of the tools of their trade underscored the cultural and economic significance of the gathering. The Hosay that year, then, was both a polycultural assertion and a labor protest, and so the plantocracy fired back with gunpower and cultural guile. Twelve people died and over a hundred suffered injuries from the police violence, but the effects of the 1884 crackdown would be much graver than that.

Faced with the combined rage of the Africans, East Indians, Chinese, and others, the colonial state moved fast to reduce contacts among them. The officials bemoaned the complexity of cultural productions such as Hosay and the "loss of culture" of the indentured workers. Since the coolies and

ex-slaves had "forgotten" their "original" cultures, the colonial state advocated the development of dogmatic religious and cultural boundaries among
peoples. Encouraged by colonial authorities, representatives of a Brahmanical orthodoxy, both the Sanathan Dharma Sabha and the Arya Samaj, came
to the Caribbean to put a stop, in effect, to polycultural practices like Hosay.[52] Clerics of Islam also traveled to the far-flung colonies in an attempt to
"reclaim the lost brethren" to the Islam of the homeland.[53] These missionaries claimed to fight against the state-supported Christian missionaries, when
in fact, apart from some Canadians, the state cleared the terrain for the swa-
mis and mullahs to create cultural fissures across the landscape of the working class. Each of these groups, for example, tried to rally East Indians from
the standpoint of an *Indian* religion and culture rather than engage them in
the polycultural practices of their new homeland. What these missionaries
did was to re-center "India" in the consciousness of the East Indians, who
sought a language, culture, and religion for their children and themselves
almost as a comfort zone in a harsh social environment.[54] Hosay was thus
curtailed, while an orthodox kind of spirituality and domesticity that did
not at all resemble everyday interactions was promoted among the East Indians. The Africans bore the weight of a bourgeois Christianity from the missionaries, who had earlier given up on the East Indians—in 1877 a planter
in Guyana noted that "if we cannot make Coolies Christians, let us build
them Hindoo temples."[55] Artistic, religious, spiritual, and social expressions
of the East Indians' everyday life experience such as the brutality of indenture, the monotony of work life on a plantation, the colonial fissures between the Africans and the Asians, the difficulty of forming family and other
social networks in the midst of the plantation, and the attempt to make the
landscape both familiar and sacred were dismissed and even feared.

As a concept, "culture" comes to us from a colonial anthropology that
defined the culture of different "civilizations" ranked by their place on the
racial hierarchy. Europeans deemed their social and cultural archive to be
the highest form of life. Colonial anthropologists evaluated the cultural features of the colonized subjects of the empire and they decided what was to
be the essence of each delimited community's culture. From the eighteenth
century onward European intellectuals accepted that ancient Asia had much
of worth, perhaps because of the Aryan kinship they claimed existed in the
ancient past. Therefore, the *real* culture of Asia was its ancient one and not
the polycultural forms created over the centuries. The stereotype of the essence of Asia and the advice of certain designated leaders (mainly orthodox
priests) defined the cultural lives for real, living East Indians. The long expe-

rience of solidarity and struggle, peasant customs, folk values, and so forth were not regarded as the culture of India. Hosay, a shared experience of poor folks, could hardly, therefore, be seen as the best representative of either Hindu or Muslim East Indian culture.[56] The pressure to separate cultural forms had an impact. A man named Bharath in Trinidad told an interviewer, long after 1884, that he played "hosay, play hosay; carnival nah cyan go dat one, dat one kaper [African] one."[57]

Nevertheless, today the collective experience of the festival remains as it must. One member of the conservative, and separatist, Hindu Sabha told anthropologist Gustav Thaiss a few years ago that Hosay is a ritual to remember the conflict between Hasan (a Muslim) and Hosayn (a Hindu), and that they "died together battling over their Faiths. People now make the tadjahs to commemorate their deaths," he said, and to "show we should all live in unity together."[58] During the Hosay these days, as the Shi'a cry out, "Hosay, Hosay," those who are not inclined toward the faith, but who are part of its polycultural universe, join in with "Hosay, I say," in rhythmic Calypso response.

In line with the fears around Hosay is the issue of interracial relationships. Historian Walton Look Lai's research shows us that between the Chinese and Africans in the Caribbean conjugal relations did not seem entirely uncommon, although most Chinese men remained formal bachelors through their lives (I suspect that further investigation would find that these men produced creative, perhaps queer, social engagements).[59] What is significant is that among the working class, a certain amount of mixedness was tolerated. For instance, the important Trinidadian labor leader of the 1920s was Charles Henry Pierre, a well-known *dougla* (the word, often pejorative, is used to index those of Afro-Indian parentage). For those who aspired to leadership over their communities within the pluralist constitutional framework, these relationships augured ill. Anthropologist Aisha Khan shows us how the bourgeois East Indians see the *dougla* as a mark of "potential engulfment of a minority," as the end to East Indian cultural coherence as such.[60] If more East Indians become *dougla* what would become of East Indian culture, what would become of the demographic category "East Indian" which gave them political power? Within pluralism, the leaders of each ethnic category often intone their "love and respect for each human being," but, as literary critic Shalini Puri rightly notes, love "must never take the form of interracial sex." Pluralism and diversity are often, then, "code words for separatism and racial purity."[61] The newly legitimized orthodoxy tried to paint the colored (Euro-Africans) and the *dougla* (Indo-Africans) with characteristics of licentiousness, as traitors to their various people. But this characterization does not accord with the facts. For instance, in 1923 the government of Trinidad was eager to mandate a language test for the franchise, with "language" meaning English. The orthodoxy of the East Indians, Africans, and Chinese greeted this literacy test with silence. The right to linguistic diversity and the right to a vote regardless of one's education should have galvanized the orthodoxy, but it was Pierre, a *dougla,* who insisted that

> I cannot for the life of me see why a person who is educated in Chinese or Hindi, who is able to work in the community and to make a position for himself and is able to follow the trend of affairs in such a way as to qualify himself as a voter should not be able to come to the polls and say I should like so and so to be returned . . . even in broken English.[62]

The orthodoxy let the "community" down, just as the *dougla* put forth a theory of linguistic diversity in keeping with the polycultural nature of working people, who, when confronted by those who do not live in their linguistic universe, in broken English and hand gestures, can often make sufficient sense of each other's joys and sorrows, and who know the words *strike* and *sardar, ganja* and *policeman.*

As the colonial state cracked down on the polycultural lives of the working people, the organizations of the latter attempted to forge unity on a political plane. Karl Marx wrote that "it is the bad side that produces the movement which makes history, by providing a struggle."[63] The actions of the colonial state and the planters, as well as those of international sugar conglomerates, moved the workers to create their representation. The first such, the Trinidad Workingmen's Association (TWA), was formed in 1897 by professional and artisanal men who felt betrayed by the empire. These professionals formed the TWA not to organize the workers, but to gain a seat before the Royal Commission which visited the British West Indies that year to assess the gravity of the sugarcane depression. The TWA's first president, a pharmacist, argued before the commission that the plantation owners and Indian indenture were the causes of the "starvation wages paid on sugar estates." Such a ungenerous attitude to the working class earned the TWA no friends among the East Indians, and the critique of the sugar interests brought them disdain from the planters. The TWA lapsed into inactivity.[64]

In 1919 the "bad side" of history made its appearance again from several quarters. The islands of the Caribbean suffered a ferocious depression after the war. Disbanded troops from the West Indian regiments experienced racism firsthand within Europe, where they spilled their blood for the empire but did not gain their humanity for it. These angry and well-organized troops found fellowship among the dockworkers whose experience came through camaraderie with the sailors of the world. The 1919 international struggle against imperialism began in Cardiff, Glasgow, and Liverpool, as Chinese, Indian, African, and Arab dockworkers and troops from the empire faced the brunt of metropolitan racism, and fought back.[65] In Trinidad the dockworkers went out on strike, then the mainly Afro-Trinidadian oil and asphalt workers, and eventually the Indo-Trinidadian workers on sugarcane plantations took to the streets. By late 1919, the historian of the TWA, Kelvin Singh, informs us that "the unrest had taken on a trans-ethnic working-class character."[66] As the state prepared its retribution, a secret dispatch revealed that the TWA had branched out to domestic workers who, led by Albertha Husbands, planned a cooks' and houseservants' strike. As well, the colonial office noted, Husbands advocated the use of poison in the households! The TWA was classed by this and other pieces of information as a seditious organization, and the state went after its six thousand members and the rest of the militant workers.[67] The strike was crushed by police violence, with leaders arrested and antistrike legislation adopted, and as the radical leadership of the TWA languished in jail, the despondent membership was taken in a "moderate" direction away from a polycultural politics by state-advised leaders. Nevertheless, the 1919 struggles terrified the planter state which saw the birth of a phenomenon it named the "Creole Coolie" who would refuse to be "manipulated as a buffer against the African." The committee that investigated the riots noted that for years the East Indian population "was looked upon as a substantial safeguard against trouble with the negroes and *vice versa*. With the abolition of immigration such a counterpoise has ceased to exist and the 'creole coolie' will either remain an interested spectator or join the mob."[68]

The TWA did not begin as an organization of all peoples, but it very soon drew in folks from the complex social world of Trinidad. From the late nineteenth century to 1913 the TWA was led by Alfred Richards, the son of Tam Chong, a Chinese indentured worker, and Margaret Richards, a black Barbadian, and from 1923 to 1934 Arthur Cipriani, a white man of French ancestry, steered the TWA. The colonial state and the planters organized the Trinidadian economy so that the Africans worked in the urban areas (as professionals and artisans), while the East Indians worked in the rural areas either on the plantations or else on their small plots. In its early years the TWA was not able to bridge the separate economic interests of these two fractions of the working class, but some of its leaders did struggle to find a common platform for this racialized workforce. In 1917 the relatively unknown TWA championed a genuine working-class political issue when it took up the cause of municipal democracy, but this did little for the rural population. The TWA's first rural measure did not befriend it to the East Indians, due to its stand against indenture. While many East Indians also deplored the brutality of indenture, few of them found the immigrants to be culpable for the woes of capital. The TWA displayed its arrogance when it blamed the indentured laborers for the chronic wage depression. Therefore it didn't try to recruit Indian workers or stand with the Indian workers in their struggle across the plantation world.[69] The experience of 1919 and after transformed the TWA, mainly when East Indians entered the organization and forced it to acknowledge their role as militant Trinidadian workers. Or else pragmatic considerations moved the TWA to embrace East Indians. During the 1928 elections, the TWA obeyed the electoral calculus to support three East Indian candidates in boroughs with a majority East Indian population (St. George, St. Patrick, and Caroni). These leaders went on to hold major roles in the union.

The entry of East Indians into the TWA was a harbinger of change for the political life of Trinidad, but in 1931 the power of the state and of the orthodoxy once more curtailed union. When a bill making divorce legal was brought before the legislators, the TWA first supported it, but then under pressure from his Catholic priests Cipriani urged the TWA to oppose it. His chief adversary on the measure was his Indian vice president Sarran Teelucksingh, who had come to the leadership as a result of the 1928 elections. Cipriani was so incensed by this public repudiation that he assaulted Teelucksingh. Eight hundred and fifty East Indians left the TWA and the blow to working-class unity was not to be undone until 1937.[70] That year, a strike for economic benefits and political power began on the oil fields, then spread rapidly to the sugarcane plantations, threatening the foundation of British rule in the region, principally due to the threat of an impending war.[71] Worker unity emerged as East Indian agricultural workers joined from the start with the mainly Afro-Trinidadian oil workers. At the leadership, three East Indian socialists who "did not separate the interest of [their] race from the larger society" made an alliance with the Grenadian Uriah Butler, the leader of the Trinidad labor movement at the time.[72] These three men, Adrian Cola Rienzi (Krishna Deonarine), F. E. M. Hosein, and Timothy Roodal, with Butler and Daisy Atwell, conceived of a society in which cultural difference would persist, but not to hold back the urges for freedom of all people. In 1938, Daisy Atwell asked Indian women to join her in the struggle, for "once we were taught to hate each other, the employers injected hatred into the minds of the two races one against the other, but now our eyes are opened, we are learning to unite."[73] These leaders, and those who pushed them to leadership, did not try to create a blueprint for cultural tolerance, for they took for granted the vibrancy and vitality of all cultures. Rather, their approach was that *in struggle* cultural forms would be reshaped to accord with the need for popular dignity. An example of this culture in struggle is the world of Rastafarianism.

Catch the Fire

The first Bob Marley album I ever heard, many years after its release, was *Catch a Fire* (1973). What was most memorable about the cover of the album was the tight shot of Marley himself, with his almost dread hair and his fingers on a fat joint at his lips. Later I read of its role as reggae's breakthrough album for the international market,[74] but right then what was most striking (after the music) was the image of the Rasta. Such pictures had not yet become commonplace in Calcutta. Marley's entire persona as a rebel for justice with his socially conscious music, the marijuana, and the long hair were very attractive. But there was something else. Marley looked like a Shaivite hermit, a devotee of Shiva, one of the godheads of the Brahmanical pantheon. Anywhere in India, one can come upon a Shaivite distinguished by his matted hair and the often glazed eyes of someone who has caught the fire of the ganja, marijuana, or hashish. The mendicants smoke ganja as they intone praise to Shiva (*Boom Shankar*) and seek release from their mortal coils. Reggae songs routinely refer to marijuana by the Hindustani word *ganja*, which is derived from Sanskrit. They also use the word *kali*, the name of the ferocious dark-skinned goddess whose temple in Calcutta is a haven for religious tourists. For years the coincidences struck me as something worth a second look.

In fact, the Jamaican use of the word *ganja*, the dreadlocks, and other little details were not coincidental. At the time I did not know that from 1834 to 1916 the British took close to half a million East Indian people to work as indentured labor in the plantations of the Caribbean and of South America. I did not know that most of these people came from eastern India, from the contemporary Indian states of Bihar, Uttar Pradesh, and Bengal. Neither in school nor from elders did I learn of the "new system of slavery" set up at slavery's end, which drew from a Trinidadian ex-indentured laborer this lament, "i no go no way again, i have to wuk, i have to slave trinidad."[75] My vision of Jamaica was of people from Africa, for few ever spoke of the forty thousand indentured laborers who went from eastern India, and also China and Cape Verde, to toil in the fields of the island, and to come into steady contact with those only recently freed from chattel slavery.

When historians Ajai and Laxmi Mansingh wrote a few suggestive pieces in the Jamaican press about the interactions of early Rastafarians and the East Indians, the criticism against them was sharp.[76] While a few scholars found some merit in what they laid out, most took pains to show that Rastafarianism had only one lineage, that from Africa.[77] But I think the Mansinghs make important connections about the way Afro-Asian communities overlapped culturally. Rastafarianism, as most accounts show us, came from a part of agrarian Jamaica mainly populated by East Indians (the rural parishes of Westmoreland, St. Thomas, and St. Catherine) and in its first urban phase, 1930–33, Rastas lived among the East Indians of western Kingston. The first Rasta commune, called Pinnacle, was surrounded by the homes of East Indians.[78] In these regions many of the practices of the dwellers drew from several heritages, not just from those of central Africa and eastern India. If one turns to the realm of the everyday working-class life, it is hard to sector out those aspects of life that are "African" or "Indian," or "Chinese," for there is much that is interwoven to produce a complex Jamaican set of social relations. Much the same can be said of life in Trinidad and Guyana, where food such as goat curry and roti, despite the Hindustani origin of the words, are eaten and cherished by all. After the arrival of the Indians to the islands, Afro-Jamaicans and Indo-Jamaicans exchanged the techniques and vocabulary of agricultural work, and in Trinidad, African and Indian women crossed paths in their door-to-door retail trade or else took routine part in petty street commerce.[79] The peoples of the Caribbean adopted vocabulary from one another and transformed grammatical structures. Thus Trinidadian Hindi ordered compound verbs in the manner of Creole English to produce what we might call a "Creole Hindustani."[80]

In Jamaica, scholarship on religious practice shows us that as the Indian indentured took root in the island with their various eastern Indian Bhakti traditions defined by a personal devotion to a preceptor or an incarnation of God, the newly freed Africans began to worship Christ in the Kumina style distinguished by the ancestor worship of the Ashanti peoples.[81] The simultaneous development of traditions that stress an unmediated relationship between the oppressed and the divine indicates that there might have been some interactions between the indentured and the former slaves, although this might be the weakest link in the Mansinghs' chain.[82] What is wrong perhaps with the Mansinghs' model is their stress on "influences," because this presupposes that the transit was one way. My interest is not so much on origins, but in the necessary connections between working people whose lives intersected and whose everyday practices, therefore, must have informed one another in some way or another. Polyculturalism does not make a strong statement about the direction of adoption, but it does indicate that those forms hitherto seen as pure are perhaps less so. So on to the Rastas.[83]

Rastafarianism emerges in the early 1930s around the time of the installation of Haile Selassie on the throne of Ethiopia. Drawing on the theosophist and theological movements of their time, four Afro-Jamaican clergymen and UNIA members—Leonard P. Howell, Robert Hinds, H. Archibald Dunkley, and Nathaniel Hibbert—preached that African people descended from the original Israelites, that Selassie was the black messiah come to take them back to freedom land, Africa. "Africa" was not just the continent, but also a state of mind, as these four men of the cloth urged a return to African ways and a rejection of Babylon (their name for capitalism). In time these African ways would be called the "Ital" route, with "Ital" drawn from vital and natural—an ecological and communitarian way to exist. But the expression and rituals of the Rastafarian movement bear considerable resemblance to those practiced by the Indo-Jamaicans. Prayer to Kali, a popular deity among the East Indians, was held mostly in isolated spots where a devotee sacrificed a goat to the chants of "*Jai Kali Mai*" ("Praise Mother Kali"), and often the revelers smoked ganja to consecrate the event. "The ceremonial rituals and prayers were restricted to devoted Hindus only," the Mansinghs note, "though some inquisitive Afro-Jamaicans would always eavesdrop at a distance in hidden places."[84] From these ceremonies, the Mansinghs emphasize four features: first that the Rastas may have cultivated the phrase "*Jah Rastafari*" from "*Jai Kali Mai*," although there is reasonable evidence that *Jah* is a shortened form of *Yahweh*, the Hebrew word for God. Second, that many Shaivites and others wear matted hair, *jata* (the people who do this are known as *jatadharis*), and perhaps the Rastas borrowed this practice. Historian Horace Campbell claimed that the custom came from the Mau Mau in the 1950s, but there is hardly more evidence for this than for that presented by the Mansinghs.[85] The third feature is perhaps the easiest place to establish the connection, the world of ganja. Religion scholar Neil Savishinsky offers us adequate evidence of widespread use of narcotics as part of faith rituals in central Africa, but he, along with scholar Kenneth Bilby, is convinced that the use of ganja "is the product of years of intercultural exchange" in Jamaica between the Africans and Indians.[86] Most scholars agree that ganja came to the islands with the East Indians, who used it as an antidote to their terrible life on the plantations.[87] From Fazal, an ex-indentured laborer, we hear that in the early years, "dem smoking ganja, singing like hell, eating like hell, eating and singing, ganja come from india an selling."[88] Ethnographers of the Rastas report that they live within a world where the East Indians smoke with them, sometimes sell them the marijuana grown on their fields, or pass on the Rasta codes for smoking "including gracing the cup before smoking."[89] A fourth feature that the Mansinghs mention and that bears some thought is the turn to vegetarianism by Rastas. One can do little more than speculate that the Indian experience of fasting and purity, some of it gendered and imbued with caste power, may have been adopted uncritically by the Rastas. As William Lewis's ethnography shows, the Rastas spoke much about freedom, but they made a doctrine of denying women moral equality with men: ideas of women's purity could have come from devout, but often misogynist, East Indian men.[90]

The Rastafarian movement draws from all manner of cultural traditions to create a coherent cultural world of its own. The life of Leonard Howell, the most spectacular character among the founders, exemplifies the polyculturalism of Rastafarianism. Born in 1898, Howell traveled far and wide, especially for a considerable sojourn in New York's Harlem, where he lived in the intellectual and political circles of Marcus Garvey and George Padmore.[91] In the United States, during the 1920s, Howell discovered Lauron William de Laurence's theosophist-inspired *Dream Book* (which some have since called the "Obeah Bible"). First published in 1904, de Laurence's work bears all the marks of the theosophist tradition of Madame Blavatsky and Colonel Olcott. Blavatsky and Olcott drew from the multifaceted wisdom of India to create an esoteric, and transnational, sect devoted to the search for the mysteries of the universe. De Laurence's treatise *The Book of Magical Art, Hindu Magic and Indian Occultism* followed Blavatsky's veneration of the "masters of *occult wisdom* on the high plateau of *Thibet*," who are only the very finest at "*telepathy, or mind-reading*," which "in *India* [is] a national characteristic."[92] Filled with talk of "adepts" and "Lamas" as well as of alchemy, the book was well known and well used among African Americans. The most popular chapter was the last one entitled "Dreams and Visions."[93] De Laurence translated dream images into numbers so that a hopeful gambler could convert his or her own dreams into bets for the next day's street lottery.

Numbers, itself, was, as journalist Roy Ottley proposed in 1943, introduced to the African American community when the Chinese Americans hired "Negro runners and collectors" to work the "Chinese Lottery."[94] Harlem in the early decades of the twentieth century was inundated by "fakirs and charlatans of every brand," people like High John the Conqueror with his love potions, Madame Fu Tuttam, "a seeress of Negro-Chinese parentage," and Rajah Rabo, a "dream book author."

> Sometimes closed motion-picture houses, empty stores, and lodge halls were converted into "temples," with announcements plastered on the buildings that were cheap and alluring, calling the citizenry to find out what trouble was brewing. The operators of these places turned neat profits from the sale of dream books, policy pamphlets, love potions, and incense to destroy evil spirits. Two questions they unfailingly answered in the affirmative: "Am I going to find work?" and "Am I going to hit the numbers?"[95]

By the 1920s, publishers produced "Dream Books" designed for African American gamblers.[96]

Inspired by de Laurence's *Dream Book*, Howell was taken by the Orientalist movement, particularly the mysterious use of "India" in the occult circles within which there is the tradition of the *Illuminati*. In 1935 under the name of Gangunguru (or G. G.) Maragh, Howell published *The Promise Key*, a work that owes as much to the 1935–36 events in Ethiopia[97] as it does to the occultist predilections he learned from de Laurence.[98] The name Howell took as his nom de plume comes from Hindustani. Gangunguru Maragh sounds like Gyanguru Maharaj ("Venerable Teacher of Knowledge"), but rather than Maharaj it might be Marg, which would give us "the Road of the Venerable Teacher."[99] Howell was not alone in his interest in the various forms of Hinduism known in the United States. In 1918, one of his associates Joseph Hibbert told his friends that he was entranced by the idea of an incarnate God (figures such as Rama and Krishna) common among the East Indian peasantry. Perhaps, he felt, people of African ancestry needed such a godhead to give them strength and inspiration and Haile Selaisse was to be that figure.[100]

With this background on the interconnected world of everyday life in Jamaica, it should come as no surprise that a few of the important producers of early ska and reggae music came from among a small Chinese community in Jamaica. When Howell and others created their Rasta commune at Pinnacle, their spiritual musician was Count Ossie, whose producer was one Prince Buster. In the 1960s, Buster joined Vincent "Randy" Chin, Charlie Moo, and Leslie Kong to produce the sound that would become vintage Bob Marley. When the planters ceased to import Chinese labor into Jamaica (partly because of a ban on emigration by the Chinese emperor), the small community on the island worked out their indentures and a section went into the small merchant trade. As shopkeepers, many Chinese merchants flourished to the extent possible in a relatively poor section of the economy, and the descendants of these traders brought the capital that enabled the production of many of the early reggae records.[101] In 1962 two of these Chinese-Jamaican businessmen produced a pair of the most powerful anti-colonial nationalist tunes: Chin with Lord Creator gave us "Independent Jamaica" and Kong with Derrick Morgan offered the ska-inflected "Forward March" (number one and number three on the Jamaican charts for the year). That same year Kong worked with one Robert Marley on the short and sweet "Judge Not," while in 1963 he coproduced "King of Kings" with Jimmy Cliff.[102] The sounds of Jamaica came, then, not just from those who claim their ancestry from Africa, but from the polycultural world of Jamaican life that seemed to find itself in the ska, roots, and dub beats.[103]

After *Coolie*

If Hosay, Rasta, and the TWA are a good examples for the practices of the polycultural working class that came under the gun of the colonial-planter state, Garveyism and Gandhianism are good examples of populism among the working class. Unable to sustain their own organizations, the polycultural working class attempted to find its vitality in the organizations set up by its middle-class representatives. The TWA tried to forge a polycultural political agenda, but it was not to be sustained in the face of imperialism. Two populist formations in this period that did create some traction against British imperialism (and did organize the polycultural working class) were led by people who attempted to organize the masses based on a racial-nationalist model. Marcus Garvey (1887–1940) and Mohandas Gandhi (1869–1948), respectively, emerged as the major leaders of the African and Indian diaspora at around the same time. Garvey was head of the Universal Negro Improvement Association, with a stress on the word *Negro*, while Gandhi became the leader of a political party founded in 1885, the Indian National Congress (INC), with a stess on the word *Indian*. The frameworks for both movements are racial-national, but neither Garvey nor Gandhi could hold back the polycultural pressures from below.

Garvey set up the UNIA in Jamaica in 1914, which he then took to the United States in 1917; Gandhi emerged at the crest of a strike wave in southern Africa in 1913, whose glory took him to the leadership of the Indian National Congress in India by 1917. As Garvey enunciated an anti-imperialism of self-rule, so too did Gandhi, and both felt a sense of unease about mass leadership of the struggle. Just as Garvey evinced regard for, but not solidarity with, East Indians, so too did Gandhi fail to fully engage in the creation of an Indian-African alliance in South Africa. Both spoke out on behalf of the struggle of each other's "people," but without too much consideration for the diverse needs of the "people."[104]

In Trinidad, for instance, Garveyism drew people into the struggle, but it also repeated the fissures of colonialism. The TWA shared some of its most important leaders with Garvey's UNIA, notably TWA secretary James Braithwaite (president of the Port-of-Spain UNIA), TWA president John Sydney de Bourg (UNIA's leader of the Negroes of the Western Provinces of the West Indies and South and Central America), and TWA's *Labour Leader* editor W. Howard Bishop (who ran stories from the UNIA's *Negro World* in the TWA's paper). In 1915, however, when the Indo-Trinidadians and the Afro-Trinidadian small peasants held joint protests against unfair cane prices, the TWA president (and UNIA member) denied that East Indians workers counted as *labor*. The working class, he felt, "was limited to the Negro element of the island."[105] But both the UNIA and the TWA could not deny its polycultural and energized base, so that its adherents had to hew the line of a multiethnic politics however much it tried to disavow itself from such a political world. In 1922 Garvey took as the editor and foreign affairs columnist of his paper *Negro World* Hucheshwar G. Mudgal, who had been born in India and come to the United States via Trinidad. One of Garvey's closest associates was Haridas T. Muzumdar, a Gandhian, who took to Garvey after he read an account of a lynching in the United States. He said of the event, "I could not eat for two days."[106] Furthermore, a "race man" like Howell hoped, in 1933, that he could become the Gandhi of Jamaica, not just the leader of his "people" but of a populist and diverse movement.[107] In 1913, in Guyana, the East Indian sugarcane workers at Rose Hall Estate struck not only against the planters, but also against their overseer, Jugmohan, whose feudal, misogynist and Brahmanical behavior rankled them. To help them came Joseph Eleazer, a black barrister, and Dr. Ram Narayan Sharma, an East Indian doctor and Hindi scholar, friends in struggle, and along the grain of the polycultural instincts of the workers.[108] The nationalist model would not know what to make of this—the sheer complexity of connections suffused with the idea of race renders the nationalist framework inadequate. Nor would it know what to make of the well-named literary and political Trinidadian magazine the *Beacon,* published from 1931 to 1934 to explore the development of a West Indian identity. Its writers included the Marxist C. L. R. James, the future Labour minister Albert Gomes, many Garveyites, as well as a regular "India Section" to engender unity.

Gandhi's political career began in South Africa, but there is only fleeting evidence that he sought to create an Afro-Asian politics or at least one that challenged the divide-and-rule policy of the government. However, only a few years into his South African career Gandhi developed a very significant friendship with the leader of the Natal "natives," Reverend John Langalibalele Dube. When Gandhi founded the Natal Indian Congress in 1894, Dube drew from this model to create the Natal Native Congress in 1900. Gandhi introduced the readers of his *Indian Opinion* to Dube as "a Negro of whom one should know," and he gave Dube access to the *Indian Opinion*'s press at the Phoenix Settlement to print Dube's English-Zulu paper *Ilange lase Natal* ("Light of Natal").[109] Both Gandhi and Dube did not react well to the famous Bambata or Zulu rebellion of 1906, and neither gave his full support to the rebels under Chief Bambata. Gandhi, in fact, offered his services to the ambulance brigade, mainly to serve the Zulu wounded (it was this act that Gandhi said "eased my conscience" and led him down the path to *Brahmacharya*, or "self-realization"[110]). In 1913, Gandhi was overtaken by the powerful upsurge of energy from among the Indian workers, whose strike consolidated the reputation of this until then unknown lawyer. Remembering the strike some years later, Gandhi wrote that "the whole community rose like a surging wave. Without organisation, without propaganda, all—nearly 40,000 —courted imprisonment. Nearly ten thousand were actually imprisoned. A bloodless revolution was effected after strenuous discipline in self-suffering."[111] The working-class, mainly Tamil, leadership was in touch with black militants, and, as South African historian Maureen Swan argues, "with the Zulu rebellion only seven years in the past, it is reasonable to suppose that there was some apprehension about the possibility of the blacks being drawn into another—possibly violent—resistance movement."[112] The fear of a rising of black workers in the south on behalf of the Indian mine workers of northern Natal and the Indian sugarcane workers of the south coast was significant pressure to cause a settlement.[113] Dr. Abdurahman, of Indian ancestry and president of the African Political Organization (a multiethnic formation), praised the passive resistance movement and extolled the "natives" to protest so that "the economic foundations of South Africa would suddenly shake and tremble with such violence that the beautiful white South African superstructure which had been built on it would come down with a crash, entailing financial ruin, such as had never been witnessed before."[114]

Dube's newly formed South African Native National Congress (later the African National Congress) did not join the struggle, mainly because Dube himself did not think it as yet possible to move the "natives" to nonviolent resistance. If the Indian and African working class did not begin its career in South Africa on a multiethnic political platform, sections of the workers did indeed experience the failures of accommodation with the apartheid regime, an insight that led independently of Gandhian-style populism into alliances of Indians with Africans.[115] In 1939, the Reverend S. S. Tema, a "native" South African, interviewed Gandhi, who told him that Indians and Africans in South Africa should work together, but not work within the same organizations—"You will be pooling together not strength but weakness." Importantly, Gandhi noted that the Indians must be urged not to "run you down as 'savages,' while exalting themselves as cultural people in order to secure concessions for themselves at your expense."[116] If Gandhi-Dube felt that unity in one organization was not to be recommended, the South African Communist Party (SACP) felt it was imperative. In 1943, the SACP formed the Non-European Unity Movement, which was a forum for Africans, Indians, and the so-called Coloureds (in alliance with white radicals) to forge unity in struggle against white supremacy.

The will of the polycultural working class, then, drew from, and exceeded, the attempts by Gandhi and Garvey to retain the boundaries set up by imperialism. The modern odyssey of the Africans and the Asians in the Caribbean and in southern Africa is enframed within the political economy of imperialism. The harsh context of expropriation and exploitation reminds us that the mutual contempt between our bedraggled peoples is not for want of empathy. Over the past fifty years and more, the descendants of the coolies and the slaves have struggled against the legacy both of social fractures and of the mobility of some at the expense of others. The brave fights have been structured between the dialectic of division and unity, of segregation and solidarity. In South Africa, the Three Doctors Pact of 1947 (signed by Dr. Yusuf Dadoo, Dr. G. M. Naicker, and Dr. A. B. Xuma—presidents of the Natal and Transvaal Indian Congresses and of the African National Congress) was the foundation for the antiapartheid struggle, which began in earnest around the June 1946 agitation against the "Ghetto Act" and took on steam with the 1952 Campaign for Defiance Against Unjust Laws. In 1952, again, Dr. Eric Williams, in Trinidad, said of the East Indians that they are a "hostile and recalcitrant minority," a phrase that undid the enthusiasm for independence in that island nation. The Purana of the coolies is still being written, caught as it is in the dialectic between the neoliberalism and racialism of Trinidad's new prime minister Basdeo Panday and the socialism of South Africa's late Chris Hani, between the urges of partition and concord. Even as the *coolie becomes cool*,[117] it is only through a genuine polycultural struggle for social justice that the coolie will cease to be *coolie*. Divisions are undone when we inhabit and struggle through them.

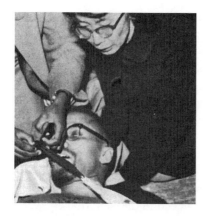

Chapter 4

The Merchant Is Always a Stranger

The Jews aren't strangers. The Jews know their history, the Jews know their culture, the Jews know their language; they know everything there is to know about themselves. They know how to rob you, they know how to be your landlord, they know how to be your grocer, they know how to be your lawyer.[1]

Malcolm's vitriolic rhetoric about the Jewish merchants stirred up Harlem, and it came along the grain of decades of tough talk from activists within the beleaguered black community. Despite the Emancipation Proclamation and the pledges of Reconstruction, black Americans remained mainly in the strata of the working class and the peasantry. Those who moved to neighborhoods like Harlem in 1901 usually worked as domestic servants and manual laborers (74 percent). A small fraction worked as artisans (10 percent), most of whom were barbers, tailors, dressmakers, and builders, and only a few were self-employed (5.5 percent).[2] Hard work seemed to bring few rewards, as Jim Crow institutions excluded African Americans from access to capital and credit, the two financial instruments crucial for advancement in a capitalist society. In 1901, W. E. B. Du Bois wrote that the color line prevented African Americans from the merchant trade. The "ever present factor of racial prejudice," he wrote, "is present to hinder or at least make more difficult the advance of the colored merchant or business man, in new or unaccustomed lines."[3] Without capital, it was not possible for the black merchant to do what many immigrant merchants had done: pool resources—money and skills—and provide special ethnic commodity needs to one's community. Historian Kevin Gaines points out that much of the African American leadership in the post-Reconstruction period married the concept of racial uplift with the accumulation of wealth.[4] Booker T. Washington worried that the black community spent its earnings elsewhere and that it did not produce a business class of its own. He was, therefore, instrumental in the creation of the New York–based National Negro Business League. The organization worked alongside the Professional and Business Men's Social Club (1890s) and the New York Colored Business Men's Association (1916) to advance the interest of black businessmen. Because of these groups, black-owned businesses flourished in the period when racist segregation was at its highest, from 1919 to 1929.[5] The Depression put an end to the gains of these years, however, and the black community was once more prey to nonblack merchants. In the early 1930s, even though Harlem was filled with Greeks, and Italian and Irish retailers, it was the Jewish merchants who faced the ire of the black community. The figure of the Jew in Harlem provides us with an avenue to discuss the "trader as stranger," the prefiguration of the Korean from the 1980s to the present. I should say right now that this chapter is not another of those self-righteous diatribes against black anti-Semitism. I am quite in line with philosopher Lewis Gordon who argues that the discourse of "black anti-Semitism," "black homophobia," and "black misogyny" appears as if there is no general problem of anti-Semitism, homophobia, and misogyny; the trope of "black pathology" makes it easy to burden blacks with these social ills, while others can rest easy in their shallow liberalism. "We," Gordon suggests to the liberal reader, "should ask ourselves about the political value of focusing our critical gaze on hatred expressed by groups who lack the institutional power to order that hatred systematically or structurally . . . It's safer to criticize the powerless."[6] In considering the "Jew," then, we need to show how capitalism operates in the United States to occlude the racism of its practices by creating social structures that pit people against one another.

In the late nineteenth and early twentieth centuries, the New York black press offered contradictory stories about the Jewish merchants within Harlem. In 1905 the *Age* called the Jews "a peculiar race. It is parasitical and predatory . . . preying upon and devouring the substance of others rather than creating and devouring the substance of itself. That is essentially the race characteristic of all parasites, all race fungi. It is the peculiarity of the Jew that if there is profit in anything he will discover it." In 1908 a story appeared in the black press that chastised a group of Jewish real estate owners for their attempt to exclude blacks from lower Harlem. The anti-Semitism, then, came alongside the racism of the Jewish propertied. And yet there were just as many stories that urged black readers to acquire "a little of the Jewish enterprise and spirit." Booker T. Washington noted that the Jews bore the weight of terrible oppression in Europe, but they were able to succeed in the United States "because the Jewish race has had faith in itself." He warned that "unless the Negro learns more and more to imitate the Jew in these matters, to have faith in himself, he cannot expect to have any high degree of success."[7] Washington's call to emulate Jews was contradictory, for while it may be seen as a form of admiration for Jewish success, it was heard as a call to arms against Jewish success on the backs of black customers. In 1889, Florence Williams, a Washingtonian, asked blacks to imitate the Jews to place their "race upon a scale of absolute independence and domination in financial circles and to compel the world to acknowledge their business genius."[8] Jews were not quite white, so their gains were more accessible to African Americans but they also weren't black and that fact made their apprent success unwelcome. Several decades later the journalist Roy Ottley would write:

> The whole business of anti-Jewish sentiment among Negroes is largely an urban manifestation and stems directly from the Negro's own depressed condition socially and economically, and is essentially an *anti-white* manifestation . . . By some unique accident, it is the Jew who is today the Negro's main point of contact with the white race—landlord, merchant, employer, and, to a small degree, professional people. Thus the treatment which the Negro experiences from the white group is mainly at the hands of Jews.[9]

Ottley prefigured James Baldwin's famous 1967 statement that "Negroes are Anti-Semitic Because they're Anti-White," that the "most ironical thing about Negro anti-Semitism is that the Negro is really condemning the Jew for having become an American white man," in other words, an oppressor in the capitalist system.[10] Of course, a host of other interactions complicate this relationship, including a shared struggle for civil rights and black liberation, the phenomenon of black Jews, the linkages of blacks and Jews in the world of jazz, and, importantly, the dialogues among black and Jewish theologians.[11] Still, the black-Jewish relationship is rather too cavalierly reduced to the experience of the (Jewish) small merchant and (black) impoverished customer.

By the early twentieth century, Jews ran many of Harlem's shops where blacks could not find employment (this may have been part of the exigency of small shops that relied upon family labor, rather than antiblack racism, but from the standpoint of a dispossessed community, the distinction is marginal). Washington's idea of "self-help" did not mean that individuals should help themselves, but that the black community should frequent only black merchants, this to use captive ethnic markets to promote a black bourgeoisie. "As long as Negroes talk race loyalty and race rights," noted Adam Clayton Powell Sr., pastor of the Abyssinian Baptist Church, "and then spend their money with white business and professional men," racism would prevail.[12] When the Depression hit, it struck the small black middle class hardest. By the 1930s, the collapsed middle class was championed by the likes of Washington and the Powells (both father and son) in customer boycotts against white, and often Jewish, stores. The Don't Buy Where You Can't Work movement began in Chicago in 1931, and it soon spread across the country, notably to Harlem, where in 1935 it led to a general uprising against the shopkeepers. Vandalism and boycotts formed the main tactics of the disorganized movement, which drew a swift response from the police and little support from Harlem's masses.[13] Nevertheless, the Harlem riot touched a nerve in the community. Well-known progressive Nannie Burroughs wrote in *The Afro-American* that

> the causes of the Harlem riot are not far to seek. They lie buried beneath
> mountains of injustices done to the colored man in every state and in
> every relationship, through years of patient sufferance on his part. In deal-
> ing with colored people, America makes void the law through custom—
> that's the deep-seated cause of the Harlem riot. Colored folks feel that
> Harlem is their last stand.[14]

Black urban folklore in Harlem saw the merchant (now mostly seen as Jewish) as the barricade against black liberation, and it was this political terrain that produced the fiery, but misguided, subaltern nationalism of the Harlem Labor Union, Inc. led by two well-known African American activists, Ira Kemp and Arthur Reed. Kemp and Reed found a kindred spirit in a man who was known to his adherents as His Holiness Bishop Amiru Al-Mu-Minin Sufi A. Hamid, head of the Universal Holy Temple of Tranquility. In Chicago, Sufi worked the South Side, where he was known as Bishop Conshankin (Buddhist missionary and Oriental magician), and before that as Eugene Brown of Lombard Street, Philadelphia.[15] The trio of Sufi, Kemp, and Reed joined together as partisans for black employment in a tight labor market.

Sufi, Kemp, and Reed wanted economic justice for blacks (with their Jobs for Negroes campaign), but they targeted their efforts at the Jewish merchants. Those merchants, however, who owned or managed small businesses in the early decades of the twentieth century worked against the tide of U.S. capitalism which ran toward large monopoly firms that cornered markets to their benefit. A small shop in Harlem was at the mercy of the banks, wholesalers, and retail outfits that worked in concert with each other (either as formal franchises or else in informal collaboration). In this market, shopkeepers tried to cultivate all manner of advantages, especially ties of ethnic solidarity. But the peril of being a small shopkeeper was only compounded if the owner was black. African American entrepreneurs could find shops to rent only in the "least desirable location," and, as we know, they could not gain access to capital funds that would permit a well-stocked store, and the wholesale merchants rarely extended them credit. "Negro merchants are so rare," Du Bois noted of Philadelphia, "that it is natural for customers, both white and colored, to take it for granted that their business is poorly conducted without giving it a trial."[16]

If black shops did not have the wherewithal to be extravagant to the consumer, black shoppers "found that they could get credit and a greater variety of goods at white-owned stores," and if they could not pay immediately, they could buy goods on an installment plan (where the merchant combined tasks of creditor and salesperson).[17] Ottley found that for the customer the "inability to meet regularly any kind of payments creates irritability; and if pressed for payment, [the customer] is stirred to anger, which is expressed in hostility to the merchant." Many of the merchants overcharged their desperate customers for second-rate goods and their customers knew it. "Because the merchants in Negro neighborhoods are mainly Jewish," Ottley argued, "the charges are placed at the Jew's doorstep. Obviously, sharp business practices are common to all merchants, gentiles as well as Jews."[18] The small merchant worked in the vise of capitalism and the American Dream: the merchant has to hew the line of profit against punitive insurance and interest regimes (as well as monopoly control by wholesalers) at the same time as the merchant desires the quick fix of the American Dream to send children to the finest colleges, to own a house, to drive a car. The dual pressure on the small merchant augments the racism experienced by the disenfranchised ghetto resident.

In 1936, the radical economics professor at Howard University Abram Harris took a nuanced position against bourgeois nationalism. Harris was close to the Communist Party which was at that time leading a strike inspired in part by the anti-immigrant and anti-Semitic practices of the W. T. Grant chain.[19]

> Denied equal competition with whites in higher positions of the capitalist
> set-up and thwarted in its ambition to develop a miniature capitalism
> within its own segregated racial domain, the Negro middle class is being
> driven into a position of extreme racial chauvinism toward other minori-
> ties . . . If there is exploitation of the black masses in Harlem the Negro
> businessman participates in it as well as the Jew, while both the Jewish busi-
> nessman and the Negro are governed by higher forces that are beyond
> their control . . . Although it is essentially the product of the revolt of the
> Negro middle class against the ever increasing restriction of their eco-
> nomic opportunities, this racial chauvanism is becoming the escape of
> the black masses bewildered by unemployment and hunger.[20]

Like Harris, the Communists recognized that structural racism was built on
historically appropriated values, that the detritus of racism rendered the
ghetto capital-denuded but work-intensive.[21] Here people labored hard to
control their destiny, but their frustrations led, in many cases, to a belabored
anger at the small merchant, the "trader as stranger."

Strange Traders, Stranger Capitalism

In 1908, the German sociologist Georg Simmel wrote an essay entitled "The
Stranger" in which he offered the tantalizing thought that "throughout the
history of economics the stranger everywhere appears as the trader, or the
trader as stranger."[22] Simmel suggested that the traders bring goods that typically emanate from outside the economic activities of an area and that the
traders' connection with these exotic goods marks them as foreign. Furthermore, "the stranger is by nature," Simmel wrote, "no owner of soil—soil not
only in the physical, but also in the figurative sense of a life-substance which
is fixed, if not in a point in space, at least in an ideal point of the social environment." The trader, then, is an outsider, one who has no title to either the
(physical) soil or the (spiritual) nation.

While Simmel's own analysis may be full of flaws, he left us with a powerful image of the the "trader as stranger." A product of his times, Simmel
captured a then-common sentiment, that the problem of working-class and
under-employed peoples stemmed from ethnic differences between customers and merchants, that anti-Semitism may find its root in the preva-
lence of Jewish merchants in gentile neighborhoods. In our own time, and
in the United States, there is the assumption that "race riots" occur because
of Asian (mainly Korean) grocers in black (and Latino) neighborhoods.
These merchants who are physically distinguishable from their customers,

who may not have been born and raised in the community are forever alien, and their alienness marks them for retribution for the widespread poverty in our urban areas.

In the United States, Simmel's stranger thesis found its domestic version in Edna Bonacich's "middleman minority" approach, in which the (mainly immigrant) minority creates a niche in "trade and commerce" as well as "other 'middleman lines' such as agent, labor contractor, rent collector, money lender, and broker."[23] The immigrant stands in the middle between the white elites, who dominate the economic system, and customers who are mainly nonwhite but who are not of the same ethnic background of the trader. The traders' ill-feeling provokes the anger of the customers; the customers' poverty produces rage against the trader. If the coolies and formerly enslaved peoples on the plantation at the very least shared deprivation, here the only thing shared is the space of commerce, with one ethnicity symbolizing demand and the other supply.

The "trader as stranger" or the "middleman minority" approach lays out some of the principal dilemmas of urban tension in the United States. Conflict is immanent in the socioeconomic relationships, so that Los Angeles or Brooklyn's Crown Heights in 1992 is not the start of the problem, but only those moments of strife that reveal a structure of class struggle. The "trader as stranger," in many of the sociological accounts, appears as a result of conscious choices among an ethnic group, who, by some sort of rational process, chooses the job of provisioning the U.S. working poor. There is little analysis of the place of the multiracist state in its guidance of the immigrants into such jobs, not just at the level of the Immigration and Naturalization Service, but also through the discriminatory credit regimes (which often favor those who are stereotyped as good business people) and racist law and order strategies (which incarcerate large numbers of black youth, thus removing them from economic activity). In 1901, a British official in East Africa noted that "on account of our Indian Empire we are compelled to reserve to British control a large portion of East Africa. Indian trade, enterprise and emigration require a suitable outlet. East Africa is, and should be, from every point of view, the America of the Hindu."[24] That is, while the British drew immense amounts of surplus from southern Asia, they recognized the need to furnish sections of the displaced southern Asian gentry and middle castes with the means of survival. In East Africa, the southern Asian merchant could then eke out a livelihood by providing goods and services to the African working class and peasantry who were also under the heel of the British. If we replace the word *British* with *American*, *East Africa* with *Har-*

lem, and *Indian* with *Korean,* we have a contemporary view of how the United States is able to stabilize its imperial role in the Koreas. Meanwhile, those who shape and mainly benefit from the economic order appear exculpated from the systematic deprivation in this country: the white elites can be liberal because they do not have to be at the front lines of class struggle. For the working poor the merchant appears to be the decisive exploiter and oppressor, while financial houses are protected by their spatial invisibility and by their crafty mechanisms that create economic distance. Because of this perverse logic, the oppressed in urban America seek to destroy the shops, if not in the name of the white elites, then certainly not in opposition to them.[25] And the idea of the "Korean," forged in the smithy of U.S. imperial policies, becomes the determinate contradiction to black liberation, while in fact it is that very conceit of imperialism that should be in the gunsights instead.

Halal in Harlem

On February 21, 1965, Malcolm X, blasted by bullets of the Nation of Islam's assassins (helped along by the convenient lapse of the U.S. state—which monitored every act of both the Nation and of the victim), fell to the stage of the famous Audubon Ballroom that graces New York's Harlem district. In the flurry after his death, a review of Malcolm's posthumously published autobiography appeared in the *New York Times,* in which he was lauded as a man who "understood, perhaps more profoundly than any other Negro leader, the full, shocking extent of America's psychological destruction of its Negroes."[26] The autobiography has since sold more than three million copies. His life has become the stuff of legend and the legacy of its last few years remains in the hearts of progressive people across the United States.

Two days before his death, Malcolm said that "it's time for martyrs now. And if I am to be one, it will be in the cause of brotherhood. That's the only thing that can save this country. I've learned it the hard way—but I've learned it."[27] How unfortunate then that more than thirty-five years after his death few Americans understand that Malcolm always already lived in a polycultural world (even if his politics did not measure up to it). Soon after Malcolm was shot, his head was cradled in the lap of his friend and comrade, Yuri Kochiyama. Born in 1921 to Japanese immigrant parents, Yuri spent World War II in an internment-concentration camp in the U.S. South. She got involved in the civil rights struggle in the 1950s, moved to Harlem in the 1960s, and was active in the liberation movement of the time, before joining the Republic of New Africa in 1969. She fought for Puerto Rican freedom as well as in the nascent Asian American movement, and despite a stroke in 1997, she continues to fight for the freedom of Mumia Abu-Jamal and other political prisoners.[28] A life of struggle was met halfway by the meteor of Malcolm X. Among radical Asian Americans the vision of Yuri holding Malcolm in her arms is by now commonplace, just as it is almost unknown among African Americans.

While Los Angeles was in flames, journalist and editor Joe Wood asked black intellectuals to "critique Malcolm X and to make sense of Malcolm X's currency among us, and to make sense of *Blackness* itself—its meaning today and its usefulness as a concept to African Americans."[29] In the 1960s Malcolm sharpened the anti-merchant ideology as he worked within the contradiction between anticapitalist and racist thought, between a visceral hatred for the merchant as merchant, and as Jew. Cultural critic Michael Eric Dyson, in a nuanced study of the X-phenomenon, shows us that the resurgence of black nationalism in the 1990s drew from Malcolm not so much for his ideological framework but for his style: the uncompromising oratory of Malcolm and his denunciation of both white supremacy and black bourgeois liberalism find a home in the hearts of those who are casualties of late capitalism.[30] Malcolm today is both an icon of blackness (illustrated by the sales of the X caps as a promotion for Spike Lee's monumental *Malcolm X*) and a mask of blackness ("You're talking Black when you wear these things," suggested Joe Wood).[31] The meaning of Malcolm which comes from a detailed account of his place in the anti-merchant struggle, then, is far more complex. Most accounts of Malcolm tend to see him as a one-dimensional black nationalist who, at the end of his life, came to a wider political vision which was not quite worked out before his death. The life and death of Malcolm, however, exudes the sort of polycultural ethos that motivates this book. Malcolm, for me, is a rich figure who cannot be seen as the possession of a people, or the posthumous leader of a territorial nationalist movement.

Most people who have read Malcolm's speeches in the last few years recognize that he had moved away from the racialism of the Nation of Islam toward a kind of antiracist socialism. To students at Columbia University on February 18, 1965, a few days before his death, Malcolm underscored the fact that "it is incorrect to classify the revolt of the Negro as simply a racial conflict of black against white, or as a purely American problem. Rather we are today seeing a global rebellion of the oppressed against the oppressor, the exploited against the exploiter."[32] But I don't want to remain with those last years to show that Malcolm's change of heart means he recognized the salience of a polyculturalist practice. Rather, I want to show that even when Malcolm was, as he put it on February 18, "asleep somewhat and under some-one else's control," he was engulfed by cultural forces that crept in mostly, but not wholly, unbeknownst to him.

When Malcolm moved to Harlem to take charge of New York City's Temple no. 7 (on Lenox Avenue and 116th Street) in 1954, he had not been a Muslim for long. Islam, like many faiths, does not only suggest a spiritual path to deliverance, but it also enjoins the believer to certain daily rituals. One of which is to eat only halal meat. In the Harlem of the 1950s, it was not easy to find a Muslim butcher, so many of the early Muslims bought their meat from kosher stores.[33] The alternative was the "Indian stores" opened by Bengali immigrants from East Pakistan (what became Bangladesh in 1971). As southern Asia won its independence from British rule, the partition of the subcontinent created the unwieldy state of Pakistan (with western and eastern provinces separated by India). East Pakistan suffered the vagaries of a sundered economy, as it lost its agricultural and industrial relationship with the rest of Bengal (now in India) and it became the junior partner to the districts of West Pakistan. Two of Pakistan's principle foreign exchange earners came from the harvests of the East, tea and jute, yet East Pakistan was already prone to food shortages.[34] Such economic pressures, combined with the cultural insensitivity of the new Pakistani regime to the Bengalis of the east, resulted in the emigration of a number of men. These men hoped to earn enough money to shore up the family economy at home, and perhaps to buy land and shift class positions. Many of them, however, remained in places like New York, where they married into the Puerto Rican and African American communities and settled into the ways of the big city. Along Lenox Avenue in Harlem, a handful of Bengali stores opened to retail all manner of goods, including the elusive halal meat. "Malcolm X apparently frequented a halal place on Lenox Ave. where he was good friends with a few of the Bengali Muslims," recounts Alaudin, the son of one of those Bengalis who came to Spanish Harlem in the 1940s and opened a small restaurant.[35] For Malcolm, these merchants enriched the community and there is no evidence of his fulminations against their class depredations. Why did these merchants not appear as strangers? What was the reason for their acceptance? Perhaps, in the words of one trader, Malcolm was "one of us," a Muslim, but also a person of color reviled by white supremacy. The shared bitterness and the shared sense of community, which the Muslims call the *ummah* ("the world of believers"), perhaps altered the image of the merchant as stranger if the merchant was a Muslim of color.

In fact, Nation of Islam founder Elijah Muhammed's closest ideological ally, formally outside of the Nation, was Pakistani immigrant Abdul Basit Naeem. Naeem worked in New York as a journalist recruited by Muhammad to produce *The Moslem World* and *The USA* in the 1950s. Aware of the problems of the racialist core of the Nation's teaching, Naeem declared that "we would rather see an all-black Moslem community in America than none at all." For his loyalty, Naeem was invited to address the 1957 annual convention of the Nation, from whose pulpit he said that Elijah Muhammad was a leader "whose teachings and messages are just about the only way I can now see of bringing the so-called Negroes into, or shall I say back into, the fold of Islam en masse."[36] Naeem was not the only South Asian to have a hand in the milieu of the Nation. Two others bear mention: W. D. Fard, the inspiration for the Nation, and Mufti Muhammad Sadiq, the missionary for the Ahmadiyya movement.

To get to Fard and Sadiq, we must go through Noble Drew Ali (Timothy Drew) and the Moorish Science Temple of America (MSTA). Founded in 1913 the MSTA drew from a number of complex traditions in its first decade such as black Freemasonry, Garvey's UNIA, Islamic ideas culled from Drew Ali's travels in the merchant marine, and marginally from "a Hindu fakir in circus shows" whom Drew Ali accompanied, and in whose company "he decided to start a little order of his own."[37] The circus was the crucial site for the transmission of a fantasy version of the "East" to most Americans.[38] For many, the "East" was a place of mysterious barbarism, but among black Americans it was often a source of wisdom and a symbol of the capacity of people of color to engender a civilization. At the 1893 Columbian Exposition in Chicago, as the sight of Muslims from the "East" amused the white spectators, a group of African American men and women took vows from them. On the basis of this encounter, they established the Ancient Egyptian Arabic Order of Nobles of the Shrine and the Daughters of Isis (later known as the black Shriners).[39] Noble Drew Ali emerged from this milieu. He forged a movement of respect and dignity, so that those who felt the indignity of being called "nigger" now appended terms of respect to their names like El and Bey (both honorific titles) and Ali (the other name for Hussain, grandson of the prophet Muhammed). Drew Ali's MSTA made its own flag, fashioned after that of Morocco, and its own identity cards. These symbols of freedom allowed the MSTA members to declare their psychological independence from Jim Crow U.S.A. Of special significance is the MSTA's claim that those whom white supremacy called "Negroes" were actually "Asiatic" peoples who claimed descent from Morocco, or, as the MSTA called them, "Moorish

Americans". The "Moorish Americans" reconstructed their racial lineage stating that "Asiatics" came from the line of Canaan and Ham and they included the Egyptians, Arabians, Japanese, Chinese, Indians, South and Central Americans, Turks, and African Americans.[40]

As the streets of black America filled up with faiths other than mainstream Christianity, some of the preachers of these faiths came from places far afield. One such person was Mufti Muhammad Sadiq, who set foot in the United States on January 24, 1920. Sadiq, a native of British India, was an Ahmadiyya missionary who came to the United States to propagate the idea that Mirza Ghulam Ahmad (1835–1908), the Punjabi visionary, was the *mahdi,* or prophet, of Islam. Persecuted in their homeland, the Ahmadiyyas sent forth missionaries to disperse and ensure the continuance of the prophecy. Sadiq was met by the immigration officials, who held him for deportation because he was accused of being a polygamist. In jail he converted a multiethnic crew of fellow deportees—four Chinese men, one American, one Syrian, one Yugoslavian—an illustration of what religious historian Richard Brent Turner calls "the *first multi-racial* model for American Islam."[41] When Sadiq gave a tender to the immigration officials that he would not preach polygamy, he was released to three years of eager and productive work during which he converted a host of Harlem residents (including women, such as Madame Rahatullah in 1921). When Sadiq moved to Chicago to open the first Ahmaddiya mosque at 448 Wabash in 1922, he drew to the movement Muslim immigrants (from Bosnia, Yemen, and Somalia, among other places) and, crucially, African Americans. (By 1940, the Ahmadiyya community in the United States numbered between five and ten thousand.[42])

In his periodical *Moslem Sunrise,* Sadiq conducted a "jihad of words," especially to argue that both the Protestant Church and Catholic Church had "failed largely to abandon racism either at the altar or through their secular policies." Furthermore, he proposed that "in the East" equality was already realized, since "in Islam no church has ever had seats reserved for anybody and if a Negro enters first and takes the front seat even the Sultan if he happens to come after him never thinks of removing him from the seat."[43] Sadiq did not stand outside the current of African American political activity, for he threw himself wholeheartedly into the world of Garveyism. One of his main converts in Chicago, James Conwell, or Brother Abdullah, was a Garveyite, and it is said that six other Garveyites wore their UNIA uniforms to the mosque. In 1923, Richard Turner records, Sadiq spoke to the UNIA of Detroit five times and converted forty members to Islam. Garvey himself was close to the Sudanese-Egyptian Muslim preacher, Duse Muhammad Ali. Sadiq urged Garvey to add "one language which would be Arabic" to the UNIA motto, One God, One Aim, One Destiny. In January 1923, Sadiq wrote an open letter to black America in the *Moslem Sunrise,* in which he condemned Christianity's failure to confront racism and he expressed outrage against "the Christian profiteers [who] brought you out of your native lands of Africa and in Christianizing you made you forsake the religion and language of your forefathers—which were Islam and Arabic."[44]

As the Nation of Islam would later do, Sadiq sought to remind African Americans about the Muslims who came to the Americas on the slave ships, people such as Yarrow Mamout, who earned his freedom and bought both a house for himself in 1819 and stock in Alexander Hamilton's Columbia Bank, as well as the Timbo (Guinean) prince Abd al-Rahman Ibrahima, who came to the United States on board a slave ship named *Africa,* won his freedom through the intervention of King Abd al-Rahman II of Morocco, and then returned to Africa as an employee of the American Colonization Society. Some scholars suggest that almost a tenth of the enslaved Africans had allegiance to Islam, while others claim that the numbers are almost as high as a fifth. Most agree that the Islam brought from Africa was lost over time as memory, and certainly as institutionalized practice.[45] Sadiq tried only to argue that despite what the trauma of slavery had wrought blacks have an ancestral connection with Islam, and that Islam as a faith pledged to equality would be a better platform for everyday dignity and the antiracist struggle.

W. D. Fard and Elijah Muhammad would go one step further. These two founders of the Nation of Islam drew from Sadiq's world and from international fascination with Martian life (and UFOs) to argue that the "Asiatic Black Man" (the "Original People") was an ancient (trillions of years old) being who was lost (due to the deviousness of the scientist Yacub) and would have to be found with the help of the Nation (hence the "Lost-Found Nation of Islam"). The Islam of Fard-Muhammad, then, would be the vehicle (along with the Mother Ship from Japan) to take the oppressed "Asiatic Black Man" to liberation.[46] Recent work on the mysterious Fard shows that he had joined the MSTA in the mid-1920s and, under the name of David Ford-el, he fought to lead the MSTA after Noble Drew Ali died in 1929.[47] While with the MSTA, Ford worshipped at the Ahmadiyya mosque in Chicago and he was involved with the UNIA. Elijah Muhammed was raised in a Garveyite family, and like Ford, he spent his formative life in the Midwest under the influence of the MSTA. Both Ford and Muhammed are genuine creatures of the milieu of nonwhite working-class life and even as they produced a form of Islam that was deeply racialist they could not help acknowledge its own polycultural roots.

Elijah Muhammad claimed that Fard was Allah, that his fair skin was irrelevant to his message that only the "Black Man" was capable of being found to liberate mankind from the designs of the evil scientist (who removed melanin from people to make them bonded to the earth and outside the web of the divine). Fard, of relatively light skin, was born in New Zealand to a father from British India, Zared Fard, and a Maori mother, Beatrice Fard. In 1913 his parents gathered enough money to send their twenty-two-year-old son to the United States. Fard probably crossed into the country through Canada without a visa and joined the undocumented working class, first as a cook and eventually as a restaurant manager. Frustrated with this sort of life, and leaving in his trail two marriages, Fard joined with a Chinese American man, Edward Donaldson, to go on the road. He worked for the Theosophist Society in San Francisco under the tutelage of Mohini Chatterjee and then for the UNIA. An FBI agent despatched to monitor the UNIA noted that

> though he claimed to be a Negro, his manner of talk, which had a little accent—not the Southern accent that is common to all Negroes, but the accent similar to that of an American-educated Hindu. He is rather small but stout. His facial color and the shape and structure of his face is also more like a Hindu than an American Negro.[48]

That Fard may have been from British India is not as important as the Indian Islamic ideas he (and the Ahmadiyyas) imported into the African American community. Richard Turner, in a very rich study, shows us that Islamic movements in the United States and their "new urban prophets" adopted the idea of "continuous prophecy" to elaborate upon the African American notion of a religious leader (the pastor of a congregation, for instance).[49] Ministers in the African American churches put great stock in the idea that they had been called to the pulpit by divine inspiration, to be in the stream of a continuous prophecy begun by Jesus Christ.[50] The idea of the continuous prophecy in terms of Islam in the United States came, in part, from the nineteenth-century founder of the Ahmadiyya movement, Mirza Ghulam Ahmad, who claimed to be the *mujahid*, ("renewer"). The idea of *mujahid* made possible the claim made by Elijah Muhammad that Fard was Allah and that he himself was both Elijah of the Bible and Muhammad of the Quran. Elijah Muhammad's closeness to Naeem and his trip to Pakistan in 1960 may be explained in part by his special fondness for the heterodox southern Asian Islam, and for the paternal homeland of his friend Fard.

By the 1940s, Harlem's streets flourished with the presence of several thousand Muslims from all across the world, but mainly from southern Asia. Without a mosque, they worshipped in their homes, but on festival days they would "don rich robes, shawls, turbans, and fezzes of their native land, and the women wear gorgeous brocades and heavy decorative jewelry." These Muslims represented the gamut of the U.S. working class—as workers in the restaurant trade, as mechanics, as janitors, as factory workers, and as students. As missionaries, many worked to convert their neighbors. "Whether they are Africans, Arabs, Tartars or American Negroes, Moors, Persians or whites," Ottley wrote in his 1943 study of Harlem, "Moslems intermarry. The racial flow back and forth defies classification."[51] Malcolm was a natural in Harlem, not only because the political events that preceded him had awakened an antiracist consciousness among the people, but also because of its place as a hive of complexity. Malcolm would have loved it, for he was not so far removed from a polycultural existence. Born of a Grenadian mother, Louise Little, Malcolm would have known, as did his brother Wilfried of one of his cousins who was an aide to Garvey and who visited the Littles often. "I'm sure from the way he looked," Wilfried told Jan Carew, "that he must have had some East Indian blood in him." On the trail of Louise Little's mother, Carew came upon a "venerable matriarch" who told him that she once heard of Malcolm's grandmother, who "musta had some coolie blood in her, or Carib in addition to the tar brush."[52] As he lay in the arms of Yuri Kochiyama in 1965, Malcolm rested in a tradition that respected the complexity of his heritage and of the kind of politics he had moved toward. As I think of Malcolm now, I cannot take this image out of my head, nor can I forget those Bengali grocers, Alaudin's father and his friends, as he taught them about racism in the United States as they taught him about halal. These are memories of genuine polycultural practice.[53]

South Central Is the *America* of the Korean

In 1991, Ice Cube self-righteously targeted Korean merchants in his song "Black Korea." "Oriental one-penny-counting motherfuckers," he called them as he demanded that they "pay respect to the black fist or we'll burn your store right down to your crisp." As Cube acted as the voice of the voiceless, he also took the opportunity to promote forty-ounce bottles of St. Ides malt liquor, a drink sold mainly by small merchants like the Korean store owners. With full-blown misogyny, Cube suggested that malt liquor will "get your girl in the mood quicker, get your jimmy thicker."[54] Cube drew upon the anger of dispossessed people who found in the Koreans a convenient scapegoat. "It's very hard to attack the establishment, or to attack the educational system, or to change the political economic structure, for someone on the street," reflected Jan Sunoo of the Federal Mediation and Conciliation Service in early 1992. "So he'll say, 'Well, maybe I can't change the world, but at least I can get this damn grocer to respect me.'"[55] Cube's hypocrisy aside, the irony of his reaction is that it comes at a time when black bourgeois political leaders had taken power, when Koreans had little political power at city hall, and when alternative political leadership was continually squashed by the U.S. state. The illusionary Chocolate City is no comfort to the exploited and oppressed whose genuine demands for freedom are met either by police force (trained, incidentally, in the manner of anti-insurgency U.S. troops in Vietnam), by the force of hard cash (to compromise leaders), or by force-fed drugs. The Koreans are part of the equation, but not even close to being the agents of bondage.

Like the story of the Nation of Islam and Malcolm X the Afro-Korean history is far more complex than we've allowed ourselves to imagine. The Koreans, like African Americans, have a relationship with the United States that results from the machinations of U.S. power rather than from Korean willfulness. Bruce Cumings's outstanding research shows us that the United States intervened in a national struggle for independence and precipitated a war that lasted from 1950 to 1953 (and which continues in a cold fashion to this day) to cost at least two million lives. The modern-day U.S. crusaders felt that they had to fend off Communism to save the world, even as they vented some vicious racist fury against both the Koreans and the Chinese. A senior officer in General MacArthur's command hoped that a harsh U.S. attack would "give these yellow bastards what is coming to them."[56] The racist hatred of the Asians took the form of ruthless destruction (this on the heels of the atomic bombs on Japan). Aerial raids on the northern part of the peninsula destroyed irrigation dams that provided water for three quarters of the North's food production. "The subsequent flash flood waters wiped out [supply routes, etc.]," the U.S. air force noted in an official report. "The Westerner can little conceive the awesome meaning which the loss of [rice] has for the Asian—starvation and slow death."[57] There was no remorse in the note.

As the war in Korea intensified, the U.S. army turned to African Americans for volunteers, but the black troops had already tasted the bitterness of the false hope of freedom in the aftermath of World Wars I and II. Paul Robeson, at a mass rally in Harlem in early July 1950, told the crowd that

> Negroes know what is happening in Korea because the same thing is happening to our people in Africa. It has to do with gold, and oil, and tin and other natural resources that the people of Korea, Africa and the West Indies and all other colonial people . . . have the right to do with as they choose. But the same men who own the cotton plantations in the South are determined to seize the riches of Korea and keep them.

Benjamin J. Davis, Communist councilman from Harlem, pointedly noted that "we want peace and freedom, and we are ready to fight for it whether in Mississippi or Harlem. If Truman, Dulles or MacArthur have ants in their pants, let them send troops into Mississippi and Georgia to fight the Ku Klux Klan." As he delivered these words, a white policeman pushed an African American woman, who reportedly turned to him and said, "If you want to fight, go on over to Korea and I wish you the worst of luck."[58] The U.S. Communist press was ruthless in its denunciation of the divide-and-rule tactic of the United States, eager to use black troops to fight for "freedom" (as it had in 1778, 1838, 1860–65, 1898, 1914–19, and 1941–45). "A reckoning with the Negro quislings of today," said an editorial in the *Daily Worker*, "is also on the Negro people's order of business. For these quislings unashamedly assert that the Wall Street leopard has changed his spots. In this way they attempt to disarm the Negro people before the onslaught of this imperialist beast."[59] African Americans, however, were deeply aware of the irony. Captain Charles Bussey, an African American commander in the Twenty-fourth Infantry Regiment in Korea, told military historians decades later, the black troops "felt they were stupid to risk their lives unduly because when they got home they didn't have the rewards citizenship should have provided . . . such as voting."[60] In February 1951, the NAACP sent Thurgood Marshall to investigate complaints from black troops in Korea, such as being sent in large numbers into treacherous combat and not being allowed to use equal facilities (the Korean War was the first time the U.S. army used integrated units). Marshall returned with extensive proof of what he called "bias," which the army disputed, but which *The Crisis* published in full.[61] Both African Americans and Koreans had a bad war, and both attempted to find better lives afterward, often in the same neighborhoods.

Battered by the shortages of foodstuffs in the southern part of the Korean peninsula, some Koreans "attached themselves to Americans by any means necessary, hoping against hope to get to America—uniformly conceived as a country where the streets were paved with gold, a fabulous PX in the sky."[62] Refugees from the North found nothing to hold them in the South, and they too made every attempt to flee to the Americans who came forth as their saviors. On the new world stage, the United States could not identity itself as the messiah and then shut the doors behind those whose lives were ruined by its supposed "goodwill." The refugee Koreans came across the waters to the United States, mostly to California. Over the decades more Koreans would join them, mainly those who continue to find it impossible to make a living in an economy dominated by vast Korean-style corporations called *chaebols* (which earn praise from U.S. management gurus).[63] In the mid-1970s, over 85 percent of the Koreans in the United States made up part of the working class, even though more than 70 percent of them came to the United States with professional qualifications.[64]

In 1967, a UCLA study of seventy-nine "ghetto merchants" (mainly Jewish, but also African American, Asian American, and Mexican American) showed that the situation for the trader "in the Los Angeles ghetto is not unlike the one faced by Chinese merchants in Malaysia or Indian merchants in Africa. In all three situations, the merchant is a member of an elite, better-educated group and resentments between merchants and customers abound."[65] The survey was already out of date, because the demographics of south-central Los Angeles shifted in the aftermath both of the 1965 Watts uprising and of the 1965 Immigration and Naturalization Act. The uprising sent a strong message against merchants who acted brazenly toward their customers, with the targets of violence frequently reserved not for one ethnic group, but for anyone who behaved inappropriately or unethically.[66]

Both the Jews and the Italians either moved their shops elsewhere or retired with the certain hope that their college-educated children, now rather firmly white, might find their destiny in the "mainstream." The 1965 immigration act, for the first time since 1924, allowed for a relatively large number of Asians to enter the United States, and of the Koreans who came, many settled in and around Los Angeles.[67] The Korean merchants actively purchased or rented their stores in the predominantly working-class black and Latino neighborhoods (while most of the Jewish and Italian merchants already owned their shops when African Americans moved into their neighborhoods).[68] Furthermore, unlike many other "outsider" ethnicities, they did not own and rent property or enter politics (perhaps they'd had too much of politics in their homeland). Instead they concentrated their efforts in small, family-run grocery-liquor stores.[69] And yet, they were unaware of the political powder keg they were about to ignite.[70]

Faced with the enormity of a white supremacist capitalism, working-class black folk have always sought means for sovereignty and dignity. One of these means is to assert one's claim to territory, to the neighborhood that is generally seen to be one's own. Ownership as self-determination is a particularly delicate subject among African Americans, whose ancestors were owned and who lost the forty acres and a mule intended to be the down payment to freedom. If there is nothing else to own, at least I own my own body and I have my 'hood. The anti-Jewish and anti-Korean tendencies in the 'hood come from this profound desire for dignity among the working class who labor for others, but who do not have the means to produce the services to run their own territory. The African American bourgeoisie dreams of a Black Belt as a captive market, but the working class wishes it both for ease of life (no need to travel miles to the store) and for self-respect (no need to bear the indignity of the petty-minded fears of the small shopkeeper for whom theft cuts into the profit margins).

The investment in territory is valid as a strategy for survival, but the African American population of South-Central (Watts), for instance, is not the first to feel that pull. In the nineteenth century many of the neighborhoods now considered to be African American had Asian populations, all of whom gathered together as a result of racist residential codes of the 1870s.[71] African Americans moved to California in large numbers only during and after the Depression, when the plutocrats of the promised land used those anti-Asian codes against them.[72] Sonora McKeller (part African American, part Mexican, part Apache, part German), the coordinator of the Watts Summer Festival in the 1960s, first visited South-Central in 1929:

> At that time Watts was all but barren land. Houses were few and far between. Japanese produce gardens were everywhere. Where today we see storm drains and cemented gullies, in those days the people of Watts fished for crawfish and catfish in mud and slime . . . in fact the section was known as Mudtown. Watts boasted one movie house, a few schools, many Chinese lottery dens where one could play such games as blackjack, chuck-a-luck, four-five-six poker, and Chinese lottery—drawings every hour on the hour.[73]

African Americans and Japanese Americans in California lived cheek by jowl. Then, in the 1940s, the U.S. state moved the latter into internment camps and opened the homes and businesses to the impoverished African

Americans indeed, most public housing in Los Angeles was built on land once home to Asians. Maya Angelou remembers the transition from her San Francisco childhood:

> The Yakamoto Sea Food Market quietly became Sammy's Shoe Shine Parlor and Smoke Shop. Yashigira's Hardware metamorphosed into La Salon de Beauté owned by Miss Clorinda Jackson. The Japanese shops which sold products to Nisei customers were taken over by enterprising Negro businessmen, and in less than a year became permanent homes away from home for the newly arrived Southern Blacks. Where the odors of tempura, raw fish and *cha* had dominated, the aroma of chitlings, greens and ham hocks now prevailed. The Japanese area became San Francisco's Harlem in a matter of months.[74]

"Why did the African Americans not protest the internment of their neighbors?" Angelou asked. "Especially in view of the fact that they (the blacks) had themselves undergone concentration-camp living for centuries in slavery's plantations and later in sharecroppers' cabins. But the sensations of common relationship were missing." The enmity has continued for nearly sixty years. In 1988 a survey of Los Angeles African Americans concluded that Asians are the least-liked ethnic group. Nativist ideas ("Koreans don't speak English") highlighted by Hollywood's unreconstructed anti-Asian imagery (*Menace II Society, Quick Change, Falling Down*) produce the idea that the immigrant is not only an alien, but also unwelcome. From the other side, surveys of Korean merchants show us that they see African Americans as "dirty," "lazy," and "uneducated," that they deploy these notions in their sometimes overzealous treatment of the working poor in their stores.[75] In April 1986, the murder of four Korean shopkeepers in south-central L.A. led to the formation of the Black Korean Alliance (BKA), of merchants, city bureaucrats, community-based organizations, the media, and the clergy. The goal of the BKA was to facilitate dialogue between the migrants to there and the earlier residents. The venture was useful, but its strategy was decidedly misguided because "dialogue" (or reconciliation, or "Can we all get along?") assumes that the problem is one of attitude or stereotype and not of a fundamental flaw in the social relations between people; the BKA, incidentally, collapsed when it could offer little in the aftermath of the 1992 uprising. Halford Fairchild, raised in the black community of Los Angeles, but child of a Japanese American mother and black father, noted that

> the terrible peril of African people places us in a position of having to do whatever we can do to survive, and a lot of times that means to steal. We have an interesting situation, where Korean-Americans are coming in as

capitalists, as merchants, as individuals who are selling goods for a profit in convenience stores and liquor stores, and I'm sure they experience theft on a regular basis. People steal because they don't have the money to buy.[76] Fairchild offers some indication of the structural problems at play in south-central L.A., one that is far removed from a simple liberal dilemma that continues to go by the name of "black-Korean relations."[77]

Los Angeles is a test case for the limits of amity within a capitalist structure that relies upon ethnicity to camouflage its power. Pyong Cap Min documents in detail the many attempts made by the bourgeois leadership of the Korean and African American communities: the BKA tried to foster dialogue, the Korean and black churches worked with each other in "sister-church" arrangements, the merchant associations tried to mediate during boycotts, and the Korean chamber of commerce even contributed toward Mayor Tom Bradley's trip to Korea in April 1991.[78] These measures attempted to create fellowship, but they did not work in 1992 when, as a reaction to police brutality and justice denied, the working-class blacks and Latinos targeted the shopkeepers, many of whom are Korean. Jan Sunoo recognized the structural element involved in the situation. "I don't think you see Korean merchants shooting blacks in middle-class neighborhoods. You don't see them shooting Latinos in middle-class neighborhoods," he noted. "I think what we're seeing is a very specific problem that happens in poverty."[79]

"Poverty" is one way to describe the devastation of south-central Los Angeles. Deindustrialization in the 1970s denuded jobs in South-Central—annual median income from 1965 to 1980 fell to $5,900, $2,500 below that of the city median for blacks—and it resulted in a community without a middle-class.[80] The economic shifts in these years did not affect only the working class, they also hit the small merchants. Once able to make a modest living as grocers and haberdashers, the small merchants in the late 1970s had to aggressively retail liquor to make a worthwhile margin (almost as high as a 25 percent profit). For this reason, there are about the same number of liquor stores in South-Central as there are in the state of Rhode Island. Kyeyoung Park reminds us, however, that the liquor store—serving as one of the few public places for people to meet—does not retail only alcohol, it retails produce as well as household goods, and, crucially, it allows customers to pay with a variety of methods (checks, welfare checks, money orders, food stamps).[81] But it would be rather unkind to blame the Korean merchants for the alcohol, for, to steal from Marx, narcotics among the poor function, like religion, as the spirit of spiritless conditions, the opium of the people.

Most Koreans don't make it, and those who own stores in low-income neighborhoods can't make the margins for the American Dream. Seven hundred Korean-owned stores opened in New York in 1994, and in the same year nine hundred Korean stores closed down.[82] Second-generation Koreans, especially those like the radical Young Koreans United (YKU), point out that "Korean Americans see a direct connection between the presence of U.S. troops in Korea and the lack of funds for domestic programs which are clearly indicated by the events in Los Angeles last April."[83] The merchants see a link between the harsh U.S. bombardment of their native land and of the LAPD's disregard for their property and bodies. LAPD chief Daryl Gates "wanted the blacks to let out their outburst toward the Koreans," said one observer, "because he knew that the blacks didn't feel very good toward the Koreans. I do believe there must have been some conscious politics, because [the police] just weren't there."[84] Baby Nerve of the Watergate-Crips Blue said after the uprising that the "government is so crooked, the Koreans don't understand—the government gave you a loan and put you in our community to set you up for this. Yes, you're in our community. You got tooken just like we got tooken."[85] What Nerve didn't get was that the Koreans may have understood what was going on, but could not find a way to control the situation, except, as continues to happen, to leave the area.[86]

But what happens when people stay and work toward Angelou's idea of a common relationship. Seattle offers us a tentative model. In the 1930s, Japanese and Chinese restaurants in the southside of Seattle welcomed black rail workers and longshoremen, and one café "near the railroad depot developed a specialized menu of soul food to entice porters and ship stewards."[87] When the Japanese were forced to leave, the African American migrants from the U.S. South, betrayed by the false promises of the First Reconstruction, for the first time had property and a taste of freedom. "Who could expect this man," asked Maya Angelou, "to share his new and dizzying importance with concern for a race that he had never known to exist?"[88] When the Japanese returned to their neighborhoods, but not to their homes, they felt from African Americans "persecution in the drawl of the persecuted."[89] Even after the loss of homes and the immanent tension of everyday life, Seattle people of color still found means to create fealty. Activists in the community formed the Jackson Street Community Council (JSCC) in 1946 "ostensibly to support community businesses and voluntary social service agencies," but the real purpose was to create "however inadvertently, a model for interethnic cooperation. Its officers rotated among its Japanese, Filipino, Chinese and African American members, as did its Man of the Year selection." The

JSCC created an integrated telephone and address directory, and in 1952 it selected four community queens, Foon Woo, Rosita DeLeon, Adelia Avery, and Sumi Mitsui, each of whom represented a section of the complex community of color.[90] This was a form of Titoist nationalism may be found up and down the West Coast until the 1960s. Even in Los Angeles the Japanese-American Citizens League, along with the Mexican American Political Association, stood together with the NAACP to oppose Proposition 14, the repeal of the Rumford Fair Housing Act which was designed to create antiracist equity in the housing market.[91] One symbol of the black-Japanese relationship was the Holiday Bowl restaurant–bowling alley on Crenshaw Boulevard. Opened in 1958, the Holiday Bowl allowed fealty between people of color to grow. Bowling leagues of the Japanese farmers bore such names as the Gardener's League, the Produce League, and the Floral League, but when the black population moved into the area, the leagues became mixed. Dorothy Tanabe of the Floral League told a reporter that "my team has one black, one Italian, another Japanese, and a Korean sponsor. We're in first place now."[92] "It's like a United Nations in there," waitress Jacqueline Sowell told another reporter. "Our employees are Hispanic, white, black, Japanese, Thai, Filipino. I've served grits to as many Japanese customers as I do black. It's much more than just a bowling alley. It's a community resource."[93] On May 7, 2000, the Holiday Bowl closed its doors. Its new owner, Axiom Real Estate Services, Inc. intends to build a strip mall on the site, another mark of the alienation induced by capitalism.[94] The story of Seattle and parts of Los Angeles is also a story of class. Roy Ottley informs us that the wealthy Japanese Americans in Los Angeles do not form close relationships with the African Americans, but the merchants and workers do.

> As neighbors, they were rather warm toward Negroes. The Japanese, who owned many business enterprises and pretty much controlled truck farming and the vending markets, employed considerable Negro help. Particularly did friendships spring up between Nisei (second-generation Japanese) and young Negroes, and intermarriage was frequent.[95]

Solidarity of the class, across color, grew not from any predisposition toward class unity, but because the Japanese and the African Americans had to live side by side, share a similar set of circumstances, and create a common cultural world. Polycultural solidarity is not the melancholic hope for unity that sometimes guides the imagination of the Left, but it is a materialist recognition that people who share similar experiences create the platform for cultural interaction. This is an indication of the common relationship wistfully hoped for by Maya Angelou.

Is "Immigrant" a Type of Race?

Customer (C): Aaay, yo.

Merchant (M): What, all oh my money grip, what's up.

C: It's me baby . . .

M: I love that type money, money coming at me . . .

C: What's going on Ackmet you'll got any good cheese steak?

M: Ackmet, what do you mean Ackmet? My brother my name is not Ackmet. My name is Raoud.

C: Oh my fault Raul, what's up baby, aaa . . . Let me get aaa . . . two Philly cheese steaks.

M: Ok.

C: Salt, pepper, ketchup, mayonnaise, fried onions . . .

M: Hold up, what type of mutherfuckin' cheese steak, what the fuck you orderin' some shit . . .

C: That's a Philly cheese steak . . .

M: I don't know that part, you put garlic, mayonnaise, bell pepper, and lettuce on a cheese steak. What, what you talkin . . .

C: No you totally off. Listen man you don't know shit about Philly, dog . . .

M: Listen don't keep . . .

C: You don't know shit about 28th and Jefferson . . .

M: I know that part, my cousin stay that part . . .

C: 21st and Sea . . .

M: My uncle build buildings there . . .

C: 10th and Park . . .

M: Construction I'm building there too . . .

C: Lehigh Avenue . . .

M: I wear Levi's. You know I wear the Levi's.

C: I said Lehigh Avenue.

M: You can't tell me where I am from, I'm from Philly . . .

C: You're not from Philly . . .

M: Philly, and a Philly top of the line steak cheese . . .

C: You're from Bangladesh or some fucking where . . .

M: No, you get the fuck out and go fight the AK . . .

C: Now you go to the AK shit again alright baby I'm gonna holler back at you . . .

M: Ok, mutherfucker money fat grip tight jeans I'm from Philly . . .

C: No Philly where we from . . .

M: No Philly is where I am from . . .

C: Remember that nigger, fuck you and that cheese steak . . . [96]

The scene is well set. A small shop in the inner city of Philadelphia, with two African American friends in search of the city's distinctive sandwich, the Philly cheese steak. They step inside and begin a conversation with a man with a strong, but not immediately placeable, Asian accent (we hear soon enough that he might be from Bangladesh). The man, early in the skit, has a name that is mistaken and then pronounced in an unidentifiable fashion. But this is commonplace banter until we get to the dispute about the recipe for the sandwich, with the merchant eager to put garlic and bell pepper, signs of spiciness. "You don't know shit about Philly," says the customer to the merchant, and they proceed to argue about locality, about the places in the city to which both claim title in different ways. The skit ends with stereotype (talk of the AK-47 and of foreignness) and with an insistence that "Philly Is Where I'm From," the title of the song that follows the skit. Against the Ruff Ryders' statement of belonging, one could pose the 1987 Eric B. & Rakim song, "It Ain't Where You're From, It's Where You're At." To walk away from origins and toward the place of residence does not, however, extricate us from the perception of foreignness and of one's title to place. When the working poor has lost every other asset, it holds on to its place of residence and life as the most precious resource ever. Bourgeois nationalism, since the nineteenth century, emphasizes a connection between blood and soil, between the idea of *jus soli* and *jus sanguinis,* descent from place and descent from blood. What we have from the Ruff Ryders is not so much this bourgeois nationalism, but a subaltern nationalism, one that demands the protection of territorial sovereignty as the only resource at one's command. When all else has been stripped away, it is land (place) that must be defended.

And it is often the immigrant who is seen as colonizer, against whom the battle rages. The immigrant of color enters the United States, vulnerable to the whims of its rulers, but eager to make a living as recompense for the sacrifices of the journey. Most of those who come upon the immigrant of color rarely fail to recognize the foreignness, to remark about the place of birth, the language or accent, sometimes the unfamiliar cultural practices. And therefore, there is a kind of fellowship among immigrants, the recognition that when we ask one another, again in our heavy accents, "Where are you from?" we're not saying, "Why don't you go back home?"[97]

In sociologist Jay MacLeod's celebrated *Ain't No Makin' It* he argues that the unemployed whites he encountered in the 1970s and 1980s seemed to live without any sense of hope for their future, whereas the African American youth felt optimistic. MacLeod contended that this disjuncture can be explained by multiple generations of failure among the white families, whereas their black neighbors had only recently won the right to the franchise and to equality.[98] Now, almost four decades after the 1965 Voting Rights Act, one might argue that the working poor born in the United States may have altogether lost any sense of the American Dream, while the immigrants of color hold on to that tarnished dream as a standard for their exertions. The immigrification of our cities has come about through minimal finances and with enormous amounts of ingenuity born from the hope that here, in this country despite its many problems, one has the capacity to succeed. Waves upon waves of immigrants bring this grand hope even though it is often vanquished. The immigrant tries, at the same time, to claim Americanness, but the native sees the immigrant of color as a settler, sojourner, perpetual foreigner. Mike Davis reports that the Latino entry into U.S. cities not only restores "debilitated neighborhoods to trim respectability," but it also means the transformation of "dead urban spaces into convivial social places."[99] One of those shops is the Quetta Halal Market opened in Philadelphia in 1975 by Wali Muhammed Scott, an African American man. That Wali Scott named his store after a town in Pakistan was perhaps a harbinger for Atiq Chaudhry, born of Pakistan, but now the owner of Pizza Pak II in Philadelphia. Chaudhry found that many of his customers over the years have been Muslims, so he pioneered the halal Philly cheese steak, and, he says, "business is getting better and better."[100] Of the hundred thousand Muslims in the city who worship at its thirty-four mosques, the retooled Philly cheese steak enables them to refashion locality in their own image. When the Ruff Ryders search for a Philly cheese steak sandwich in today's Philadelphia, there is a good chance that they'll have to get it from Atiq Chaudhry—and it'll be halal.

When Atiq Chaudhry is told that he's not from Philadelphia, perhaps he should in the future tell his angry customer of Paul William Quinn (1800–73), who was a leading member of the African Methodist Episcopal Church in Pennsylvania, and who earned his title to the region by his commitment to justice. Quinn was an extraordinary man, bishop in the AME, which gave him the strength to fiercely combat racism. Slavery, he argued, is a "sin against God and man. On occasion he would denounce the slaveholder in his sermons; and he generally climaxed his remarks with his favorite expression,

'May God have mercy on him; I never will.'"[101] At the 1851 AME conference, Quinn noted that "nine times out of ten when we look into the face of a white man we see our enemy. A great many like to see us in the kitchen, but few in the parlor. Our hope is in God's blessing on our own wise, strong, and well-directed efforts."[102] When he was heckled by racist slavers, he physically threw them out of his presence. What is so astounding about Quinn is that while he was a senior member of the AME and a fierce antiracist, he was an immigrant from southern India. Evidence for this is faint, but respectable. In 1854, Quinn "declared himself a British subject by birth."[103] "It was generally known in this community," wrote the historian of the AME, "that Paul Quinn was of foreign birth, but many of his forbears [sic], having no knowledge of an India in Asia, believed him to be a West Indian." One source says that he was born in Calcutta, India. The *Richmond Telegram* (February, 28 1873) says that "his father and uncle were mahogany merchants, the latter being very wealthy. From infancy the cruelties practiced by the Hindus upon each other, both in peace and war, were revolting to him and this repugnance was strengthened at about the age of 17 years by hearing Elizabeth Walker, a Quakeress who went from England on a mission to India." Quinn followed Walker, came to England, then to the United States where he moved to East Point, Pennsylvania, and "was received in the local AME Church."[104] Quinn, a native of India, is now absorbed into the historical memory of African Americans and given title to Pennsylvania principally because of his strong commitment to justice for those who lived around him. If to assimilate (literally, to make similar) means to conform and to lose one's sense of where one comes from, then assimilation is not only impossible, but it is unpalatable. To assimilate, to me, is close to the word *habituate,* to bring the body into another disposition: to struggle with those around one to make one's social ecology conform to one's values. Quinn habituated into the hearts of his fellows. This is a worthy, if dated, example.

The contribution of immigrants like Chaudhry, Quinn, and countless others, however, is rarely acknowledged. Instead, most immigrants experience sharp xenophobic sentiment in the manner of what Albert Memmi calls the "racism of the impoverished" and what Etienne Balibar calls "working-class racism."[105] It is the working class that comes into contact with those relatively noncosmopolitan sections of the immigrants of color, and it is this conclave of difference in a time of deindustrialization and NAFTAization that sparks economic resentments, cultural fears, and social anxiety.

On April 29, 2000, for example, Richard Baumhammers went on a killing spree.[106] In the space of two hours he shot his Jewish neighbor (Nicki

Gordon), two workers at the Ya Fei Chinese Restaurant (Ji-ye Sun and Thao Pham), one African American (Garry Lee) who was in a storefront karate school, and one Indian man (Anil Thakur) who was inside the India Grocers. Another Indian man (Sandip Patel) was grievously injured. Chief Paul Wolf of the Allegheny County Police in Pennsylvania noted immediately that "we are taking the tack of ethnic intimidation, a hate crime." Mr. Baumhammers's lawyer took a different approach. "He clearly has an extensive history of mental illness," said William H. DiFenderfer, the well-named advocate. Yes, without a doubt Mr. Baumhammers is sick. But he is not sick in the manner portrayed by his lawyer, or by a section of the media. He is sick with the disease of racist xenophobia that permeates our country and its system, especially when promoted by politicians who use fear as a tactic to gain votes. Guard the borders, expel unwanted immigrants. Send in the INS, the migra. When the California right wing put forward Proposition 187, the number of its anti-immigrant plebiscite is the same as the police code for murder. Proposition 187 means both physical and social death for the immigrant. The state wants us to work here, but it does not recognize us as human beings. It wants our expertise, our patience, but it doesn't want smelly food and dusky faces.

There is no "safe haven" in the United States as long as racist xenophobia is not tackled at multiple levels. From Queens, New York, to Scott, Pennsylvania, xenophobia is at large. The 1996 Immigration Act, the New York City administration's anti-immigrant approach to taxi drivers and street vendors, the U.S. coast guard and INS's use of the so-called drug war to stand aside as vigilante groups kill exploited Mexicans in border states: these are all indications of widespread state-sanctioned racist xenophobia. Mr. Bauhammers, an immigration lawyer and second-generation Latvian immigrant, simply took some of the federal signals to their extreme.

There is and has always been a glimmer of hope. Seattle's history offers hope, the evolution of Malcolm X's message offers hope, and among immigrants of color the process of habituation offers hope. During the 1935 Harlem uprising, a sign was posted in the window of a Chinese laundry shop which read Me Colored Too.[107] Three decades later, in Watts, a shopkeeper posted a sign that read Me Chinese, but Me Blood Brothers Too.[108] And, then three decades later, after the Diallo verdict, Dong Lee, a Korean store owner in the Bronx, put a sign in his window that read Stop Police Brutality. Four Cops Murdered Diallo. Weak Prosecution and Wrong Judgement.[109] Malcolm X recalled being with his friend Shorty Henderson on Seventh Avenue, in reminiscence of riots such as these: "And we laughed about the scared little

Chinese whose restaurant didn't have a hand laid on it because the rioters just about convulsed laughing when they saw the sign the Chinese had hastily stuck on the front door: 'Me Colored Too.'"[110] The solidarity of fear was insufficient to young people like Malcolm X, since their notion of colored and blood brothers was not simply about skin or ethnicity, but as well a factor of class. Those who can lay claim to being "blood" should also be able to show that their only possessions in life are their chains, those clods of iron that fetter their destiny and that they would willingly cast off even for the saturnalia of violence (if not a more organized revolution).

The immigrant attempts to habituate through solidarity for the woes of those who are one's customers, but also those who are now one's neighbors. Despite the weight of structural forces that tend toward division (such as the role of the stranger as merchant and the tendency toward the racist denial of capital to the native working class), one can find many creative attempts at solidarity that are not simply about the opportunistic protection of one's property during a riot. At these moments, with a sign in one's window, the merchant says, I am also like you. Even if this is an inaccurate sentiment (for the merchant at least has a shop), it is a gesture of oneness that offers the presumption of something more than foreigness. The "race of immigrant" offers solidarity. At least this can be read from "Me Colored Too."

Chapter 5

Kung Fusion
Organize the 'Hood Under I-Ching Banners[1]

Although hot and humid as usual 1974 was not just another year for us in Calcutta. The railway workers across India had been on strike and their boldness worried the complacency of the elite. The short Maoist insurgency called Naxalism came and went like a whirlwind. The Communist movement grew apace and three years later would come to power over the state administration and stay there winning six separate elections. And, across from the New Market, Globe Cinema Hall showed *Enter the Dragon* starring Bruce Lee.

There was something extraordinary about Bruce Lee. He was the "foreign" version of our own Amitabh Bachchan, the Big B, who that year gave us such classics as *Benaam* and *Roti Kapada aur Makaan,* and who would in the next year star in the greatest spaghetti Eastern of all time, *Sholay.* As far as those foreign heroes were concerned (and *foreign* simply refers to English-language films), my friends and I supped on James Bond with some satisfaction. *Enter the Dragon*, however, was something else. I saw the movie several times, blown away by the beautiful acrobatics of the celluloid freedom fighter. Bond thrilled us with his gadgets, but we did not take kindly to his easy victories against his adversaries who seemed to be either Asian or Eastern European, straw figures standing in for Communists from Vietnam to Poland. Bond was the agent of international corruption manifest in the British MI-5, while Bruce stood his ground against corruption of all forms, including the worst of the Asian bourgeoisie, Mr. Han. With his bare fists and his *nanchakus,* Bruce provided young people with the sense that we, like the Vietnamese guerrillas, could be victorious against the virulence of international capitalism. He seemed invincible. We did not know that he was already dead.

Born in San Francisco on November 27, 1940, the Year of the Dragon, Bruce made his first U.S. film, *Golden Gate Girl,* at the age of three months. A child of Chinese opera stars (although his mother was a fourth German), he moved to Hong Kong in his childhood, where he starred in over twenty films, before returning to the United States as an undergraduate at the University of Washington. In Seattle, Bruce threw himself into the Asian American world, working in Chinatown as a busboy and as a teacher of his favorite art, kung fu in the sticking hands method. He left college to marry Linda Emery, a white American of Swedish English ancestry, against her family's wishes. They soon had a son, Brandon, and a daughter, Shannon. When asked about "racial barriers," he told a Hong Kong journalist in 1972 that "I, Bruce Lee, am a man who never follows those fearful formulas . . . So, no matter if your color is black or white, red or blue, I can still make friends with you without any barrier."[2] In fact, Bruce was one of the first martial arts *sifus* ("masters") to train non-Asians, including people such as Chuck Norris, Roman Polanski, and Kareem Abdul-Jabbar.

The anti-racism of Bruce was not matched by the world in which he lived. "I am a yellow-faced Chinese, I cannot possibly become an idol for Caucasians."[3] Since the late eighteenth century, when the first Asians arrived in the Americas, the white patriarchs found their presence foul. Deemed to be nothing but labor (as coolies), they came to be seen as fundamentally alien rather than as assimilable immigrants. Representations of these foreigners exaggerated certain attributes to render them not only strange, but also inferior. In the minstrel shows, Jim Crow and Zip Coon were joined by John Chinaman. As historian Robert Lee notes, "Unlike the minstrel characterization of free blacks, who were represented as fraudulent citizens because they were supposed to lack culture, the Chinese were seen as having an excess of culture."[4] What was this excess of culture? If the republic saw itself as virtuous and industrious, then it saw the Chinese, who themselves formed a crucial part of the working class, as oozing cultural sloth mainly through their language, food, and hair (the queue, or long ponytail). These cultural stereotypes enabled the mockery of a people by suggesting that they could never be part of the republic, since they had too much alien culture. This was to change somewhat in the 1960s, as social movements against racism and state management of these movements helped produce what we know today as multiculturalism. U.S. television, with *The Green Hornet,* 1966–67, embraced Bruce to play the Asian, just as the state acknowledged the role of Asians in the creation of a cold war United States. The passage of the 1965 Immigration Act signaled a shift in U.S. racism from outright contempt for Asians, as evinced in the 1924 Immigration Act, to one of bemused admiration for their technical and professional capacity. In the throes of the cold war, and burdened by the lack of scientific personnel, the U.S. state and privileged social forces concertedly worked to welcome a new crop of Asians whose technical labor was to be their crucial passport to this New World. This is not to say that Asians found life easy or that the U.S. state was the paragon of generosity. Nevertheless, the opening afforded by the U.S. state's needs allowed immigrant Asians to imagine ways to import elements from their diverse Asian societies into their new homes. The Asian American movement, in tandem with the civil rights and other minority movements fought for this cultural wedge. Yet, when Bruce's bravado took him to Hollywood in 1966 to play Kato in *The Green Hornet,* his role did nothing to challenge the legendary stereotypes of the alien "Heathen Chinee" within America.[5] As Kato, Bruce was welcome to be the mysterious clown, and sidekick. "Hollywood sure as heck hasn't figured out how to represent the Chinese," Canadian journalist Pierre Berton said to Bruce, who replied that "you better believe it, man. I mean it's always the pigtail and the bouncing around, chop-chop, you know, with the eyes slanted and all that."[6] *The Green Hornet* ended production in July 1967 with a special program in which the champion crime fighters teamed up with Batman and Robin. The script had the four heroes fight one another to a draw, then join efforts to defeat the villainous Colonel Gumm. Bruce, nonplussed, "maintained an icy silence, but his eyes burned through the holes in the mask he wore." With the cameras on, he menacingly stalked Burt Ward, who played Robin. Ward tried to plead that it was only a TV show, but Bruce ignored him, and only when he was disturbed by a noise off-stage did he back off and exclaim, "Lucky it is a TV show."[7] But of course it was more than that. Kato was still the Heathen Chinee. The Green Hornet, Batman, and Robin respected his martial skills, but still they could allow him neither to win nor be their equal. The cultural hierarchy of race set in place for over a hundred years was not to be swept away by the entry of a talented young Chinese American actor.

It is hardly a surprise then that in 1971, the studio considered Bruce to play Caine in the television show *Kung Fu* (then called *The Warrior*), but then rejected him as "too Chinese." The dismissal sent Bruce packing to

Hong Kong and into history. *Kung Fu,* on the other hand, became all that Bruce disavowed. Set in the nineteenth century, the show has Caine (half Chinese, half white) taking on racism by his own individual, superhuman initiative; other Asians appear passive or as memories of a grand era long past and always exotic. The half-white man, a leftist Chinese American periodical argued, is guided by "the feudal landlord philosophies of ancient China," and even nineteenth-century China "is pictured as a place abstracted from time and place." The Taiping and Boxer revolts have no room in what is essentially a very conservative view of China and of social change.[8] Bruce would not have played Caine in this light. "It was hard as hell for Bruce to become an actor," remembers Jim Kelly, the African American kung fu star of *Enter the Dragon:*

> And the reason why was because he was Chinese. America did not want a
> Chinese hero, and that's why he left for Hong Kong. He was down and out.
> He was hurt financially. He told me that he tried to stick it out, but he
> couldn't get the work he wanted. So he said, "Hey, I'm gone." My under-
> standing, from talking to Bruce, was that the *Kung Fu* series was written
> for him, and Bruce wanted to do that. But the bottom line was that the net-
> works did not want to project a Chinese guy as the main hero. But Bruce
> explained to me that he believed that all things happened for a reason.
> Even though he was very upset about it, he felt that everything would
> work out. He wasn't going to be denied. I have so much respect for Bruce,
> because I understand what he went through just by being black in Amer-
> ica. He was able to find a way to get around all those problems. He stuck
> in there, and wouldn't give up. He knew my struggle, and I knew his.[9]

Bare Feet and Naked Hands

> *They say, Karate means empty hands,*
> *So it's perfect for the poor man.*[10]

In the early 1970s, every "Oriental" was a "gook." Born in the U.S. mendacity against the Philippines and Latin America in 1898, the word *gook* was applied equally to the Vietnamese guerrillas and to those Asian Americans drafted into the U.S. army. During basic training, an instructor pointed to twenty-year-old marine corps recruit Raymond Imayama from Los Angeles and said, "This is what the Viet Cong looks like, with slanted eyes. This is what a gook looks like, and they all dress in black."[11] "Japs are the next lowest thing to niggers," one fellow U.S. army recruit said to twenty-year-old Marcus Miyamoto.[12] Miyamoto, born in the Manzanar internment camp in 1945, was in the U.S. Marines in Danang in 1965–66. Imayama and Miyamoto are two of many marines of color pushed to the front lines to fight a racist war. So the war was racist, then, not just in its virulent attack on the Vietnamese, but also in the way the United States Army used Asian and African Americans as cannon fodder.[13]

Steve Sanders, one of the founders of the Black Karate Federation (BKF) in 1968 and a co-star of *Enter the Dragon*, learned his art as a marine on Okinawa before being shipped off to Southeast Asia.

> I didn't enjoy being over there. Anybody who says he did is either a nut who enjoys seeing people killed or a liar. I really don't know why I was there in the first place. I didn't hate the North Vietnamese or the VCs. They looked the same as the South Vietnamese who we were supposed to be helping. How can you like one and hate the other? As far as I'm concerned, those people just want to be left alone to do their own thing.[14]

Sanders is not alone in this view. Certainly we all remember Muhammad Ali's public stance—I ain't got no quarrel with them Vietcong[15]—but less public figures also saw the irony and vigorously protested against serving the U.S. government. In 1966 three army privates associated with the Communist Party refused to ship out to Vietnam. James Johnson (African American), Dennis Mora (Puerto Rican), and David Samas (Lithuanian Italian), in a joint statement, noted that "Negroes and Puerto Ricans are being drafted and end up in the worst of the fighting out of proportion to their numbers in the population; and we have first hand knowledge that these are the ones who have been deprived of decent education and jobs at home." Furthermore, "We were told that you couldn't tell [the Vietnamese] apart—they looked like any other skinny peasant," but "the Viet Cong obviously had the moral and physical support of most of the peasantry who were fighting for their independence."[16] Known as the Fort Hood Three, they represented many troops who felt, in their skin, the horror of the war.

In April 1967, the year Bruce made his mark on television, Martin Luther King Jr. stood before a congregation at Riverside Church in New York City and broke his silence about Vietnam.[17] "We were taking the black young men who had been crippled by our society and sending them eight thousand miles away to guarantee liberties in Southeast Asia which they had not found in southwest Georgia and East Harlem," he said. "If America's soul becomes totally poisoned, part of the autopsy must read Vietnam. It can never be saved so long as it destroys the deepest hopes of men the world over."[18] To speak out against the Vietnam War, to kick it against international corruption—this was what it took to be a worthy nonwhite icon. And Bruce did it without guns, with bare feet and fists, dressed in the black outfits associated with the North Vietnamese army. For U.S. radicals, the Vietnamese became a symbol of barefoot resistance. Early issues of the farm workers' newspaper *El Malcriado* called President Johnson the "Texas grower" and the Vietnamese, "farm workers," to make the transcontinental links that would give the Mexican workers hope.[19] Frustrated by her contemporary social movements in 1968, Marilyn Webb of DC Women's Liberation applauded the "Vietnamese woman [who] has literally won her equality with a weapon in her hand and through the sheer strength of her arms."[20] The Black Panthers, of course, recognized this aspect of the Vietnamese struggle. Connie Matthews, a Black Panther from San Jose, was eloquent on this theme at the Vietnam moratorium demonstration in October 1969. "The Vietnamese are a good example of the people being victorious," she said. "Because with all of America's technology and her greatness she has been unable to defeat the Vietnamese. Every man, woman and child has resisted."[21]

The Vietnamese seemed like the only force capable of being brave before nuclear imperialism. As the "Man," imperialism appeared untouchable to millions of youths across the planet. How could the bare feet of the world trounce B-52s, Agent Orange, fleets of destroyers, nuclear bombs, the military-industrial powerhouse of the United States. Each time a people made the attempt, from the Congo to Chile, the CIA's technological sophistication put paid to their efforts. The cultural symbol of the CIA was James Bond, that overarmed agent of U.S.–UK imperialism, and he had to answer Bruce's *Enter the Dragon* with *The Man with the Golden Gun* (1974).[22]

U.S. imperialism was like a poison. Apart from napalm, the United States used its arsenal of finance capital to undermine the sovereignty of the nations of the Third World. From 1965 to 1973, aggregate manufacturing profitability in the advanced industrial countries began to decline, a phenomenon that was assisted by the oil shocks of this period. One of the strategies for recovery conceived by the managers of the Group of 7 nations was to export the crisis, to conduct the structural adjustment of the newly independent nations, and to subsume all the economies of the world under the Dollar-Wall Street regime.[23] Robert McNamara, fresh from his post sending B-2 bombers to Vietnam, went to the World Bank, where he provided vast funds to bolster new authoritarian regimes such as Indonesia, Brazil, and the Philippines.[24] The debt of the entire Third World has increased from $100 billion in 1970 to $1.3 trillion in 1990. Whatever limited sovereignty was produced by the newly independent nations (and their import substitution strategy) was usurped by multinational firms (who enjoyed the corporate welfare of the IMF) and by the parasites who ruled the new nations. From 1962 to 1974 the register of revolutions held only one entry, South Yemen, but "in 1974 the dam had burst." In the next six years revolutionary movements took power in at least fourteen states, from the overthrow of Haile Selassie in Ethiopia to the victory of the New Jewel Movement (Grenada) and the FSLN (Nicaragua), in 1979.[25] The dollar wars against the currencies of the poor increased the sense of powerlessness. Big capital wrenched the reins of history from artisans and peasants, who saw technology as the enemy rather than as the puppet of financiers and plutocrats. Bruce, on the screen, seemed to be able to ward off the evil of iron and steel, of dollar and debt, with his bare hands.[26]

What appealed to many young people, men and women, was the "simplicity, directness and nonclassical instruction" of kung fu. "Ninety percent of Oriental self-defense is baloney," Bruce said, "It's organized despair."[27] Kung fu, in Bruce's vision, revoked the habit of hierarchy that swept up most institutions. Frustrated with what his student Leo Fong called "chop suey masters" who created an art for recompense, Bruce eagerly developed his kung fu (in the wing chung style, which he called jeet kune do) against the style of his fellow teachers whom he described as "lazy. They have big fat guts. They talk about *ch'i* power and things they can do, but don't believe in."[28] Instead Bruce used weights and drank high-protein weight-gain drinks (blended with ginseng, royal jelly, and vitamins). His virtuoso approach to perfection, and culture, came across in his delicate fierceness on the screen. If the *sifu* rejected the authority that came with the *sifu*'s position and instead fought for authority based on skill, then this was itself a rejection of the hierarchy of tradition. Bruce did not claim his power from his inherited kung fu lineage (his teacher, Yip Man, was master of the "sticking hands" method of wing chung), but he wanted others to bow to his street-fighting prowess. When asked if he was a black belt, Bruce was forthright. "I don't have any belt whatsoever. That is just a certificate. Unless you can really do it—that is, defend yourself successfully in a fight—that belt doesn't mean anything. I think it might be useful to hold your pants up, but that's about it."[29] In other words, anyone with dedicated tutelage can be a master, can be a *sifu*.

Kung fu gives oppressed young people an immense sense of personal worth and the skills for collective struggle. Kung fu, Bruce pointed out in his sociology of the art, "serves to cultivate the mind, to promote health, and to provide a most efficient means of self-protection against any attacks." It "develops confidence, humility, coordination, adaptability and respect toward others."[30] Words like *respect* and *confidence* jump out at me immediately, for one hears the former from working-class youth and the latter from their hardworking, but beleaguered teachers. These youth live within a calculus of respect and disrespect, wanting the former, but alert to challenge the latter. Their teachers want them to be confident. Kung fu allows for both and don't the kids know it. They are there on the weekends, for no "credit." And they fight not just for anything, but for righteousness.[31]

The notion that anyone can be a *sifu* was powerful, and it became the basis for the turn of many working-class youth to the martial arts. In the ghettos of the United States, dojos and kung fu schools opened to eager students. Cliff Stewart's dojo opened in Los Angeles in the late 1960s. Stewart, a founder of the BKF, set up the dojo for "the kids in our neighborhood. Most of them couldn't afford to travel to dojos in other parts of the city," nor could they afford the equipment required to participate in most sports except basketball.[32] Karate requires no fancy equipment, just a small space, bare feet, and naked hands. The youth in the ghetto took refuge, said Steve Sanders, in "pills and pot for a long time. Some were stealing to keep up their habits. So I made a deal with them. I told them if they kept away from drugs, they could come to my classes and train for nothing."[33] Many came and excelled.

Fred Hamilton organized All-Dojo Karate Championships at places like the Manhattan Center in New York City or at the Fordham University Gymnasium in the Bronx, where, for a few dollars, entire families could sit and watch the black belts demonstrate their rough poetry in motion.[34] By then most young African Americans knew of the deeds of the BKF (and its founders, Steve Sanders, Jerry Smith, Cliff Stewart, and Don Williams). Staff Sergeant George Harris was the first African American judo champion for the air force. In 1971, *jujitsu* artist Moses Powell was the first African American to perform at the United Nations and by 1973 became a featured performer in Aaron Banks's Oriental World of Self-Defense. That same year, Howard Jackson from Detroit, Michigan, took the world of kung fu by storm, winning the Battle for Atlanta and becoming the first African American to be ranked number one in the sport's history. Tayari Casel, a student of Jimmie Jones of Chicago, later, experimented with *kupiganangumi*, a "rhythmical and acrobatic martial art developed by African slaves and their descendants and ch'ang ch'uan," when he won the Battle of Atlanta in 1976.[35] Each of these men continue to develop their martial arts skills to build community power. Powell has developed a style known as sanuces-ryu (he works with "ex-offenders, teaching them self-respect, self-control and honesty through the martial arts" and he works "with disadvantaged youth and senior citizens").[36] Meanwhile, Mufundisi Tayari Casel trains young people in Maryland in the arts of *kupigana ngumi,* a Swahili phrase that means "way of fighting with fist." He urges the development of a healthy lifestyle, discipline, and community values.[37] The Black Karate Federation continues to preach the path of karate as the path to a disciplined and just community. It seeks to "faciliate a sense of unity among a diverse community, provide leadership and guidance for youth and their families, narrow the gap between cultures, gender and age groups, create a greater sense of awareness of both physical and mental health."[38]

What was astounding about the BKF and several other U.S. dojos was their openness to women. Bruce himself was not keen on women in the dojos. Of women fighters he said that "they are no match for the men who are physiologically stronger, except for a few vulnerable points. My advice is that if they have to fight, hit the man at his vital points and then run. Women are more likely to achieve their objectives thorough feminine wiles and persuasion."[39] You can imagine what Pauline Short thought of these words. Called the "Mother of American Karate," Short opened her first karate school in Portland, Oregon, in 1965, which catered entirely to women. Or one can sense the fury of Ruby Lozano, the Filipina, who won one of the twelve awards for Outstanding Filipinos Overseas from the government of the Philippines in 1974 for her karate prowess. And what about the fiery reaction from Graciela Casillas, born in Bellflower, California, in 1956 and karate champion by the late 1970s. And, finally, what of Judith Brown's suggestion that women should live in all-female celebate communes and practice karate, a weapon in the arsenal of a strong, liberated woman.[40] The BKF welcomed women into the schools, just as the black kung fu movies took pains to represent women as fighters in their own right.[41]

In addition to the master of the local dojo, there were black kung fu heroes like Jim Kelly, bigger than life on the movie screen, tangling with women just as fierce as he. Born in Paris, Kentucky, in 1946, Kelly came to kung fu through karate, and by the 1970s Kelly cemented his place among the top rank of martial artists at Ed Parker's famous tournaments (where Bruce first did an exhibition in 1964). When they worked together on *Enter the Dragon,* Kelly's skills impressed. Bruce admired the soul that Kelly put into his *chi'i* and let him choreograph his own fights (others tended to make martial arts entirely mechanical if they were not supervised).[42] The ability to transmit "soul" was central to Kelly, whose mix of pleasure and skill had thrilled young aficionados in his day. Consider the famous act of bluster from Kelly (as Williams) in *Enter the Dragon*. When the evil Han asks Williams about his fear of defeat, he responds that "I don't waste my time. When it comes, I won't even notice. I'll be too busy lookin' good." You can imagine entire sections of the theater breaking into spontaneous applause. As writer David Walker recounts in his essay "Jim Kelly and Me,"

> I wanted to be Jim Kelly. Sure I wanted to be Bruce Lee too, but I wasn't Chinese and that seemed like an obstacle that I wouldn't be overcoming anytime soon. I promptly began growing my hair into an Afro. "Man, you come right outta some comic book" became my catch phrase. And once Halloween rolled around, I slipped into yellow pajamas, pencilled in some sideburns, and I hit the trick-or-treat trail decked out as my main man.[43]

With plots that revolved mainly around efforts to smash unjust power lords, Kelly's bare-fisted bravado was at its best. When a white supremacist organization plans to poison African Americans through the water supply, Kelly is onto them (*Three the Hard Way*, 1974). As Black Belt Jones, Kelly first takes on the Mob and a corrupt city government. Two years later, in *Hot Potato*, he goes after a corrupt wing of the U.S. military. In *Black Samurai* (1977), Kelly is Bond (*Goldfinger*, 1964)—as he infiltrates a secret island getaway of a crime syndicate to rescue his girlfriend.[44] Of course in *Black Belt Jones*,[45] Gloria Hendry, who plays the lead, Sidney, is a *sifu* in her own right. When Jones (Kelly) gets a message that the bad guys are on the move, he gets ready to leave Sidney to do the dishes as he goes off to do combat. Sidney, incensed by his sexism, borrows his gun and "does" the dishes with a round of well-aimed fire. This is the film of black liberation.[46]

Panthers and Dragons

Liberation wasn't restricted to the screen. From 1968 until the late 1970s, the terrain of left political struggle in the U.S. was populated by energetic organizations formed to combat the problem of racism and its effect on communities. In 1967, Stokely Carmichael and Charles Hamilton's manifesto *Black Power* argued that just coalitions can be built only if each party within the compact is empowered—"*before a group can enter an open society, it must first close ranks*"[47]—Oppressed groups were to form their own organizations to hold discussions that could not be held before the eyes of all people, and to forge the strength for mutual respect in broad coalitions.[48] While some activists in the late 1960s took the position that the most oppressed must lead the movement, most of those among the oppressed, as a prelude to a united front, created organizations under the banner of the Third World. Inspired in part by the struggles of others in China, Vietnam, and Africa, the Black Panther Party for Self-Defense, formed in 1967, led the way, but right on their heels came groups such as the Young Lords Organization (which began in 1956 as a gang before being rectified by Cha Cha Jiménez in 1967), the Brown Berets (a Chicano formation in 1968), the American Indian Movement (formed in Minneapolis in 1968), the Red Guard Party (a group of Chinese Americans in San Francisco in 1969), and the I Wor Kuen (from New York's Chinatown in 1969).[49] Poor white folk formed the Patriot Party. In 1968 Bernardine Dohrn of Students for a Democratic Society (SDS) was of the view that "the best thing that we can do for ourselves, as well as for the Panthers and the revolutionary black liberation struggle, is to build a fucking white revolutionary movement."[50] Against the liberalism of support came the revolutionary instinct of self-interest politics here in the guise of the Weather Underground. Four other women of the SDS sounded the clarion call for an autonomous women's organization when they wrote in mid-1967 that "we find that women are in a colonial relationship to men and we recognize ourselves as part of the Third World."[51]

If the Black Panthers inspired the multicolored Left, they in turn had been inspired by Chinese Communism.[52] When Bobby Seale and Huey P. Newton formed the Black Panthers in October 1966 they took much inspiration from Mao's radical critique of imperialism. The Chinese Communists, during the Yenan period (1937–46), learned that the party must harness the strength of the people and allow creative popular energy to determine social organization. "Our culture is a people's culture," noted Mao in 1944. "Our cultural workers must serve the people with great enthusiasm and devotion, and they must link themselves with the masses, not divorce themselves from the masses."[53] Such values motivated Bobby Seale and Huey Newton, and they also had an impact on Amiri Baraka, who knew of the Black Panthers during a teaching assignment at San Francisco State in 1967. Baraka founded the Congress of African Peoples on Maoist principles; in 1978, as the Revolutionary Communist League [Marxist-Leninist], it merged with the I Wor Kuen and the Chicano August Twenty-Ninth Movement to create the ill-fated U.S. League for Revolutionary Struggle.[54] For Seale and Newton, furthermore, Maoism provided a way to raise easy cash: they went to Chinatown, ordered and bought boxes of Mao's Red Book, took them over to the UC Berkeley campus, and sold them for a profit. This money enabled them to buy guns and other equipment for the party. Mao was in the Black Panthers, just as the Black Panthers opened themselves up to other organizations.

And each of these organizations did more than just recognize an affinity. They worked closely with one another in a piecemeal coalition. The Young Lords worked in close concert with I Wor Kuen, and in 1971 Central Committee member Juan Gonzalez traveled to San Francisco's Chinatown to meet with Asian revolutionaries and others.[55] When Native American radicals took Alcatraz in 1970, a detachment of Japanese American radicals unfurled a huge banner that read Japanese Americans Support Native Americans, painted signs that said This Is Indian property and Red Power, and brought them food.[56] The Palestine Liberation Organization offered their solidarity with Native Americans too; Stokely Carmichael offered the keynote statement at the Arab Student Convention in 1968; the Black Panthers took up the cause of the forty-one Iranian students set for deportation from the United States because of anti-shah activities; and the Wei Min made liberation struggles of the Ethiopian Students Union of Northern California their common cause. It was a vibrant world of internationalism through nationality, in other words, of a *particular universalism*.[57] When DeAnna Lee asked Bobby Seale in 1970 if he had a message for Asians, he said that "I see the Asian people playing a very significant part in solving the problems of their own community in coalition, unity and alliance with Black people because the problems are basically the same as they are for Brown, Red and poor White Americans—the basic problem of poverty and oppression that we are all subjected to."[58] Amy Uyematsu at UCLA had an even larger worldview, declaring in 1969 that "yellow power and black power must be two independently-powerful, joint forces within the Third World revolution to free all exploited and oppressed people of color."[59] These movements acknowledged the strategic importance of unity, and they knew that unity could not be forged without space for the efflorescence of oppressed cultures and the development of their leadership.

Of course, an alliance of blacks and Asians was sometimes resisted. Moritsuga "Mo" Nishida was raised in Los Angeles, joined a gang (the Constituents from the westside on Crenshaw), and moved into the orbit of black radicalism. But he was not welcomed: "We ain't black so we get this, especially from non-California bred blacks who don't understand the Asian oppression and struggle, so to them, if you're not black then you're White. So we getting all kind of bullshit like that."[60] Yet, the complexity of segregated neighborhoods in the United States meant that the idea of an exclusive nation could not always be actively sustained. Asians along the West Coast of the United States lived among blacks, so that when the Black Panther Party was formed, Asians gravitated to it (in much the same way as Asians of another generation worked within the civil rights ambit). Yuri Kochiyama had already made contact with Malcolm X, and in the late 1960s, several Asians joined the Panthers, including Richard Aoki (made immortal by Bobby Seale as "a Japanese radical cat," who "had guns for a motherfucker"[61]), the Chinese Jamaican filmmaker Lee Lew-Lee, and Seattle activist Guy Kurose.[62] Aoki, raised in the Topaz Concentration Camp and then in west Oakland with Huey Newton and Bobby Seale, was a charter member of the Black Panthers and its field marshal, who went underground into the Asian American Political Alliance at UC Berkeley. Three decades later, Aoki said that "if you are a person of color there's no other way for you to go except to be part of the Black liberation struggle. It doesn't mean submerge your own political identity or your whatever, but the job that has to be done in front, you got to be there. And I was there. What can I say."[63]

One of the classic examples of this alliance is the relationship between the Red Guard and the Black Panthers. According to former Red Guard member Alex Hing, Asian women from San Francisco's Chinatown made the Black Panthers in Oakland aware of the disaffected young people from their neighborhood, many of whom assembled at a pool hall owned by a cooperative called Leway (or Legitimate Ways).[64] The Panthers visited them, and worked alongside some of them to create a radical nucleus that would, in 1969, emerge as the Red Guard.[65] In Los Angeles, similar developments among lumpen Asian youth led to the creation of two formations, the Yellow Brotherhood and Asian Hardcore,[66] while in New York City the I Wor Kuen emerged as a Maoist outfit of Chinatown.[67] Radical Chinese youth on both coasts renamed 1969 (the Year of the Rooster) the Year of the People Off the Pigs, a salute to the style of the Black Panthers and against the oppression within Chinatown. Always restricted to not more than a few hundred youths, the Red Guard tried to develop some programs to reach out to the community in a manner similar to that of the Black Panthers. The Guard attempted to make commercial street fairs into community fairs. They tried to dethrone the dominance of the right-wing leadership within Chinatown, they created a Breakfast for Children program and when this did not work began to feed elders in Portsmouth Square Park. They fought against the oppressive police and worked hard to undercut the racism of the white teachers and tourists. They fought to maintain a tuberculosis center and a Buddhist temple, and set up a legal clinic (Asian Legal Services). At the same time the Guard publicized the efforts of other politicized communities and distributed propaganda on behalf of the Cultural Revolution in China, against the Vietnam War, and in favor of the Black Panthers.[68] The Red Guard, unlike many of the campus-based groups, "was born out of the poverty and repression of the ghetto,"[69] which enabled it to make connections with the other antipoverty, anticapitalist organizations that struggled among the working class and working poor in their communities.

The milieu of the Red Guard, the Brown Berets, and the Black Panthers was one of an enchanted solidarity against capitalism. Since the economic system was prone to crisis, Alex Hing of the Guard told Asian students at UCLA in 1970 that Asians must prepare for its eventuality. Since Asians are only a small population in the United States, and since "most Asians don't know the front end from the back end of a gun," an alliance with the oppressed working class seemed the only avenue for the "survival of Asians."[70] If ethnicity was not sufficient in tactical terms for survival, in strategic terms to bind around ethnicity would make it hard to be critical of "Uncle Charleys" like Dr. S. I. Hayakawa, president of San Francisco State, as well as of the right-wing Chinatown leadership. Jack Wong, of Chinatown, said that Hayakawa's obdurate stand against the students of color during the 1968 strike at the school was "just another instance of a yellow man being used by the whites."[71] A critique of the Asian Right from within the Asian community facilitated Black Panther David Hilliard's comment that "we can run Hayakawa not only off this campus, but we can run him back to imperialistic Japan. Because the man ain't got no motherfucking power. He's a bootlicker." Not only could Hilliard make this statement thanks to the opening afforded by the Red Guard's critique of Hayakawa, but in response to Kim Il Sung's call to combat imperialism and the "ideological degeneration" among the oppressed peoples.[72] The Guard produced a space for the Left to undertake a clear distinction between an antiracist nationalism and one that protected the Right from any criticism on the grounds of national assertion. But, as many people have said in retrospect, the Guard failed to create a mass base, perhaps mainly due to its views of the Guard as an army, but also because of the tendency among the Chinese Americans to withdraw from engagement with the state—in New York and in San Francisco, the Asian Left had to deal with the military formations of the police as well as of the Asian middle class, such as the right-wing Chinatown elite's gangs, the Flying Dragons and the White Shadows.[73]

Army machismo came in part from the Black Panthers, but also from the widespread sense of wonder that the Vietnamese forces could penetrate the defenses of the U.S. army during the famous 1968 Tet offensive. With Tet, young Asian Americans ceased to feel the burden of a stereotypical submissiveness, and many of them refashioned themselves around the symbols of

Asian resistance to imperialism, particularly those of the Cultural Revolution—the Mao jackets, the Red Book, the slogans. The U.S. army's attempt, after Tet, to retake control over the war led to a genuine moral failure (in the village of Ben Tre a U.S. major provided the famous line, "It was necessary to destroy the city in order to save it"). Disgusted by this, many young Americans turned to the struggles within that omnibus category the Third World to find the agent of revolutionary struggle (Cuba, Vietnam, Algeria), and they drew upon that category to create the tentative united front for their own struggles at home. In 1970, the U.S. People's Anti-Imperalist Delegation traveled to North Korea and Vietnam under the leadership of Eldridge Cleaver, minister of information of the Black Panther Party. Two Asians made up the ten delegates: Pat Sumi, a member of the Movement for a Democratic Military, and Alex Hing, of the Red Guard. Writing of their experiences in Asia, Sumi and Hing noted that the struggle in the United States had to be moved from being antiwar to antiimperialist, from one that wanted to "bring the troops home" to one that opened "up the resources of Amerika to the rest of the world."[74]

Two years later, Bruce Lee would give us the perfect allegory both of Asian American radicalism and of the Vietnam War with *The Way of the Dragon* (also called *Return of the Dragon*). Here Bruce (as Tang Lung, or China Dragon) works at a Chinese restaurant (the ultimate stereotype of skillful servileness), but in the back alley he trains the waiters in martial arts to repulse the thugs whose harassment has hurt business. The godfather of the thugs hires a few heavies to deal with Bruce, a *hapkido* expert (Wong In Sik) and two U.S. karate champions (Bob Wall and Chuck Norris, now Walker-Texas Ranger). He dispatches both Wall and In Sik, representatives perhaps of the ordinary U.S. soldier and of the South Korean army. With Norris (named Colt—45 perhaps?), Bruce takes his time, but as he demolishes him, the fight, set in the Coliseum in Rome, becomes a battle between Western civilization and Chinese civilization, between the paper tiger of U.S. imperialism and the rising tide of the Red East.[75] Bruce, in the context of the Red Guards and of the North Vietnamese army, appeared on the screen to young Asian Americans as "the brother who showed [America that] Asian people can kick some ass."[76]

From Baku to Bandung: Third World Solidarity

When Bruce planned *Way of the Dragon*, he told his mother, "Mom, I'm an Oriental person, therefore, I have to defeat all the whites in the film."[77] At the time, the United States had dropped eight hundred thousand tons of bombs on Cambodia, Laos, and Vietnam. Bruce's victory over Norris/Colt would be an act of solidarity with the army in black pajamas. In June 1972, in Bombay, in another show of unity, a group of Dalits formed the Dalit Panthers. Named in honor of the Black Panthers, they hoped to celebrate and emulate the ethic of the panther, who, as they argued, *fights without retreat*. The Dalit Panther manifesto offers an immense sense of political comradeship:

> Due to the hideous plot of American imperialism, the Third Dalit World, that is, oppressed nations, and Dalit people are suffering. Even in America, a handful of reactionary whites are exploiting blacks. To meet the force of reaction and remove this exploitation, the Black Panther movement grew. From the Black Panthers, Black Power emerged. The fire of the struggles has thrown out sparks into the country. We claim a close relationship with this struggle. We have before our eyes the examples of Vietnam, Cambodia, Africa and the like.

When representatives of the Black Panther Party (David Hillard and Elbert Howard) met the representatives of the National Liberation Front of Vietnam in Montreal, the Vietnamese said, "He Black Panther, we Yellow Panther!" and the Black Panthers replied, "Yeah, you're Yellow Panthers, we're Black Panthers. All power to the people!"[78]

To appreciate the vitality of the idea of Third World solidarity, we will need a detour into its modern history. That Ho Chi Minh once hung out in Garveyite halls in Harlem should perhaps be part of this story, as should the Maoist inflections in both the National Liberation Front (of Vietnam) and Black Panther politics. In 1965, Ho Chi Minh and the black radical Robert F. Williams spent an evening together during which they "swapped Harlem stories; Ho recounted his visits to Harlem in the 1920s as a merchant seaman and claimed that he had heard Marcus Garvey speak there and had been so inspired that he 'emptied his pockets' into the collection plate."[79] The story could very well be about the conversations between Nkrumah of Ghana and Stokely Carmichael or any other black radical who visited the Ghanaian leader, who had also spent a formative period of his life in Harlem and Philadelphia.[80] The radical visions that emerged in the twentieth century enabled the sense of enchanted comradeship of the 1960s and 1970s, a legacy worth revisiting in this new century.

Talk of Ho Chi Minh and Robert Williams leads me toward Lenin's famous articles from the early 1900s that exalted the Asian rebellions, this in light of Japan's defeat of the Russians in the 1904 war. "There can be no doubt

that the age-old plunder of India by the British, and the contemporary struggle of all these 'advanced' Europeans against Persian and Indian democracy,
will *steel* millions, tens of millions of proletarians in Asia to wage a struggle
against their oppressors which will be just as victorious as that of the Japanese. The class conscious European worker now has comrades in Asia, and
their number will grow by leaps and bounds."[81] The internationalism of the
world Communist movement produced several institutions dedicated to
building solidarity across the world, the First Congress of the Peoples of the
East in Baku (1920), the Indian School at Tashkent which became the Institute of the Study of the East (1921) and then the University of the Toilers
of the East, the League Against Imperialism (1924), the Conference of the
Oppressed People in Brussels (1927), and then into the 1940s, the various
peace and youth festivals.[82]

Intellectuals of the Afro-Asian world found immense political, moral,
and intellectual resources in the tradition of Marxism and Communism,
something that has been wonderfully catalogued in recent years.[83] The depth
of this connection is forgotten or else minimized by the example of George
Padmore's resignation from the CPUSA or Aimé Cesaire's celebrated letter
to Maurice Thorez resigning from the Communist Party of France. Cesaire
wrote in that letter, "What I want is that Marxism and Communism be harnessed into the service of colored people, and not colored people into the
service of Marxism and Communism." There is a falseness to this statement
because Marxism and Communism both emerged from the labors of "colored people" (whether as the materials for Marx's analysis of the world system or at the debates in the Comintern between the Indian Communist
M. N. Roy and Lenin or else in the developments of communisms outside
Europe whose heritage continues till this day). But what those who quote
from Cesaire fail to reveal is that in the very same letter he wrote, "There
exists a Chinese communism. Though I have no first hand acquaintance
with it, I am strongly prejudiced in its favor. And I expect it not to sink into
the monstrous errors that have disfigured European communism."[84]

"Black Maoism," whose contours we traced earlier, was enabled by the
strong antiracist position taken by Mao's China: as the Communists took
power over China, the party abolished the idea of "race," suspended anthropology departments (which had a propensity toward a racist form of physical
anthropology), and proscribed them until 1952. In 1963, at the urging of his
guest Robert Williams, Mao offered a strong statement in favor of the black
liberation movement to call on "the workers, peasants, revolutionary intellectuals, enlightened elements of the bourgeoisie, and other enlightened

personages of all colours in the world, white, black, yellow, brown, etc., to unite to oppose the racial discrimination practiced by U.S. imperialism and to support the American Negroes in their struggle against racial discrimination."[85] The Chinese Communist position reveals for us the centrality of political engagement over cultural history.[86]

During the onrush of anticolonial national liberation (which began with India and Pakistan in 1947), African and Asian leaders spoke in glowing terms of their need to cooperate. In late 1946, Nehru wrote to six East African leaders in solidarity with their struggles ("the voice of India will always be raised in the cause of African freedom") and he suggested that "African students should come to the universities and technical institutes of India."[87] Indeed, Nehru was instrumental in putting Indian resources at the service of African independence, whether these were economic or political.[88] In the 1940s and 1950s, Nehru was a regular speaker at historically black colleges in the United States, where in tribute his suit became the vogue (only when Nkrumah came to these colleges wearing the same suit was its name changed from the Nehru jacket to the Nkrumah jacket).

With the Communists in power from 1949, the new Chinese republic attempted to solidify its relationship with Africa. In the early 1960s, political scientist Immanuel Wallerstein noted that

> The Soviet Union is to Africans, particularly black Africans, simply
> another part of the Western world. It is China, not the USSR, that fasci-
> nates. China is not a white nation. It is more militant than the USSR on
> colonial questions. It is a poorer country, and its efforts at economic devel-
> opment are more relevant to Africa's problems, the Africans think. Above
> all, China has been a colony of the West, or at least a semi-colony.[89]

From 1959, the Peoples' Republic of China began to offer technical assistance to and cooperative market arrangements with a number of African nations (as well as military training to those who still fought colonial powers). Guinea was the first country to create close economic ties with the PRC through interest-free loans and instruction in rice-growing techniques.[90] The African reaction to Chinese Communism is best captured in President Julius Nyerere's 1965 speech to welcome Chou En-lai to Dar es Salaam. After praising the Long March, Nyerere noted that both China and Africa are on a joint long march, "a new revolutionary battle—the fight against poverty and economic backwardness." But the war was not only economic, because, said Nyerere, Tanzania had to defend against neocolonialism, and carefully take assistance from others, for "neither our principles, our country, nor our freedom to determine our future are for sale."[91] China was well aware of this,

for when Chou and President Mobido Keita of Mali signed the "Eight Principles" of aid in 1964, point four specifically stated that "the purpose of the
Chinese government's foreign aid is not to make the recipient countries dependent on China but to help them embark on the road to self-reliance and
independent economic development step by step."[92] Assistance from India
or China came only because, as Nkrumah made clear during his 1958 trip to
India, the struggle for Indian independence was longer and the people were
able to prepare themselves for it. In Ghana, "the change was comparatively
sudden" and "we had to start from scratch to manage our own affairs."[93]

The links between Asia and Africa in the middle of the previous century
came on the terrain of a sort of anti-colonial solidarity. In 1955, representatives from twenty-nine African and Asian nations gathered together in the
small Indonesia town of Bandung to celebrate that heritage.[94] There were
also representatives from the United States. Flushed with success from the
ongoing anticolonial movement, a community of leaders, behind whom
stood masses of people, came together with a loose agenda, but with considerable self-confidence. President Sukarno of Indonesia noted that the partic-
ipants are united "by a common detestation of colonialism in whatever form
it appears. We are united by a common detestation of racialism." Furthermore, Sukharno pointedly noted that unity at Bandung was not one of race
or religion, since "conflict comes not from variety of skins, nor from variety
of religion, but from variety of desires." Therefore the anticolonial heritage
and suspicion of neocolonialism was the principle ethic for unity.[95] Bandung
left an impressive mark on peoples of Africa and Asia, despite the impossi-
bility for such a platform to mean much in the intense suspicion of the
cold war era. Ideological differences between countries (variety of desires)
and the arrangements made by nations with the superpowers prevented any
combined action, except occasionally at the United Nations (for crucial anticolonial votes, on world disarmament as a moral force, for aid to newly free
countries, and decisively, through agencies to ameliorate or check the multinational corporations).[96]

At Bandung, Nehru remembered the centrality of the Middle Passage
to any project to craft solidarity across the tide of color.

> There is nothing more terrible, there is nothing more horrible than the
> infinite tragedy of Africa in the past few hundred years. When I think of it,
> everything else pales into insignificance; that infinite tragedy of Africa ever
> since the days when millions of them were carried away in galleys as slaves
> to America and elsewhere, the way they were treated, the way they were
> taken away, 50 percent dying in the galleys. We have to bear that burden,

all of us. We did not do it ourselves, but the world has to bear it. We talk
about this country and that little country in Africa or outside, but let us
remember this Infinite Tragedy.[97]

Nehru's contribution continued the anticolonial relationship of Indian nationalism with the U.S. black left, one that was wiped out by the U.S. state
in the 1950s.[98]

However, U.S. black representatives failed to grasp the depth of struggle
as they perversely defended the U.S. record on civil rights and attacked
China's communism. From the mid-1940s, the U.S. state department cultivated certain African American artists and writers to muddy the critiques of
U.S. racism that mainly came from the USSR.[99] Several black artists and
writers colluded with the U.S. government out of fear or to gain access to
the world stage. At Bandung, African Americans such as Congressman Adam
Clayton Powell Jr. and Max Yergan vigorously praised the U.S. governmental
system, perhaps to shore up their own political futures upon return. Even
arch anti-Communists among the Asians, such as Sir John Kotelawla of Ceylon, held their tongues as Chou En-lai took a conciliatory position. But Powell and Yergan let loose much to the consternation of their Asian allies.[100]
Richard Wright, like Yergan, had been a Communist in his youth. In the
1950s he joined with the liberal anti-Communist wing (and contributed to
their celebrated collection *The God That Failed*), but, unlike Yergan, Wright
was always an unpredictable political writer. At Bandung he was not taken
by Powell and Yergan, yet he too seemed to miss the point when he claimed
that Sukarno was "appealing to race and religion" or when he wondered how
Chou felt "amidst the ground swell of racial and religious feeling."[101] But
by the Vietnam War, a conflict with no forseeable ending, black and Asian
American activists would become more radical and more united than they
had ever been, finally empowered by a sense of Third World solidarity.

Everybody Was Kung Fu Fighting, ca. 1974

As *Enter the Dragon* came to us in Calcutta, a song also broke through the
tedium offered by Musical Bandbox, a Sunday afternoon program on All-
India Radio. It was a rather trite song: Everybody was kung-fu fighting,
hunh, Those cats were fast as lightning, hunh. Nothing to it, really. But
Biddu, an exemplary Indian who lived in England and produced Tina
Charles's *Disco Fever* and Nazia Hasan's *Disco Dewanee*, wrote the tune,
hence its appearance on Indian radio. Sung by Carl Douglas, an African
American whose entire career was forged around the gimmick of kung fu

music ("Dance the Kung Fu" and "Shanghai D"), the song belongs in my memory bank alongside an atrocious tribute to Muhammad Ali with that infectious line from the master, "Fly like a butterfly, sting like a bee."[102] Tripping on Carl Douglas and Biddu, we read the papers for news of the impending fight between Muhammad Ali and George Foreman in Zaire, the famous "Rumble in the Jungle" in the autumn of that year.[103] "From slave ship to championship," the promoters declaimed. "We were taken from Africa as slaves and now we're coming back as champions." Ali was only thirty-two, a year younger than Bruce. And Ali was as politically incensed about racism and imperialism as Bruce was. Bruce was trained to hate white supremacy in the hovels of Hong Kong. Ali's life in the U.S. South prepared him to strike tough jabs for the Black Power movement. It was Ali, after all, who denounced the U.S. imperialist engagement in Southeast Asia with the memorable line, "No Vietcong ever called me nigger." Although Bruce Lee was also a boxing champ in Hong Kong (and the 1958 Crown Colony Cha-Cha Champion), he spent much of the 1960s watching films of Ali boxing. "An orthodox boxer, Ali led with his left hand. Since Bruce was experimenting with a right lead stance he set up a mirror so that he could watch Ali's movements and practice them the appropriate way."[104] In an instance of classic cross-fertilization, the great boxer Sugar Ray Leonard told an interviewer in 1982 that "one of the guys who influenced me wasn't a boxer. I always loved the catlike reflexes and the artistry of Bruce Lee and I wanted to do in boxing what he was able to do in karate. I started watching his movies before he became really popular in *Enter the Dragon* and I patterned myself after a lot of his ways."[105]

So what are the implications of the world of polycultural kung fu? Color-blind capitalists wish to make a profit from its appeal, often by the opportunistic combination of ethnic niche markets (when Jackie Chan and Chris Tucker appear together in the 1998 *Rush Hour,* and soon in *Rush Hour II,* or else when Sammo Hung and Arsenio Hall did time in CBS's *Martial Law,* or the ultra-commodified Tae-Bo of Billy Blanks[106]). Primordialists (and "perfectionists") argue that the artistry originates in either Africa or Asia. "It was Africa and not Asia that first gave martial arts to the world," wrote Afrocentric scholar Kilindi Iyi, "and those same African roots are deeply embedded in the martial arts of India and China."[107] Iyi looks at ancient murals from Beni Hasan, Egypt, to make his claim, but he could equally make the point that the similarities between Capoeira Angola and kung fu can be traced to those enslaved Africans who created the Brazilian art in the 1500s, nurtured it in the *senzalas* ("slave houses"), and developed it into a symbolic as well as a physical response to the atrocity of a racist slavery. The language of Capoeira, indeed, is replete with Bantu words, and the movements of Capoeira resemble the southern Angolan dance of *n'golo* ("zebra dance").[108]

If Iyi looks to Africa for the origins of martial arts, others do the same with Asia. Most histories of kung fu tell the story of Bodhidharma, an itinerant Buddhist monk who introduced the monks of the Shaolin Temple in China to the martial arts of his homeland, southern India. Bodhidharma may be the son of the King of Kancheepuram in the region of today's Tamil Nadu (as some Japanese manuscripts claim), and it is said that he imported the arts of Kalarippayattu to China from Kerala, in the southwest of India.[109] Bodhidharma's *Hseih Mai Lun* ("Treatise on the Blood Lineages of True Dharma") lays out a philosophy of the *ch'i* ("life force"), and how it must be kept active to ensure that monks don't sleep during meditation.[110] The desire to seek origins in what might be complex cultural diffusion or else independent creation is certainly not of much help. However, we might say that the martial arts traditions such as kung fu developed in a manifold world that involved, in some complex way, Kalarippayattu of Kerala, Capoeira Angola of Brazil, and the various martial arts of Africa. Kung fu is not far from Africa, nor from the *favelas* ("slums") of Brazil.[111]

Iyi, along with Afrocentric historians Wayne Chandler and Graham Irwin, makes the mistake of finding *racial* links when I am more tempted to avoid that complex soup of "descent," whatever that may mean. They argue, for instance, that Buddha, the man whose tradition produces kung fu, was of African "descent."[112] The school of Kamau Ryu System of Self-Defense claims that Bodhidharma was "black with tightly curled knots of hair and elongated ear lobes which are traditional African traits."[113] The incessant interest in origins bespeaks a notion of culture as an inheritance that is transmitted across time without mutation, and is the property of certain people. There are numerous reasons to claim origins and to mark oneself as authentic if one belongs to an oppressed minority. Minority groups may mobilize around the notion of an origin to make resource claims, to show that despite the denigration of the power elite, the group can lay claim to an aspect of civilization and the cultural currency attached to it. Furthermore, to demarcate oneself from the repressive stereotypes, the oppressed frequently turn to their "roots" to suggest to their children that they have a lineage that is worthy despite racism's cruelty. These are important social explanations for the way we use both origins and authenticity (to protect our traditional forms from appropriation by the power elite). As defensive tactics these make sense, but as a strategy for freedom they are inappropriate. In a prosaic moment in 1919, W. E. B. Du Bois wrote of the "blood of yellow and white hordes" who "diluted the ancient black blood of India, but her eldest Buddha sits back, with kinky hair."[114] Du Bois's gesture toward Buddha was not necessarily a claim to the *racial* or *epidermal* lineage of Buddha, but it was a signal toward some form of solidarity across the Indian Ocean and between Asians and Africans in diaspora. In his 1928 novel *Dark Princess,* the Indian Kautilya seals her bond with the African American Matthew through a ruby that is "by legend a drop of Buddha's blood"; in time, their child, "Incarnate Son of the Buddha," will rule over a kingdom fated to overthrow British rule.[115] Matthew, for Du Bois, was a symbol of anti-imperialist solidarity, and the claim to Buddha indicated a search for the cultural roots of solidarity not too dependent on the mysterious world of biology.

In our own day, community scholars like Q-Unique of the Arsonists come at kung fu from the lens of hip-hop. He believes that Bruce Lee should be remembered as "the first to teach non-Asians Martial Arts and to be the first big Asian actor," and "that right there is enough to tell me that you should be able to believe in yourself to be able to climb the highest mountain. Or just go against whatever is thrown your way. You should be able to look at adversity in its face and believe in yourself to get what you want. And that's what Bruce Lee ultimately taught me: What I do with my MCing skills is sort of like what he did with his Martial Arts. You study everybody's techniques and you strip away what you don't find necessary and use what is necessary and you modify it. You give it your own twist. He used Jeet Kune Do. Mine is Jeet Kune Flow."[116] The polycultural view of the world exists in the gut instincts of many people such as Q-Unique. Scholars are under some obligation to raise this instinct to philosophy, to use this instinct to criticize the diversity model of multiculturalism and replace it with the antiracist one of polyculturalism. Culture cannot be bounded and people cannot be asked to respect "culture" as if it were an artifact, without life or complexity. Social interaction and struggle produces cultural worlds, and these are in constant, fraught formation. Our cultures are linked in more ways than we could catalog, and it is from these linkages that we hope our politics will be energized. The Third World may be in distress, where the will of the national liberation movements has put the tendency to anti-imperialism in crisis, and where the Third World within the United States has often been overrun by the dynamic of the color blind and of the desire to make small, individual gains over social transformation. Nevertheless, the struggle is on, in places like Kerala and Vietnam, but also within the United States as the Black Radical

Congress greets the Asian Left Forum, the Forum of Indian Leftists, the League of Filipino Students (among others), and as all of them join together against imperialism, against racism. History is made in struggle and past memories of solidarity are inspiration for that struggle. Indeed, the Afro-Asian and polycultural struggles of today allow us to redeem a past that has been carved up along ethnic lines by historians. To remember Bruce as I do, staring at a poster of him ca. 1974, is not to wane into nostalgia for the past. My Bruce is alive, and like the men and women before him, still in the fight.

Notes

The Forethought: Raw Skin

1   Tony Kushner, *Angels in America. Part Two: Perestroika* (New York: Theater Communications Group, 1996), 14.

2. The winter/spring 2001 (no. 13) issue of *SAMAR: South Asian Magazine for Action and Reflection* is entitled "Come Africa" and offers a partial inventory of the links between Asia and Africa. This magazine, this book, and many other such attempts point to a tendency among scholars to map out a terrain that is already being hewed in practice by young activists who walk quite confidently between these identities.

3. Vijay Prashad, *Karma of Brown Folk* (Minneapolis: University of Minnesota Press, 2000).

4. I am drawing freely from a distinction imbedded in LeRoi Jones (Amiri Baraka), *Blues People* (New York: Morrow Quill, 1963), notably in chapter 9. Thanks to Nikhil Pal Singh for a discussion on this theme.

Chapter 1: The Strange Career of Xenophobia

1   K. M. Panikkar, *Asia and Western Dominance. A History of the Vasco Da Gama Epoch of Asian History, 1498–1945* (New York: John Day, 1953).

2. Alfred W. Crosby, *Ecological Imperialism: The Biological Expansion of Europe, 900–1900* (Cambridge: Cambridge University Press, 1986), 113–119.

3. Sanjay Subrahmanyam, *The Career and Legend of Vasco da Gama* (Cambridge: Cambridge University Press, 1998), 112. On pages 121–128, Subrahmanyam effectively demolishes the idea that the pilot who took da Gama to Calicut was the legendary Ibn Majid (also in Crosby, *Ecological Imperialism*, page 120); whoever the pilot may have been, he was clearly an Arab, an African, or an Indian.

4. K. N. Chaudhuri, *Trade and Civilisation in the Indian Ocean. An Economic History from the Rise of Islam to 1750* (Cambridge: Cambridge University Press, 1984), 20–21.

5. Janet Abu-Lughod, *Before European Hegemony. The World System* A.D. *1240– 1350* (New York: Oxford University Press, 1989), 263–67; and Shereen Ratnagar, *Encounters: The Westerly Trade of the Harappan Civilisation* (Delhi: Oxford University Press, 1981).

6. Abu-Lughod, *Before European Hegemony,* 199. Canton was closed to trade after the attack, but was shortly reopened in 792, not to be disturbed as such until the arrival of the gunboats much later.

7. Amitav Ghosh, *In an Antique Land* (New Delhi: Ravi Dayal, 1992), 286.

8. Ibid., Ghosh wonderfully captures the twelfth-century relationship of Abra-

ham Ben Yiju (based in Mangalore, on the southwestern coast of India) and Khalaf ibn Ishaq (based in Aden). This is but one example of the multifaceted relationships among merchants who came from discrete communities but who developed a sense of cosmopolitanism that we can glean in the documents they have left for us.

9. S. B. Kaufmann, "A Christian Caste in Hindu Society: Religious Leadership and Social Conflict Among the Paravas of Southern Tamil Nadu," *Modern Asian Studies* 15, no. 2 (1981): 203–34; C. R. DeSilva, "The Portuguese and Pearl Fishing off South India and Sri Lanka," *South Asia* 1, no. 1 (1978): 14–28; David Sopher, *The Sea Nomads: A Study of the Maritime Boat People of Southeast Asia* (Singapore: National Museum, 1977).

10. Sudipta Kaviraj, "The Imaginary Institution of India," in *Subaltern Studies,* Vol. 8, ed. Partha Chatterjee and Gyanendra Pandey (New Delhi: Oxford University Press, 1992), 20–33.

11. Anthony Pagden, *The Fall of Natural Man: The American Indian and the Origins of Comparative Ethnology* (Cambridge: Cambridge University Press, 1986), 129. For a full discussion, see Ivan Hannaford, *Race: The History of an Idea in the West* (Baltimore: Johns Hopkins University Press, 1996), 20–28 (on the Greeks), and 73–85 (on the Romans).

12. The idea of "Aryan" is deeply controversial, as I shall show later in the chapter. British scholars from the late eighteenth century assumed that the "Aryans" were a race of people, when the evidence suggests only that "Aryan" meant noble people and referred to an esteemed people who spoke a language in common. As we'll see below, the Aryans probably shared ancestry with those whom they called Dasas, although this too is hard to establish from the scant materials at our disposal. In Sanskrit the word *barbara* is used to describe stammering speech, while the Sumerians used the word *barbar* to speak of those foreign to them.

13. Romila Thapar, *Ancient Indian Social History: Some Interpretations* (New Delhi: Oxford University Press, 1978), 159–92; and Aloka Parasher, *Mlecchas in Early India* (Delhi: Munshiram Manoharlal, 1991).

14. Suvira Jaiswal, *Caste. Origin, Function and Dimensions of Change* (Delhi: Manohar, 1998), 144–45. The controversy over the entry of these people from central Asia is discussed at length in Romila Thapar [interviewed by Parita Mukta], "On Historical Scholarship and the Uses of the Past," *Ethnic and Racial Studies* 23, no. 3 (May 2000): 595–616. Compelling evidence for the migrations can be found in Asko Parpola, *Decipering the Indus Script* (Cambridge: Cambridge University Press, 1994); and Ram Sharan Sharma, *Advent of the Aryans in India* (Delhi: Manohar, 1999).

15. Michael Weiner, "The Invention of Identity. Race and Nation in Pre-War Japan," in *The Construction of Racial Identities in China and Japan,* ed. Frank Dikötter (Honolulu: University of Hawaii Press, 1997), 100.

16. Frank Dikötter, *The Discourse of Race in Modern China* (Stanford: Stanford University Press, 1992), 2.

17. Frank Snowden, *Before Color Prejudice. The Ancient View of Blacks* (Cambridge: Harvard University Press, 1983), 74 and 133.

18. Christine Obbo, "Village Strangers in Buganda Society," in *Strangers in African Societies,* ed. W. A. Shack and E. P. Skinner (Berkeley: University of California Press, 1979), 232–33.

19. Enid Schildkrout, "The Ideology of Regionalism in Ghana," in *Strangers in African Societies,* 185.

20. John Middleton, *The World of the Swahili. An African Mercantile Civilization* (New Haven: Yale University Press, 1992), 12. The Afro-Sharazi Party in Zanzibar, ally to Nyerere, draws its heritage from here.

21. Monica Wilson, "Strangers in Africa: Reflections on Nyakyusa, Nguni and Sotho Evidence," in *Strangers in African Societies,* 52–53.

22. Derek Nurse and Thomas Spear, *The Swahili: Reconstructing the History and Language of an African Society, 800–1500* (Philadelphia: University of Pennsylvania Press, 1985), 25.

23. Louise Levathes, *When China Ruled the Seas: The Treasure Fleet of the Dragon Throne, 1405–1433* (New York: Oxford University Press, 1995); and J. J. L. Duyvendak, *China's Discovery of Africa* (London: Arthur Probsthain, 1949).

24. Crosby, *Ecological Imperialism,* is right that it is Zheng He who should be seen as "the first great figure of the age of exploration," for his fleet was bolder than that of Bartholomew Diaz, conventionally thought to be the pioneer (106).

25. Levathes, *When China Ruled the Seas,* 37–38; Duyvendak, *China's Discovery,* 13–14; G. S. P. Freeman-Grenville, *The East African Coast: Select Documents from the First to the Earlier Nineteenth Century* (Oxford: Clarendon Press, 1962), 8.

26. Al-Mas'udi's text is in Freeman-Grenville, *The East African Coast,* 14–16; and Duyvendak, *China's Discovery,* 16–17.

27. In Japanese the word is *kirin,* and beer drinkers will recognize this as the name of one of the premier lagers of Japan (whose label bears an image of the giraffe-unicorn).

28. Duyvendak, *China's Discovery,* 32–34; and Levathes, *When China Ruled the Seas,* 140–43 and 172–73.

29. Chaudhuri, *Asia Before Europe,* 126.

30. Levathes, *When China Ruled the Seas,* 195–203. For references to the Bajuni, without any mention of their possible heritage, see Middleton, *The World of the Swahili.*

31. Christopher Ehret, *An African Classical Age: Eastern and Southern Africa in World History, 1000 B.C. to A.D. 400* (Charlottesville: University Press of Virginia, 1998), 277–81.

32. Michael N. Pearson, *Port Cities and Intruders: The Swahili Coast, India, and Portugal in the Early Modern Era* (Baltimore: Johns Hopkins University Press, 1998), 21–22.

33. Asiff Hussein, "From Where Did the Moors Come," *Sunday Observer* (Colombo, Sri Lanka) 25 June 2000.

34. Shanti Sadiq Ali, *The African Dispersal in the Deccan: from Medieval to Modern Times* (New Delhi: Orient Longman, 1996); R. R. S. Chauhan, *Africans in India: From Slavery to Royalty* (New Delhi: Aryan, 1994); Omar Khalidi, "African Diaspora in India: The Case of the Habashis of the Dakan," *Hamdard Islamicus* 4 (Winter 1988): 3–22; Vasant D. Rao, "The Habshis: India's Unknown Africans," *Africa Report* 18, no. 5 (September–October 1973): 35–38; D. K. Bhattacharya, "Indians of African Origin," *Cahiers D'Études Africaines* 40 (1970): 579–82. For a contemporary look, see Kenneth J. Cooper, "Within South Asia, A Touch of Africa," *Washington Post,* 12 April 1999, A16. Two ongoing research projects on this interchange will help us a great deal, one by Araafat Valiani at Columbia University on the Siddis and the other by Nolen Carter on the Habshi Sultans.

35. Joseph E. Harris, *The African Presence in Asia: Consequences of the East-African Slave Trade* (Evanston, Ill.: Northwestern University Press, 1971); and Graham W. Irwin, *Africans Abroad* (New York: Columbia University Press, 1977).

36. Vijay Prashad, *Karma of Brown Folk* (Minneapolis: University of Minnesota Press, 2000), 158–62.

37. Huan Ma, *Ying-Yai Sheng-lan* [The Overall Survey of the Ocean's Shores, 1433], ed. and trans. Feng Ch'eng Chun (Cambridge: Hakluyt Society at the University Press, 1970), 160 (Bengal), 174 (Mecca), and 124–25 (Ceylon).

38. Frank Dikötter, *The Discourse of Race,* 13, mistakes the evidence in my opinion in what is otherwise a very fine book (after the first few chapters).

39. Beth Notar, "Wild Histories: Popular Culture, Place and the Past in Southwest China" (Ph.D. diss., University of Michigan, 1999), 53–55; and Christian Pelras, *The Bugis* (Oxford: Blackwell, 1996), 75.

40. Ghosh, *In an Antique Land,* 260. But see evidence of prejudice among the Swahili regarding enslaved peoples, Middleton, *The World of the Swahili,* 116–18.

41. Bernard Lewis, *Race and Slavery in the Middle East: An Historical Enquiry* (New York: Oxford University Press, 1990), 62–71. For an incisive critique of Lewis, see C. M. Naim, "The Outrage of Bernard Lewis," *Ambiguities of Heritage. Fictions and Polemics* (Karachi: City Press, 1999), 195–204.

42. Duyvendak, *China's Discovery,* 23–24.

43. Lewis, *Race and Slavery,* 12.

44. Ibid., 86.

45. Ibid., 31. Lewis's depiction of this section as a satire cuts both ways. The piece he cites from Jahiz on page 32 might equally be the satire, and the one I quote from above might be the one that gives us a clue to this intention.

46. Irwin, *Africans Abroad,* 151.

47. Snowden, *Before Color Prejudice,* 70. To reduce all forms of slavery to the bondage of one person by another is to reduce the effects of Atlantic slavery in which a dominant power rendered a people into slaves and built an economic system on the backs of the enslaved workforce. The edifice of modern capital-

ism was built upon slavery and on the serfdom of the plantation worker in the colonies of Europe (such as India, Indonesia, and much of Africa as well as of Europe's semi-colonies, like China). In 1847, Marx was on point with his observation that "direct slavery is just as much the pivot of bourgeois industry as machinery, credits, etc. Without slavery you have no cotton; without cotton you have no modern industry. It is slavery that gave the colonies their value; it is the colonies that created world trade, and it is world trade that is the precondition of large-scale industry. Thus slavery is an economic category of the greatest importance." Karl Marx, *The Poverty of Philosophy* (Moscow: Progress Publishers, 1955), 97.

48. Joseph P. Harris, *Africans and Their History* (New York: New American Library, 1972), 55.

49. Abdul Sheriff, *Slaves, Spices and Ivory in Zanzibar* (Dar es Salaam: Tanzania Publishing House, 1987), 33–73.

50. Jaiswal, *Caste*, 61.

51. Ronald Inden, *Imagining India* (Oxford: Blackwell, 1990), 56–66.

52. Prashad, *Karma of Brown Folk,* 97; and B. R. Ambedkar, *Who Were the Shudras? How They Came to Be the Fourth Varna in the Indo-Aryan Society* (Bombay: Thacker and Co., 1946), 75–79.

53. Dikötter, *The Discourse of Race,* 5.

54. Snowden, *Before Color Prejudice,* 63.

55. Ibid., 83.

56. Ibid., 63 and 77.

57. Dikötter, *The Discourse of Race,* 10–11.

58. Prashad, *Karma of Brown Folk,* 98.

59. Details of these wars and of their impact upon Europe can be found in Richard Bonney's encyclopedic *The European Dynastic States, 1494–1660* (Oxford: Oxford University Press, 1991). On the Ottoman campaign in the waters, see Bonney, *The European Dynastic States,* 292 and André Clot, *Suleiman the Magnificent* (New York: New Amsterdam Books, 1992), 194–96. Hannaford's vast survey of the idea of race follows my general argument: "In the sixteenth century dynastic ambitions and religious issues were of such great consequence that there was little room for the growth of a conscious idea of race as we understand it today." (*Race,* 182).

60. Chaudhuri, *Trade and Civilization,* 65.

61. Middleton, *The World of the Swahili,* 46–47.

62. R. W. Southern, *Western Views of Islam in the Middle Ages* (Cambridge: Harvard University Press, 1980), 37. A parenthetical example of cultural interchange: Before the thirteenth century, it was commonly believed in Christian theology that in paradise the blessed souls would see God. Avicenna (Ibn Sina, 980–1037) had argued that this was not possible, and God and the created are conceptually separate. In reply to Ibn Sina, Thomas Aquinas, in 1250, took his arguments from Averroes (Ibn Rush, 1128–98), and so R. W. South-

ern notes, "on a central theological issue Western theologians of all shades of opinion in the mid-thirteenth century did not scruple to re-examine traditional views in the light of Islamic philosophy, or at least to restate traditional views in the language of these philosophers" (55). Dante's *Divine Comedy*, it is also suggested, drew some of its principle themes from an Arabic text.

63. Eliyahu Ashtor, *Levant Trade in the Later Middle Ages* (Princeton: Princeton University Press, 1983).

64. On the 1490s tussle, see Subrahmanyam, *The Career and Legend*, 110–11; for the cannon, see J. J. L. Duyvendak, "Desultory Notes on the Hsi-Yang Chi," in *T'oung Pao Archives*, vol. 42 (Leiden: E. J. Brill, 1954), 18–20.

65. Subrahmanyam, *The Career and Legend*, 112.

66. Audrey Smedley, *Race in North America: Origin and Evolution of a Worldview* (Boulder: Westview, 1993), 68. For details of the Inquisition and for a reevaluation of the place of Jews in the early 1600s (which proves Smedley's point), see Bonney, *The European Dynastic States*, 131–33 and 458–63.

67. Noel Ignatiev, *How the Irish Became White* (New York: Routledge, 1995).

68. Smedley, *Race in North America*, 103 and 60–61.

69. In the early 1500s, the armies of Cortés, Pizarro, and Almagro held enslaved people, but only "after the development of Portuguese Luanda in the 1570s important contingents of slaves from the Congo and Angola began arriving" in the Americas. Herbert S. Klein, *The Atlantic Slave Trade* (Cambridge: Cambridge University Press, 1999), 22.

70. Theodore W. Allen, *The Origin of Racial Oppression in Anglo-America*, vol. 2 of *The Invention of the White Race* (New York: Verso, 1997), 122; and Jacqueline Jones, *American Work: Four Centuries of Black and White Labor* (New York: Norton, 1998), 23–54.

71. Michael Goldfield, *The Color of Politics: Race and the Mainsprings of American Politics* (New York: The New Press, 1997), 42–43.

72. Winthrop Jordan, *White Over Black* (Chapel Hill: University of North Carolina Press, 1968), 100.

73. Ibid., 96.

74. Panikkar, *Asia and Western Dominance*, 111.

75. Snowden, *Before Color Prejudice*, 84.

76. Hannaford, *The Idea of Race*, 203.

77. Bonney, *The European Dynastic States*, 360.

78. Hannaford, *The Idea of Race*, 203–4; Jordon, *White Over Black*, 217–18; Smedley, *Race in North America*, 163–64.

79. Thomas Trautmann, *Aryans and British India* (Berkeley: University of California Press, 1992), 52.

80. "I have declared again and again and again that if I say Aryas, I mean neither blood nor bones, nor hair nor skull; I mean simply those who speak an Aryan

language. I assert nothing beyond their language when I call Hindus, Greeks, Romans, Germans, Celts and Slaves; and in that sense, and in that sense only, do I say that even the blackest Hindus represent an earlier stage of Aryan speech and thought than the fairest Scandinavians . . . To me an ethnologist who speaks of Aryan race, Aryan blood, Aryan eyes and hair, is as great a sinner as a linguist who speaks of doliochephalic dictionary or brachyce-phalic grammer." F. Max Müller, *Biographies of Words and the Home of the Aryas* (Oxford: Clarendon, 1888), 120.

81. Raymond Schwab, *The Oriental Renaissance: Europe's Rediscovery of India and the East, 1680–1880* (New York: Columbia University Press, 1984), 59 (Goethe), 71 (von Schlegel).

82. Leon Poliakov, *The Aryan Myth* (London: Sussex University Press, 1974), 194.

83. Blumenbach, years before, felt that the women of the Caucasus were the most attractive in the world, so he was eager to select this region as the cradle of civilization!

84. Albert Étienne Jean-Baptiste Terrien de Lacouperie, *Western Origins of the Early Chinese Civilisations from 2300 BC to 200 AD* (London: Asher, 1884), translated by Jiang Zhiyou in *New People's Journal*, October 1903–January 1905. Dikötter, *The Discourse of Race*, 119. In 1933, Wei Juxian argued that the Xia ("similar to those of the Aryan race") mixed with the Yin ("red barbari-ans" from Sichuan) to produce the "Yellow Han" (Dikötter, *The Discourse of Race*, 132). In the late nineteenth century, Tang Caichang advocated the amalgamation of the White and the Yellow races through "racial communi-cation" to create a better, healthier people: a form of eugenics with a nod to these origin myths, perhaps? (Dikötter, *The Discourse of Race*, 87.)

85. Anything good in the world came either from the diffusion of Greek culture or through a common European ancestor. This point bespeaks the conde-scension of Euro-American scholars and the insecurity of non-Europeans who continue to tussle over whom to accord priority for scientific and philo-sophical developments. Did Greece come before India, or Africa, and vice versa? Such questions obscure the cultural and epistemic differences between zones of the world, and it undermines the disparate and dialectical structures that give rise to genuine innovations in science or mathematics or mythologi-cal thought itself.

86. Romila Thapar, *Interpreting Early India* (New Delhi: Oxford University Press, 1992), 8. In the early 1900s, D. L. Roy wrote a wonderful little verse: "*Moksha-muller bolechhe arya, tai shune mora cherechi karya*" ("Max Müller called us Arya, so we have given up work"). Thanks to Srilata Gangulee, dean at Uni-versity of Pennslyvania, for this nugget.

87. Kanzuki Sato, "'Same Language, Same Race': The Dilemma of *Kanbun* in Modern Japan," in Weiner, *Construction of Racial Identities*, 125. My colleague Duncan Williams tells me that there was also a long-standing notion among some Europeans that the Japanese were "the lost tribe" of the Jews, a view that emerges occasionally to explain why the Japanese are seen as superior to other Asians.

88. Bipinchandra Pal, *The New Spirit* (Calcutta: Sinha Sarvadhkari & Co., 1907), 112–16.

89. B. G. Tilak, *The Arctic Home of the Vedas* (Poona: Kesari, 1903), 464. The idea of an Arctic *Urheimat* was from Baillay, against whom Kant posited a Tibetan *Urheimat*. Chetan Bhatt, "Primordial Being: Enlightenment, Schopenhauer, and the Indian Subject of Postcolonial Theory," *Radical Philosophy* 100 (March–April 2000): 31.

90. Ambedkar, *Who Were the Shudras?*, 76.

91. On Diop, see Stephen Howe, *Afrocentricism. Mythical Pasts and Imagined Homes* (London: Verso, 1998), 163–92.

92. The stage for much of this was set by the planetary attack on the commons by an energetic capitalism during the eighteenth century, as documented by E. P. Thompson, "Custom, Law and Common Right," in his *Customs in Common. Studies in Traditional Popular Culture* (New York: The New Press, 1991).

93. Paul Gilroy, *Against Race. Imagining Political Culture Beyond the Color Line* (Cambridge: Harvard University Press, 2000), 208–37; Chetan Bhatt, *Liberation and Purity: Race, New Religious Movements and the Ethics of Postmodernity* (London: UCL Press, 1997) and his "Ethnic Absolutism and the Authoritarian Spirit," *Theory, Culture, & Society* 16, no. 2 (April 1999): 65–85.

94. Gilroy, *Against Race*, 62–63.

95. Edward Said, *The Question of Palestine* (New York: Vintage, 1979), 138; Mahmood Mamdani, *Politics and Class Formation in Uganda* (New York: Monthly Review Press, 1976), 305. From Golwalkar, we hear that "there are only two courses open to the foreign elements, either to merge themselves in the national race and adopt its culture [assimilation] or to live at the sweet will of the national race." M. S. Golwalkar, *We, Or Our Nationhood Defined*, 3^d ed. (Nagpur: Kale, 1945), 52.

96. The notion of "authoritarianism" is rather a waste here, since it ideologically links fascism with communism without any sense of the gap that separates the two political systems. Bobbio is correct to show us how the Left and the Right are divided along the axes of liberty and equality. There is a Right and a Left that takes a hard position on liberty ("liberty above all else"), but it is only the Left that is able to take a strong position on equality. Given the Left's determination to make an equal world, there is a section of the Left that would be willing to constrain liberty for equality, but this is hardly the same as fascism (with its attendant racist, militaristic and hierarchical core). Norberto Bobbio, *Left & Right. The Significance of a Political Distinction* (Cambridge: Polity Press, 1996).

97. Miles Fletcher, "Intellectuals and Fascism in Early Showa Japan," *Journal of Asian Studies* 39, no. 1 (November 1979): 39–63. I tend to accept the view that what we have in Japan is something in between a "military fascism," an "Emperor-System fascism," and, in sum, a "fascism from above." The Japanese leadership set in motion the revolutionary reconstruction of society in a manner similar to its German and Italian allies, but it was not identical to that which swept through central Europe. Stanley G. Payne, *A History of Fascism, 1914–1945* (Madison: University of Wisconsin Press, 1995), 328–37.

98. Christophe Jaffrelot, *The Hindu Nationalist Movement in India* (New York: Columbia University Press, 1996), 11–79; and Marzia Casolari, "Hindutva's

Foreign Tie-Up in the 1930s: Archival Evidence," *Economic & Political Weekly* 35, no. 4 (22 January 2000): 218–28. Savarkar approved the German occupation of the Sudentenland, a position that earned him a feature in the Nazi Party's *Völkischer Beobachter*, Nicholas Goodrick-Clarke, *Hitler's Priestess: Savitri Devi, the Hindu-Aryan Myth, and Neo-Nazism* (New York: New York University Press, 1998), 59.

99. O. Tanin and E. Yohan, *Militarism and Fascism in Japan* (New York: International Publishers, 1934); Sandra McGhee Deutsch, *Las Derechas: The Extreme Right in Argentina, Brazil and Chile, 1890–1939* (Stanford: Stanford University Press, 1999), 141–42 and 244–47; and Patrick J. Furlong, *Between Crown and Swastika: The Impact of the Radical Right on the Afrikaner Nationalist Movement in the Fascist Era* (Hanover: Wesleyan University Press, 1991), 87–96.

100. A. James Gregor and Maria Hsia Chang, "*Nazionalfascismo* and the Revolutionary Nationalism of Sun Yat-sen," *Journal of Asian Studies* 39, no. 1 (November 1979): 21–37. Maria Chang denies that Chang Kai-shek's Blue Shirts Society was fascistic, since it was principally concerned with the renaissance of China. Her material, however, suggests that the Blue Shirts are not far from other mono-colored sartorial military formations, such as the Black and Brown Shirts. Maria Hsia Chang, "The Blue Shirts Society: Fascism and Development Nationalism" (Ph.D. diss., University of California, Berkeley, 1983).

101. A very competent synthesis on fascism can be found in Payne, *A History of Fascism*, 487–95, but he does neglect the economic causes of 1930s fascism.

102. Dikötter, *The Discourse of Race*, 67–71.

103. Richard Siddle, *Race, Resistance and the Ainu of Japan* (London: Routledge, 1996), 11–13; H. H. Smythe, "Note on Racial Ideas of the Japanese," *Social Forces* 31, no. 3 (March 1953).

104. V. D. Savarkar, *Samagra Savarkar Wangmaya*, vol. 4, ed. Hindu Rashtra Darshan (Pune: Maharashtra Prantik Hindusabha, 1964), 320.

105. Ibid., 284.

106. Weiner, "The Invention of Identity," 102–3; Ian J. Neary, *Political Protest and Social Control in Pre-war Japan: The Origins of Buraku Liberation* (Manchester: Manchester University Press, 1989); and Siddle, *Race, Resistance and the Ainu.*

107. Zionism's reduction to the flagship of U.S. imperialism is another example, as is Idi Amin's ire at the Asians while he allowed the real owners of capital, British firms, to remain intact in Uganda (for which, see Mahmood Mamdani, *Politics and Class Formation in Uganda*, 307–8).

108. On Jews and Japanese thought, see David Goodman with Masanori Miyazawa, *Jews in the Japanese Mind: The History and Uses of a Cultural Stereotype* (New York: The New Press, 1995); and Isaiah Ben-Dasan, *The Japanese and the Jews* (Tokyo: Kenkyusha, 1972).

109. Anna Davin, "Imperialism and Motherhood," *History Workshop Journal* 5 (1978): 9–65; and Stefan Kühl, *Nazi Connection: Eugenics, American Racism*

and German National Socialism (New York: Oxford University Press, 1994). One should not, I suspect, forget the miscegenation worries in the British Empire (as catalogued in Kenneth Ballhatchet, *Race, Sex and Class Under the Raj: Imperial Attitudes and Policies and Their Critics, 1793–1905* [New York: St. Martin's Press, 1980]) and in Italy's Ethiopian Empire (as described in Alberto Sbacchi's "Racism Italian Style," in *Ethiopia Under Mussolini. Fascism and the Colonial Experience* [London: Zed, 1985]).

110. Dikötter, *The Discourse of Race,* 174–90.

111. Golwalkar, *We, Or Our Nationhood Defined,* 40–41 and 54. "We are an old nation," Golwalkar writes ominously, "and let us deal, as old nations ought to and do deal, with the foreign races, who have chosen to live in our country" (53).

112. Zenji Suzuki, "Geneticists and Eugenics Movement in Japan and America: A Comparative Study," *XIVth International Congress of the History of Science, Proceedings no. 3* (Tokyo and Kyoto: Sciences Council of Japan, 1975), 68–70.

113. Elise K. Tipton, "Ishimoto Shizue: The Margaret Sanger of Japan," *Women's History Review* 6, no. 3 (1997): 337–55.

114. Barbara Ramushuck, "Embattled Advocates: The Debate over Birth Control in India, 1920–40," *Journal of Women's History* 1, no. 2 (1989): 34–64.

115. W. G. Beasley, *Japan Encounters the Barbarian: Japanese Travelers in America and Europe* (New Haven: Yale University Press, 1995), 66.

116. Marius B. Jansen, *Japan and Its World: Two Centuries of Change* (Princeton: Princeton University Press, 1980), 47.

117. Siddle, *Race, Resistance and the Ainu,* 94–96.

118. Ibid.

119. Jawaharlal Nehru, *The Discovery of India* (New Delhi: Oxford University Press, 1981), 85 and 152. The failure of unanimism in southern Asia, to some extent, should be put to the sheer density of difference in the region, where, in the 1990s, the Anthropological Survey of India counted at least 4,635 discrete endogamous groups (while scholars at the Centre for Ecological Science found the number to be about 50,000 to 60,000). M. Gadgil et al., "Peopling of India" in *The Indian Human Heritage,* ed. D. Balasubramaniam and N. Appaji Rao (Hyderabad: Universities Press, 1997), 100–129.

120. Dikötter, *The Discource of Race,* 136.

121. Colin Mackerras, *China's Minorities* (Hong Kong: Oxford University Press, 1994), 59–60.

122. John Talbot Gracey, *India: Country, People, Missions* (Rochester: J. T. Gracey, 1884), 11; and William Butler, *The Land of the Veda* (New York: Eaton and Mains, 1906), 19.

123. Thomas Dyer, *Theodore Roosevelt and the Idea of Race* (Baton Rouge: Louisiana State University Press, 1980), 27, 48, 67.

124. Adolf Hitler, *Mein Kampf* (Boston: Houghton Mifflin, 1943), 158 and 639–40.

125. Ibid., 290–91. David H. Pierce very insightfully noted, "In Germany the Negro is presented as an inferior breed of humankind. The Japanese, on the contrary, are lauded because the Germany and Japan have designs on the Soviet Union. Otherwise Japan would be relegated by Hitler's pseudo–scientists to the inferior breeds." "Fascism and the Negro," *The Crisis* (April 1935): 107.

126. Hitler, *Mein Kampf*, 656–58.

127. Ibid., 388–89.

128. Gerald Horne led me to Dennis whose papers are ensconced in the Hoover Institution. A useful oral history with Dennis ("The Reminiscences of Lawrence Dennis") done in 1967 is housed in the Oral History Research Library, Columbia University.

129. Lawrence Dennis, *Is Capitalism Doomed?* (New York: Harper Bros., 1932) and *The Coming American Fascism* (New York: Harper Bros., 1936). For an analysis of Dennis's place in U.S. fascism, see Ronald Radosh, *Prophets of the Right: Profiles of Conservative Critics of American Globalism* (New York: Simon & Schuster, 1975), 275–322.

130. Dennis, *Is Capitalism Doomed?*, 85–86.

131. Lawrence Dennis, *The Dynamics of War and Revolution* (New York: The Weekly Foreign Letter, 1940), 120.

132. Ibid., 130.

133. Ibid., 213 and Dennis, "Propaganda for War: Model 1938," *American Mercury* 44, no. 173 (May 1938): 7, quoted in Radosh, *Prophets*, 280.

134. Dennis, *The Dynamics*, 17 and 204.

135. Lothrop Stoddard, *The Rising Tide of Color Against White World Supremacy* (New York: Scribner, 1920); *The Revolt Against Civilization: The Menace of the Underman* (New York: Scribner, 1922); finally, the famous debate between Du Bois and Stoddard on the question "Shall the Negro Be Encouraged to Seek Cultural Equality?" held on March 17, 1929, and published by the Chicago Forum Council in 1929 (available at the Schomburg Center for Research in Black Culture in the Schomburg Negro Collection in Series 1, no. 7205).

136. Robert Hess, *Italian Colonialism in Somalia* (Chicago: University of Chicago Press, 1966), 25; and Saadia Touval, *Somali Nationalism* (Cambridge: Harvard University Press, 1963), 42–43.

137. Dikötter, *The Discourse of Race*, 159; and S. K. B. Asante, *Pan-African Protest: West Africa and the Italo-Ethiopian Crisis, 1934–1941* (London: Longman, 1977), 11. In 1904 a Chinese intellectual wrote that the "Chinese are less than black slaves," for at least the Africans fought for their freedom. Dikötter, *The Discourse of Race*, 156.

138. Zhangshan is quoted in I. Spector, *The First Russian Revolution* (Englewood Cliffs, N. J.: Prentice Hall, 1962), 8; Jawaharlal Nehru, *Towards Freedom* (New York: John Day, 1941), 29. News of Japan's role reached as far off as the villages of Bihar and eastern U. P., as reported by G. Pandey, "The Revolt of August 1942 in Eastern UP and Bihar," in *The Indian Nation in 1942,* ed. G. Pandey (Calcutta: K. P. Bagchi, 1988), 154–55. The year 1904 truly changed the tenor

of Japan, since in 1884, one leading Indian intellectual called the Japanese *tattoos,* or ponies, and joked about how even the "midget Japanese" have tried to become modern, while the Indians remain prone before the British. Of course the writer insulted the Japanese to salt the comparison with the defeated Indians. Bhartendu Harischandra quoted by Gyanendra Pandey, *The Construction of Communalism in Colonial North India* (Delhi: Oxford University Press, 1990), 273.

139. George Padmore, "Ethiopia and World Politics," *The Crisis* (May 1935), 157. A young Indonesian man told Richard Wright that "the biggest event of the twentieth century was the defeat of Russia by Japan in 1905. It was the beginning of the liberation of the Asian mind." Richard Wright, *The Color Curtain. A Report on the Bandung Conference* (Cleveland: The World Publishing Company, 1956), 60. What is extraordinary about this statement is that it comes not a decade after Japan's ruthlessness in the islands was put to a stop. The memory of 1905 outlived the atrocities of the Japanese imperial forces.

140. Anthony Mockler, *Haile Selassie's War: The Italian-Ethiopian Campaign, 1935–1941* (New York: Random House, 1984), 16.

141. Reuben S. Young, "Ethiopia Awakens," *The Crisis* (September 1935): 262.

142. Padmore, "Ethiopia and World Politics," 157.

143. J. A. Rogers, "Italy Over Abyssinia," *The Crisis* (February 1935): 50.

144. Winston James, *Holding Aloft the Banner of Ethiopia* (London: Verso, 1998).

145. A number of new studies cover this ground in greater detail than I do. Marc Gallicchio, *The African American Encounter with Japan and China: Black Internationalism in Asia, 1895–1945* (Chapel Hill: University of North Carolina Press, 2000); and Gerald Horne, "Tokyo Bound: Japan and African Americans Confront White Supremacy" (talk at the Blacks and Asians: Revisiting Racial Formations conference at Columbia University, New York, November 10, 2000).

146. William H. Ferris, "Gandhi, Garvey and De Valera: Martyrs in Jail for Justice," *Negro World,* 25 August 1923, 10.

147. W. E. B. Du Bois to Harry F. Ward, October 7, 1937, *The Correspondence of W. E. B. Du Bois,* Vol. 2, ed. Herbert Aptheker (Amherst: University of Massachusetts Press, 1976), 147. *The Crisis* carried a number of notices on events from China and India on anti-imperialist resistance from as early as 1913.

148. Marcus Garvey, "Race Discrimination Must Go," *Negro World,* 30 November 1918; *Marcus Garvey and the Universal Negro Improvement Association Papers,* Vol. 1, ed. Robert A. Hill (Berkeley: University of California Press, 1983), 304–5.

149. Roy Ottley, *"New World A-Coming." Inside Black America* (Cleveland: The World Publishing Company, 1945), 334–35. Much of my discussion relies upon the following two articles by Ernest Allen Jr., "When Japan Was 'Champion of the Darker Races': Satokata Takahashi and the Flowering of Black Messianic Nationalism," *Black Scholar* 24, no. 1 (winter 1994): 23–46; "Waiting for Tojo: The Pro-Japan Vigil of Black Missourians, 1932–1943," *Gateway Heritage* 16, no. 2 (fall 1995): 38–55; George Lipsitz, *The Possessive Investment*

in Whiteness (Philadelphia: Temple University Press, 1998), ch. 9; and Gallicchio, *The African American Encounter with Japan and China.*

150. Ottley, *"New World A-Coming,"* 335.

151. Cheryl Greenberg, "Black and Jewish Responses to Japanese Internment," *Journal of American Ethnic History* 14, no. 2 (winter 1985), 19.

152. Robin D. G. Kelley, "'This Ain't Ethiopia, But It'll Do': African Americans and the Spanish Civil War," in his *Race Rebels* (New York: Free Press, 1994).

153. Mike Masaoka with Bill Hosokawa, *They Call Me Moses Masaoka: An American Saga* (New York: William Morrow, 1987), 143–44.

154. Harry Haywood, *Black Bolshevik. Autobiography of an Afro-American Communist* (Chicago: Liberator, 1978), 459.

155. Karl Evanzz, *The Messenger. The Rise and Fall of Elijah Muhammad* (New York: Pantheon, 1999), 105–12. Evanzz's account is largely based on FBI files. Gallicchio notes that Takahashi was a Canadian national whose name was Nakane Naka. Gallicchio, *The African American Encounter with Japan and China,* 95–96.

156. Evanzz, *The Messenger,* 106.

157. Allen, "When Japan Was," 32.

158. Hyman Kublin, *Asian Revolutionary. The Life of Sen Katayama* (Princeton: Princeton University Press, 1964); and Karl G. Yoneda, "The Heritage of Sen Katayama," *Political Affairs* 14, no. 3 (March 1975): 38–57.

159. "Report by Special Agent P-138," in *Marcus Garvey and the Universal Negro Improvement Association Papers,* Vol. 2, ed. Robert A. Hill (Berkeley: University of California Press, 1983), 546.

160. Mark Solomon, *The Cry Was Unity. Communists and African-Americans, 1917–1936* (Jackson: University of Mississippi, 1998), 41.

161. Harry Haywood, *Black Bolshevik. Autobiography of an Afro-American Communist* (Chicago: Liberator, 1978), 656. Claude McKay was no less effusive:

> Sen Katayama was the Japanese revolutionist . . . He was a small, dark-brown, with intensely purposeful features which were nevertheless kindly. I met him when I was working on *The Liberator.* He dropped in one day and introduced himself. He took me to lunch at a Japanese restaurant, and at another time to a Chinese, and introduced me to the Indian rendezvous restaurant in the theatre district [of New York]. His personality was friendly but abounding in curiosity—a sort of minute methodical curiosity . . . And like a permanent surprise he invaded my rooms at all hours and talked in his squeaky grandmotherly voice about Negro problems. He demonstrated a vast interest and sympathy for the Negro racialists and their organizations. I liked Sen Katayama immensely. I was fascinated by his friendly ferreting curiosity . . . He had more real inside and sympathetic knowledge and understanding of American Negroes than many of the white American Communists who were camping in Moscow [for the Comintern meetings].

A Long Way from Home (New York: Harcourt Brace, 1970), 164–65. McKay corroborates Haywood on Katayama's role in Moscow on the Black Belt question (*A Long Way,* 180).

162. Evanzz, *The Messenger,* 108.

163. "The Mikado's administrators govern with iron hands, the brown-skinned subjects of the Pacific mandates," so, Harold Preece noted, one should be wary of Japan's role as "friend of the colored races." Harold Preece, "War and the Negro," *The Crisis* (November 1935): 338.

164. W. E. B. Du Bois, "Inter-racial Implications: A Negro View," *Foreign Affairs* 14, nos. 1–4 (October 1935–July 1936): 88–89.

165. Ibid.

166. William R. Scott, *The Sons of Sheba's Race. African Americans and the Italo-Ethiopian War, 1935–1941* (Bloomington: Indiana University Press, 1993); and Joseph E. Harris, *African American Reactions to War in Ethiopia, 1936–1941* (Baton Rouge: Louisiana State University Press, 1994).

167. "Is Japan Friendly Toward Colored Peoples of World?" *The Daily Gleaner,* 16 May 1934.

168. "Not Like Negroes," *The Afro-American* (4 November 1933) and "Japan Protests Against Nazi Race Discrimination," *The Daily Gleaner,* 31 October 1933.

169. In 1934 a Japanese training ship, *Iwate,* docked in Baltimore harbor. Commander Althiro Sito told his mainly African American guests that Japan was against racism, that three hundred blacks lived happily in Japan, and that he was pleased with the agility of Jesse Owens. "Japanese Commander Opens Ships to Colored Visitors," *The Afro-American* (29 August 1936).

170. "The Rediff Interview with Professor Sanjay Subrahmanyam," available at the rediff.com Website at www.rediff.com/news/jun/09gama2.html.

171. Rushdie set the final scene in *al-Andalus,* the world of Moorish Spain, to indicate the confluence of forces that ended the cosmos of the Indian Ocean (the Inquisition, the expulsion of the Moors, the entry of Vasco into the ocean). *Al-Andalus* left us such complex social documents as Ghalib ibn Ribah al-Hajjam of Toledo's eleventh-century offering entitled "The Stork": "She is an immigrant from other lands/When she stretches out her ebony wings/shows her ivory body/opens her sandlewood beak/and laughs with great guffaws/it's a sign of good weather." *Poems of Arab Andalusia,* trans. Cola Franzen (San Francisco: City Lights Books, 1989), 20.

172. Salman Rushdie, *The Moor's Last Sigh* (London: Vintage, 1996), 414.

Chapter 2: The American Ideology

1. W. E. B. Du Bois, *The Souls of Black Folk* (New York: Random House, 1996), xxiii.

2. David Levering Lewis, *W. E. B. Du Bois: Biography of a Race, 1868–1919* (New York: Henry Holt, 1993), 248.

3. Kwame Nkrumah, *Neo-Colonialism: The Last Stage of Imperialism* (New York: International Publishers, 1965), xi.

4. In the mountains of southeastern Mexico, Subcomandante Insurgente Marcos offered the final address for the First Intercontinental Encounter for Humanity and Against Neoliberalism, during which he said: "Millions of

women, millions of youths, millions of indigenous, millions of homosexuals, millions of human beings of all races and colors only participate in the financial markets as a devalued currency worth always less and less, the currency of their blood making profits. The globalization of markets is erasing borders for speculation and crime and multiplying them for human beings. Countries are obligated to erase their national borders when it comes to the circulation of money but to multiply their internal borders. Neoliberalism doesn't turn countries into one country, it turns each one of them into many countries" (August 3, 1996).

5. Neil Gotanda, "A Critique of 'Our Constitution Is Color-Blind,'" *Stanford Law Review* 44, no. 1 (November 1991): 37–52; Kimberlé Williams Crenshaw, "Color Blindness, History and the Law," in *The House That Race Built,* ed. Wahneema Lubiano (New York: Vintage, 1998), 280–88.

6. Michael Eric Dyson, *I May Not Get There with You: The True Martin Luther King, Jr.* (New York: Free Press, 2000), 35.

7. The standard text is Masatoshi Nei and Arun Roychoudhury, "Genetic Relationship and Evolution of Human Races," *Evolutionary Biology* 14, no. 1 (1982): 1–59; and L. Luca Cavalli-Sforza, Paolo Menozzi, and Alberto Piazza, *The History and Geography of Human Genes* (Princeton: Princeton University Press, 1994), 16–20 and 266–67.

8. On white supremacy, among others, see Jessie Daniels, *White Lies: Race. Class, Gender and Sexuality in White Supremacist Discourse* (New York: Routledge, 1997). On neo-conservative, gloves-off racism, see Jean Hardistry, *Mobilizing Resentment: Conservative Resurgence from the John Birch Society to the Promise Keepers* (Boston: Beacon Press, 1999), 126–61.

9. Stanley Fish, "Boutique Multiculturalism," in *Multiculturalism and American Democracy,* ed. Arthur Melzer, Jerry Weinberger, and M. Richard Zinman (Lawrence: University of Kansas, 1998), 69–88.

10. Fish, "Boutique Multiculturalism," 76.

11. Gary Peller, "Race Consciousness," *Duke Law Journal* 4 (September 1990): 758–847; Stephen Steinberg, "The Liberal Retreat from Race During the Post-Civil Rights Era," in Lubiano, *The House That Race Built,* 13–47.

12. H. B. Schonberger, *Aftermath of War, 1945–1952* (Kent: Ohio State Press, 1989); T. Cohen, *Remaking Japan: The American Occupation as New Deal* (Berkeley: University of California Press, 1987); and John W. Dower, *Embracing Defeat: Japan in the Wake of World War II* (New York: The New Press, 1999), 525–46.

13. Ann Seidman, "Post World War II Imperialism in Africa," *Journal of Southern African Affairs* 2 (October 1977): 409. South Africa was the most profitable country for U.S. investment, as shown by Ann Seidman and Neva Seidman, *South Africa and US Multinational Corporations* (Dar es Salaam: Tanzania Publishing House, 1977), 96.

14. Nathan Glazer and Daniel P. Moynihan, "Why Ethnicity?" Commentary 58, no. 4 (October 1974): 34.

15. Nathan Glazer, *Affirmative Discrimination: Ethnic Inequality and Public Policy* (New York: Basic Books, 1975), 75–76. Also see the influential report by

Richard Neuhaus and Peter Berger, *To Empower People: The Role of Mediating Structures in Public Policy* (Washington: American Enterprise Institute, 1975).

16. Thomas Sowell, "Colleges Are Skipping over Competent Blacks to Admit 'Authentic' Ghetto Types," *New York Times Magazine*, 13 October 1970, 49.

17. Angelo N. Ancheta, *Race, Rights and the Asian American Experience* (New Brunswick: Rutgers University Press, 1998), 158.

18. Daniel P. Moynihan, "The New Racialism," *Atlantic Monthly*, August 1968, 40. The word *blunt* seems to imply some kind of racism is about to make its appearance from the Right: consider Joe Gelman, office manager for Proposition 209 in California, who noted of Ward Connerly that "to be blunt the fact that he was black was very important. It's like using affirmative action to defeat affirmative action. It's slightly unprincipled, but the fact was he brought some positive things like the full weight of the governor's office." Lydia Chávez, *The Color Bind: California's Battle to End Affirmative Action* (Berkeley: University of California Press, 1998), 74.

19. David Bell, "The Triumph of Asian Americans," *The New Republic*, 15–22 July 1985, 25; Dinesh D'Souza, *Ronald Reagan: How an Ordinary Man Became an Extraordinary Leader* (New York: The Free Press, 1997).

20. William Wei, *The Asian American Movement* (Philadelphia: Temple University Press, 1993), 157.

21. Alice Amsden, *Asia's Next Giant: South Korea and Late Industrialization* (Oxford: Oxford University Press, 1992).

22. Francis Fukuyama, "Social Capital and the Global Economy," *Foreign Affairs* 74, no. 5 (September–October 1995): 93.

23. "Up from Inscrutable," *Fortune*, 6 April 1992, 120.

24. Vijay Prashad, "Anti-D'Souza: The Ends of Racism and the Asian American," *Amerasia Journal* 24, no. 1 (1998): 23–40; and Vijay Prashad, *Karma of Brown Folk* (Minneapolis: University of Minnesota Press, 2000).

25. William McGurn, "The Silent Minority," *National Review*, 24 June 1991, 19–20.

26. Kenneth Lee, "Angry Yellow Men," *The New Republic*, 9 September 1996, 11. We heard this first from Dinesh D'Souza, *Illiberal Education* (New York: Free Press, 1991), 50, but also from such stalwarts as Arthur Hu, "Education and Race," *National Review* 49, no. 17 (15 September 1997): 52–56, and Peter Shaw, "Counting Asians," *National Review* 48, no. 17 (25 September 1995): 50–54.

27. Lance T. Izumi, "There are Asians, and Asians," *National Review*, 1 July 1996, 25.

28. Chávez, *The Color Bind*, 117.

29. James Carroll and Frank Wu, "Anything for the Cause," *Asian Week* 19, no. 14 (20–26 November 1997).

30. Lucia Hwang, "A House Divided: Asian Americans and Affirmative Action," *Third Force* 4, no. 5 (November/December 1996), provides the start of an explanation.

31. Chavez, *The Color Bind*, 236.

32. Emil Guillermo, "White Asian Americans," *Asian Week*, 28 July 1995.

33. Wei, *Asian American Movement*, 155–56.

34. George Lipsitz, *The Possessive Investment in Whiteness* (Philadelphia: Temple University Press, 1998), 222.

35. Max B. Baker, "Bill Would Bar 'Legacy' Admissions," *Fort Worth Star Telegram*, 4 January 1999, 1.

36. In 2001 Representative Burhman put two bills forward. The first, House Bill 954: College Admissions Fairness Act, whose main provision is as follows:

    > An institution of higher education, in making a decision relating to the admission of an applicant to the institution or to a college, school, or degree program, including a graduate or professional school, may not consider whether the applicant: (1) is related by consanguinity or affinity to another person who attends or has attended the institution or a college, school, or program of the institution; or (2) has made a donation to the institution or is related by consanguinity or affinity to another person who has made a donation to the institution.

    The second, House Bill 953 asks that the government order the University of Texas to remove "from public view" all statues of Confederate officers from their campuses. Thanks to Naila Ahmad who works for Burnham, and keeps me uptodate on the activities of this people's emissary.

37. J. Morgan Kousser, *Colorblind Injustice. Minority Voting Rights and the Undoing of the Second Reconstruction* (Chapel Hill: University of North Carolina Press, 1999), notably chs. 7–9.

38. Lipsitz, *Possessive Investment in Whiteness*, 1–23.

39. Joel Bleifuss, "Etc.," *In These Times* 19, no. 26 (13 November 1995): 10–11.

40. Vijay Prashad, "No Sweat," *Public Culture* 10, no. 1 (fall 1997): 193–99 and "Mit den Dow Joneses mithalten: Sorgen und Kämpfe in den USA," *Marxistiche Blätter*, 3–01, Mai/Juni 2001: 27–34.

41. Kavaljit Singh, *Taming Global Financial Flows: Challenges and Alternatives in the Era of Globalization* (London: Zed Books, 2000) and Biplab Dasgupta, *Structural Adjustment, Global Trade and the New Political Economy of Development* (London: Zed Books, 1999).

42. Joel Kotkin, *Tribes: How Race, Religion, and Identity Determine Success in the New Global Economy* (New York: Random House, 1993), 4.

43. Aidan Southall, "The Illusion of Tribe," in *The Passing of Tribal Man in Africa*, ed. Peter Gutkind (Leiden: Brill, 1970), 28–51. The debate on primordialism is ongoing, for which, see J. D. Eller and R. M. Coughlan, "The Poverty of Primordialism: The Demystification of Ethnic Attachments," *Ethnic and Racial Studies* 16, no. 2 (April 1993): 183–202.

44. Kotkin, *Tribes*, 8. For the place of the book, see Arjun Appadurai, *Modernity at Large: Cultural Dimensions of Globalization* (Minneapolis: University of Minnesota Press, 1996), 170.

45. Jim Naureckas, "Media on the Somali Intervention: Tragedy Made Simple," *Extra!*, March 1993; and Jane Hunter, "As Rwanda Bled, Media Sat on Their Hands," *Extra!*, July/August 1994.

46. On the logic of partition, see Radha Kumar, *Divide and Fall? Bosnia in the Annals of Partition* (London: Verso, 1997). On the new "humanism," see Noam Chomsky, *The New Military Humanism: Lessons from Kosovo* (Monroe: Common Courage Press, 1999). Indeed, NATO peacekeepers have been deployed in the former Yugoslavia to *keep people ethnically segregated*, a phenomenon formally illegal in most NATO countries! "Albanians Again Confront NATO Troops in Mitrovica," *New York Times*, 9 August 1999, A8.

47. Vijay Prashad, "NGO Anthropology," *Left Curve* 23 (1999): 77–78.

48. Independent Commission on International Humanitarian Issues, *Indigenous Peoples. A Global Quest for Justice* (London: Zed Books, 1987), 8. Incidentally, without using the phrase "indigenous peoples," the International Labor Organization provided an early definition for it in 1957 in Convention no. 107 (concerning the Protection and Integration of Indigenous and other Tribal and Semi-Tribal Populations in Independent Countries).

49. Claude Lévi-Strauss with Didier Eribon, *Conversations with Lévi-Strauss* (Chicago: University of Chicago Press, 1988), 153.

50. Wazir Jahan Karim, "Anthropology Without Tears: How a 'Local' Sees the 'Local' and the 'Global,'" in *The Future of Anthropological Knowledge*, ed. Henrietta Moore (New York: Routledge, 1996), 131. The balanced account by Tsering Shakya on Tibet acknowledges that traditionalists worry about the secular values that attract the youth, so that were the Chinese army to withdraw from Tibet the conflicts in the country would be vast. So much for the ahistorical indigenousness of the Tibetian people! Tsering Shakya, *The Dragon in the Land of Snows: A History of Modern Tibet Since 1947* (London: Pimlico, 1999), 420. Smart accounts of the naïveté of the pro-Tibet forces can be found in Margaret McLagan, "Mobilizing for Tibet: Transnational Politics and Diaspora Culture in the Post-Cold War Era" (Ph.D. diss., New York University, 1996); and Eric McGuckin, "Postcards from Shangri-La: Tourism, Tibetan Refugees, and the Politics of Cultural Production" (Ph.D. diss., City University of New York, 1997).

51. Indeed, Rajshekar informs the "Communists of the outside world" that "the Indian Untouchables are like dynamite. Their body is like steel and their mind a volcano. They are an explosive commodity. They would burn the whole land, once ignited." V. T. Rajshekar, *Dalit: The Black Untouchables of India* (Atlanta: Clarity Press, 1995), 85. The prairie fire envisaged by Rajshekar would be in a "caste war," not in a class war that is aware of and grounded in the problems of caste oppression. Caste solidarity, without a scrupulous analysis of class, and class solidarity, without a careful watch on Brahmin supremacy, are both inadequate. I've worked out some of this in summary in "The Soul of Soulless Conditions: Dalits in Contemporary India," *ColorLines* 3, no. 2 (summer 2000): 9–11.

52. Runoko Rashidi, "Looking at India Through African Eyes," E-mail on the Black Radical Congress listserver (May 1999); www.cwo.com//ucmi/india3.html.

53. "Dr. Ambedkar Award for Runoko Rashidi," *Dalit Voice*, 1–15 January 2000.

54. Rajshekar, *Dalit*, 35 and 43.

55. Wahneema Lubiano, "Black Nationalism and Black Common Sense: Policing Ourselves and Others," in Lubiano, *The House That Race Built*, 233. Wilson Jeremiah Moses, *Afrotopia: The Roots of African American Popular History* (Cambridge: Cambridge University Press, 1998).

56. Stephen Howe, *Afrocentrism: Mystical Pasts and Imagined Homes* (London: verso, 1998); and Moses, *Afrotopia*.

57. Runoko Rashidi, "Blacks as a Global Community" (reproduced in Rajshekar, *Dalit*, 86); and Wayne Chandler, "The Jewel in the Lotus: The Ethiopian Presence in the Indus Valley Civilization," in *African Presence in Early Asia*, ed. Ivan Van Sertima and Runoko Rashidi (New Brunswick: Transaction Books, 1985).

58. Vijay Prashad, *Untouchable Freedom. The Social History of a Dalit Community* (Delhi: Oxford University Press, 2000), 83–84.

59. David Frawley, *The Myth of the Aryan Invasion of India* (New Delhi: Voice of India, 1994). Frawley, who goes by the Brahmanical name of Swami Vamdev Shastri, runs the American Institute of Vedic Studies and is part of the U.S.-based detachment of the Hindu Right.

60. The claim on Buddhism may come from the link made by Dr. B. R. Ambedkar and the Dalit movement with Buddhism (Ambedkar converted to the faith in 1956). Chandler, "The Jewel in the Lotus," 88–104; and C. A. Winters, "The Dravidian Language and the Harappan Script," *Archiv Orientalni* 58 (1990): 301–09.

61. Asko Parpola, *Deciphering the Indus Script* (Cambridge: Cambridge University Press, 1994); Gregory Possehl, *Indus Age: The Beginnings* (Philadelphia: University of Pennsylvania Press, 1999). Cultural connection refers to the theory of joint and combined cultural development, the creation of cultural forms in conversation between groups. The theory of cultural origins, like racialist theory in general, assumes that a people are delimited and that they create their cultures out of whole cloth, and not in cultural conversation with others. It is an ahistorical approach to culture.

62. The adherence to raciology leads to a general racist stereotyping, as with Rajshekar: "because of the tremendous physical stamina of the Negroes, they have produced outstanding athletes, cricketers, singers and dancers. They have actors, writers, and many creative thinkers. Black is Beautiful." Rajshekar, *Dalit*, 53. What is striking about this is that Rajshekar is well aware of the dangers of fascist thought (V. T. Rajshekar, *Brahmanism: Father of Fascism, Racism, Nazism* [Bangalore: Dalit Sahitya Academy, 1994]), yet he trades in an epistemology that shares far too much with a fascistic racism.

63. Rashidi is quoted by Rajshekar, *Dalit*, 44. George Washington Williams anticipated Rashidi with his suggestions that the "Negro race" is a very "cosmopolitan people" who are perhaps the ancient "race" of India. G. W. Williams, *History of the Negro Race in America from 1619–1880* (New York: G. P. Putnam, 1883), 17–19.

64. Rajshekar, *Dalit*, 52. In Dalit studies, the debate over the relations between Dalits and non-Dalits is fraught with discord. See Robert Deliège, *The Untouchables of India* (London: Berg, 1999).

65. Interview with Runoko Rashidi, December 22, 1999. For a critique of epidermal determinism and more on the Afro-Dalit thesis, Vijay Prashad, "Badge of Color: An Afro-Dalit Story," *The Toronto Review* 18, no. 3 (summer 2000): 17–21; *Z Magazine* (March 2000): 8–10; *Little India* (February 2000); *Dalit Voice* 19, no. 13 (16–30 June 2000): 19–21; and at several Internet sites. The essay earned some marginal notoriety when Mr. Thomas Mountain, an Afrocentric activist from Hawaii, threatened me with libel.

66. Walter Rodney, *The Groundings with My Brothers* (London: Bougle-l'Ouverture, 1969), 31. In memory of this history, Ambalavaner Sivanandan (editor of *Race & Class*) says, in his brilliant spoken word piece, "Black is not just the color of our skins. It is the colour of our politics." Asian Dub Foundation, "Colour Line," *Community Music* (London: Virgin France/Virgin Benelux, 2000).

67. For a people as subjugated in modern times as the Africans, the question of the subject of history has been fraught with controversy. Is the subject of the continent's history the African? Are the Egyptians Africans? What makes an African? Is it a continental matter? If so, do those of "African descent" in the Americas count as part of African history? What then is the meaning of the African Diaspora? Are those of "Indian descent" in Africa part of African history? Or are they part of the history of Africa, of the continent, which itself is different from African history, the history of a distinct people? How do we determine who is African? Must we follow the protocols of racial science? However, were there Africans only after racism? Was there no notion of Africa prior to race science? There are, of course, no easy answers to these questions. I recommend as a start V. Y. Mudimbe, *The Idea of Africa* (Bloomington: Indiana University Press, 1994). The problem here is similar to that of Levinas's perceptive statement that the "Jews" preexisted anti-Semitism (this in response to Sartre's *Réflexions sur la question juive,* (Paris: Morihien, 1940)), on which see Jean-François Lyotard, "Jewish Oedipus," trans. S. Hanson, *Genre* 10, no. 3 (fall 1977): 395–411. Thanks to Dr. Tsenay Serequeberhan for leading me to this.

68. When John Speke went in search of the Nile in 1859, he was led by ancient Indian and Egyptian texts as well as by the advice of "the Hindu traders" who "had a firm basis to stand upon from their intercourse with the Abyssinians" about the geography of eastern Africa. John Hanning Speke, *Journal of the Discovery of the Source of the Nile* (London: J. M. Dent, 1906), 216.

69. Mahmood Mamdani, *From Citizen to Refugee* (London: Frances Pinter, 1973), 39.

70. Ibid., p. 52.

71. In Hartford, CT, for instance, the organization Hartford Area Rallys Together (HART) is seen by many white liberals as a "grassroots" outfit because it has many black and Puerto Rican members. That these members are from the middle class and that their agenda is frequently in opposition to the Puerto Rican and black working poor is neglected. The idea of the "grassroots," in this case, enables exploitation to go by under the guise of a kind of nationalism.

72. Frantz Fanon, *The Wretched of the Earth* (New York: Grove Press, 1963), 164;

and Randall Robinson, *Defending the Spirit: A Black Life in America* (New York: Dutton, 1998), 265.

73. Jonathan Chait, "Prophet Motive," *The New Republic*, 31 March 1997, 21–24; and Vijay Prashad, "May Days of Mayavati," *Economic & Political Weekly*, 10 June 1995, 1357–58.

74. This is clearly illustrated by Ma Tomah Alesha, "Blacks of the World Must Fight the Aryan Plague," *Dalit Voice*, 16 November 1992, 9; and C. A. Winters, "African Origins of Glorious Dalits," *Dalit Voice*, 16 September 1985.

75. For a philosophical critique of authenticity, see Lewis R. Gordon, *Bad Faith and Antiblack Racism* (Atlantic Highlands: Humanities Press, 1995), 59–63.

76. B. R. Ambedkar, *Who Were the Shudras?* (Bombay: Thacker & Co., 1946), xii. Du Bois shares much the same kind of approach to "race," as is discussed in Manning Marable, *W. E. B. Du Bois: Black Radical Democrat* (Boston: Twayne, 1986), 36–38.

77. Pauli Murray, *The Autobiography of a Black Activist, Feminist, Lawyer, Priest and Poet* (Knoxville: University of Tennessee Press, 1987), 329–30.

78. David Chioni Moore, "Local Color, Global 'Color': Langston Hughes, the Black Atlantic, and Soviet Central Asia, 1932," *Research in African Literatures* 27, no. 4 (winter 1996): 64.

79. At the start of European colonial rule in India, in the late 1700s, the Abbé Dubois was pleased to see the Dalits in southern India under the twin yoke of Brahmanism and British colonialism. "I am persuaded that a nation of Pariahs [*Paraiyars*] left to themselves would speedily become worse than the hordes of cannibals who wander in the vast waste of Africa and would soon take to devouring each other." Without the "moral restraint" of caste and colonial violence, the Dalits would "abandon themselves to their natural propensities," their "natural predilections and sentiments." Abbé J. A. Dubois, *Hindu Manners, Customs and Ceremonies* (Oxford: Clarendon Press, 1906), 28. The denial of humanity to Dalits and Africans produced similar outrageous structures to render them unfree, one along the lines of "race" (as in the United States, southern Africa, and in the Congo) and the other along the convoluted logic of the colonial caste system. My understanding of the logic of this caste regime can be found in the first three chapters of Prashad, *Untouchable Freedom*.

80. Prashad, *Untouchable Freedom*, 40.

81. Jotibai Phule, "Gulamgiri (1873)," in *Collected Works*, vol. 1 (Bombay: Government of Maharashtra, 1991), xxix.

82. "The Far Horizons," *The Crisis* 35 (January 1928): 34.

83. "Gandhi Hits U.S. Bar," *The Afro-American*, 16 June 1934, 1.

84. Lajpat Rai, *Unhappy India* (Calcutta: Banna, 1928), 104.

85. Sudarshan Kapur, *Raising Up a Prophet: The African-American Encounter with Gandhi* (New Delhi: Oxford University Press, 1992), 64.

86. Ibid., 82.

87. Martin Luther King Jr., "My Trip to the Land of Gandhi," in *A Testament of Hope: The Essential Writings and Speeches of Martin Luther King, Jr.,* ed. James M. Washington (San Francisco: Harper, 1986), 27–28.

88. Y. N. Kly's foreword to Rajshekar, *Dalit,* 11 and the preface from the publisher, 4. Also see Prashad, "Badge of Color," 20, for the assessment of the former *Washington Post* bureau chief in New Delhi Kenneth Cooper.

89. Asian Dub Foundation, "Jerico," *Fact and Fiction* (Tokyo: London Records, 1995).

90. Details for these histories can be found in the many wonderful short articles collected by Sukanta Chaudhuri in *Calcutta. The Living City,* 2 vols. (Calcutta: Oxford University Press, 1990).

91. Dhriti Kanta Lahiri Choudhury, "Trends in Calcutta Architecture, 1690–1903," *Calcutta* 1 (1990): 157.

92. Sumanta Banerjee, "The World of Ramjan Ostagar, The Common Man of Old Calcutta," *Calcutta* 1 (1990): 82.

93. Karl Marx, "On the Jewish Question," in *Collected Works,* vol. 3 (Moscow: Progress Pub. 1975). 153.

94. Ibid., 157.

95. Around the calculus of *mestisaje,* although this is more developed in the Central American and Mexican context: in South America there is an extensive racial lexicon, with such terms as *mestizo* or *caboclo,* in Brazil, *mulatto, zambo, cholo,* and so on. For a fine introduction to race in Latin America, see Peter Wade, *Race and Ethnicity in Latin America* (London: Pluto Press, 1997), but for a special study into the trials in two emblematic nation–states, see Michael Hanchard, ed. *Racial Politics in Contemporary Brazil* (Durham: Duke University Press, 1999); and Winthrop R. Wright, *Café Con Leche: Race, Class and National Image in Venezuela* (Austin: University of Texas Press, 1990).

96. Fred Halliday, "Students of the World Unite" and Gareth Stedman-Jones, "The Meaning of the Student Revolt," in *Student Power,* ed. Alexander Cockburn and Robin Blackburn (London: Penguin, 1969); and Tariq Ali and Susan Watkins, *1968: Marching in the Streets* (New York: The Free Press, 1998).

97. Karen Umemoto, "'On Strike!' San Francisco State College Strike, 1968–69," *Amerasia Journal* 15, no. 1 (1989): 3–41.

98. Linda Hamilton, "On Cultural Nationalism," in *The Black Panthers Speak,* ed. Philip S. Foner (New York: De Capo, 1995), 152. The Black Panther Party quickly seized upon the contradictions within Black Power, and its links to Nixon's theory of "Black Capitalism": Reginald Major, *A Panther Is a Black Cat* (New York: William Morrow, 1971), 102; and Robert L. Allen, *Black Awakening in Capitalist America: An Analytic History* (New York: Doubleday Anchor, 1970), 46–65.

99. On the labor movement, see Kim Moody, *An Injury to All. The Decline of American Unionism* (London: Verso, 1988), 83–94; on overproduction and the crisis of 1967, see Robert Brenner, "The Economics of Global Turbulence," *New Left Review* 229 (May/June 1998): 95–111.

100. Joseph Turow, *Breaking Up America: Advertisers and the New Media World* (Chicago: University of Chicago Press, 1997), 45.

101. Don Peppers and Martha Rogers, *The One to One Future* (New York: Doubleday, 1993), 383–87.

102. Walden Bello, *Dark Victory. The United States, Structural Adjustment and Global Poverty* (Penang, Malaysia: Third World Network, 1994), 11.

103. Naila Kabeer, *Reversed Realities. Gender Hierarchies in Development Thought* (London: Verso, 1994), 71.

104. Angela Y. Davis, "Gender, Class and Multiculturalism: Rethinking 'Race' Politics," in *Mapping Multiculturalism*, ed. Avery F. Gordon and Christopher Newfield (Minneapolis: University of Minnesota Press, 1996), 44. The point is also made strongly by Paul Gilroy, *Against Race: Imaging Political Cultural Beyond the Colar Line* (Cambridge: Harvard University Press 2000), 270.

105. Michael Eric Dyson, "Bush's Black Faces," *The Nation* 272, no. 4 (29 January 2001): 5.

106. Davis, "Gender, Class and Multiculturalism," 44; and Cynthia Hamilton, "Multiculturalism as Political Strategy," in Gordon and Newfield, *Mapping Multiculturalism,* 173.

107. Slavoj Zizek, *The Ticklish Subject. The Absent Center of Political Ontology* (London: Verso, 1999), 216.

108. R. Radhakrishnan, *Diasporic Mediations: Between Home and Locations* (Minneapolis: University of Minnesota Press, 1996), 210–11.

109. Appadurai, *Modernity at Large,* 12.

110. Gayatri Chakravorty Spivak, *A Critique of Postcolonial Reason: Toward a History of the Vanishing Present* (Cambridge: Harvard University Press, 1999), 397. On the point about the colonization of our social imaginary, see John Tomlinson, *Cultural Imperialism* (Baltimore: Johns Hopkins University Press, 1991), 163.

111. Susan Moller Okin et al., *Is Multiculturalism Bad for Women?* (Princeton: Princeton University Press, 1999), 9. For an excellent overview of the issues at stake in this debate, see Leti Volpp, "Blaming Culture for Bad Behavior," *Yale Journal of Law and Humanities* 12, no. 89 (2000): 109–16.

112. Davis, "Gender, Class and Multiculturalism," 41; and Elizabeth Martinez, *De Colores Means All of US: Latina Views for a Multi-Colored Century* (Boston: South End Press, 1998), 129.

113. Davis, "Gender, Class and Multiculturalism," 47.

114. This is a point made endlessly, but most effectively by Nira Yuval-Davis, "Fundamentalism, Multiculturalism and Women," in *"Race," Culture and Difference,* ed. James Donald and Ali Rattansi (London: Sage, 1992); and Kumkum Sangari, "Politics of Diversity: Religious Communities and Multiple Patriarchies," *Economic and Political Weekly* 30, no. 51 (23 December 1995): 3287–3310 and no. 52 (30 December 1995): 3381–89.

115. Homi Bhabha, "Liberalism's Sacred Cow," in Okin et al., *Is Multiculturalism Bad*, 80.

116. This is well laid out in several essays from Kumkum Sangari, *Politics of the Possible. Essays on Gender, History, Narrative, Colonial English* (Delhi: Tulika, 1999).

117. Homi Bhabha rightly notes that "the representation of difference must not be hastily read as the reflection of *pre-given* ethnic or cultural traits set in the fixed tablet of tradition," *The Location of Culture* (London: Routledge, 1994), 2. And yet, it so often does, as is shown for the world of music by John Hutnyk, "Hybridity Saves? Authenticity and/or the Critique of Appropriation," *Amerasia Journal* 25, no. 3 (1999/2000): 39–58. Hutnyk's complete argument is made in *Critique of Exotica* (London: Pluto, 2000).

118. Daryl Lindsey, "The stakes are a bit higher for us," http://www.salon.com/news/feature/2000/02/16/naacp/index.html.

119. Cyrus Patell suggests "cultural polygenesis," but then holds back because he feels that the term "brings with it the same philological baggage that 'hybridity' does." I tend to think that the problem here is with "genesis" and not with "poly," as shall become clear. Cyrus R. K. Patell, "Comparative American Studies: Hybridity and Beyond," *American Literary History* 11, vol. 1 (spring 1999): 184.

120. Robin D. G. Kelley, "People in Me," *ColorLines Magazine* 1, no. 3 (winter 1999): 5–7.

121. Gerd Baumann, *The Multicultural Riddle. Rethinking National, Ethnic and Religious Identities* (London: Routledge, 1999), 95.

122. "Ganesh Rao to the Editor," in *Marcus Garvey and the Universal Negro Improvement Association Papers*, vol. 4, ed. Robert H. Hill (Berkeley: University of California Press, 1983), 495–96.

123. Prashad, *Karma*, 173.

124. Tu-Wei Ming, ed., *Confucian Traditions in East Asian modernity: Moral Education and Economic Culture in Japan and the Four Mini-Dragons* (Cambridge: Harvard University Press, 1996); and Lionel M. Jensen, *Manufacturing Confucianism: Chinese Traditions and Universal Civilizations* (Durham: Duke University Press, 1997).

125. Gauri Viswanathan, *Masks of Conquest: Literary Study and British Rule in India* (New York: Columbia University Press, 1989); and Sangari, *Politics of the Possible*, 96–183.

126. Prashad, *Karma of Brown Folk*, 14.

127. For the Eurasian case, see R. I. Moore, "The Birth of Europe as a Eurasian Phenomenon," *Modern Asian Studies* 31, no. 3 1997: 583–601; and Sanjay Subrahmanyam, "Connected Histories: notes towards a Reconfiguration of early modern Eurasia," *Modern Asian Studies* 31, no. 3 (1997): 735–62.

128. Donald A. Grinde Jr. and Bruce E. Johansen, *Exemplar of Liberty: Native America and the Evolution of Democracy* (Los Angeles: American Indian Studies Center, UCLA, 1991); on science and math, see Toby Huff, *The Rise of Early*

Modern Science: Islam, China and the West (New York: Cambridge University Press, 1993).

129. Chetan Bhatt, *Liberation and Purity. Race, New Religious Movements and the Ethics of Postmodernity* (London: UCL Press, 1977), 255–64 and Meera Pandya, "Ethical Economics," *Hinduism Today* (March 1998).

130. The argument for authenticity led to the denial of tenure to Dr. Cynthia Mahabir at San Jose State University on the grounds, she (and the university, which settled with her) argues, that the chair of her department noted that "African American Studies has no room for an Indian." Dr. Mahabir is from Trinidad and considers herself of Indo-Caribbean descent. Michele N-K Collison, "The 'Other' Asians," *Black Issues in Higher Education* 16, no. 25 (3 February 2000): 21.

131. David Hilliard, "Black Student Unions," *The Black Panthers Speak,* 125–26.

132. Volpp, "Blaming Culture," 112.

133. Fish, "Boutique Multiculturalism," 82.

134. Etienne Balibar and Immanuel Wallerstein, *Race, Nation & Class* (London: Verso, 1991), 223.

135. Che Guevara, *Socialism and Man in Cuba* (New York: Pathfinder, 1989), 5.

136. Louis Althusser, "Marxism and Humanism," *For Marx* (London: Verso, 1990), 247.

Chapter 3: Coolie Purana

1 Sunaina Maira, "Identity Dub: The Paradoxes of an Indian American Youth Subculture (New York Mix)," *Cultural Anthropology* 14, no. 1 (1999): and Amy Otchet, ed., "Youth's Sonic Force," *The UNESCO Courier* (July–August 2000):21–56.

2. Thomas C. Holt, *The Problem of Freedom: Race, Labor and Politics in Jamaica and Britain, 1832–1938* (Baltimore: Johns Hopkins University Press, 1992).

3. "The bourgeoisie sees in the workers only 'hands' and they call them 'hands' to their faces. As Carlyle says, the middle classes can conceive of no relationship between human beings other than the cash nexus." Friedrich Engels, *The Condition of the Working Class in England* (Stanford: Stanford University Press, 1968), 312.

4. Harish Puri, *Ghadar Movement* (Amritsar: Guru Nanakdev University Press, 1993), 136.

5. Jan Breman, "Introduction," in *Imperial Monkey Business. Racial Supremacy in Social Darwinist Theory and Colonial Practice*, ed. Jan Breman (Amsterdam: VU University Press, 1990), 4.

6. Hugh Tinker, "Into Servitude: Indian Labour in the Sugar Industry, 1833–1970," in *International Labour Migration*, ed. Shula Marks and Peter Richardson (London: Maurice Temple Smith, 1984), 80; and Anil Sookdeo, "Problems of Labor and Freedom in Trinidad's Transition to a Post-Emancipation Society, 1808–1888" (Ph.D. diss., Johns Hopkins University, 1996).

7. Thomas R. Metcalf, *The Aftermath of Revolt. India, 1857–1870* (Princeton: Princeton University Press, 1964), 196.

8. Jean Chesneaux, *Peasant Revolts in China, 1840–1949* (London: Thames & Hudson, 1973).

9. Walton Look-Lai, *Indentured Labor, Caribbean Sugar: Chinese and Indian Migrants to the British West-Indies, 1838–1918* (Baltimore: Johns Hopkins University Press, 1993), 62. On South Africa, see Maureen Swan, "Indentured Indians: Accommodation and Resistance, 1890–1913," in *Essays on Indentured Indians in Natal,* ed. Surendra Bhana (Leeds: Peepal Tree Press, 1990), 121–23. On Fiji, see John D. Kelly, " 'Coolie' as a Labour Commodity: Race, Sex and European Dignity in Colonial Fiji," *Journal of Peasant Studies* 19, nos. 3–4 (1992): 246–67.

10. Ronald Takaki, *Iron Cages: Race and Culture in 19th Century America* (Seattle: University of Washington Press, 1982), 217.

11. Look-Lai, *Indentured Labor,* 119.

12. Noor Kumar Mahabir, ed., *The Still Cry. Personal Accounts of East Indians in Trinidad and Tobago During Indentureship, 1845–1917,* (Tacarigua: Calaloux, 1985), 166.

13. *Report by the Honourable E. F. L. Wood on His Visit to the West Indies and British Guiana* (London: HMSO, 1922), 62; and Governor Wilson quoted in Kelvin Singh, "Indians and the Larger Society," in *Calcutta to Caroni. The East Indians of Trinidad,* ed. John Gaffar La Guerre (St. Augustine, Trinidad: University of West Indies, 1985), 47.

14. Mahabir, *The Still Cry,* 167.

15. Naomi Zack, "The American Sexualization of Race," in *Race/Sex. Their Sameness, Difference, and Interplay* (London: Routledge, 1997), 148–52.

16. Brij V. Lal, "Kunti's Cry: Indentured Women on Fiji Plantations," *Indian Economic and Social History Review* 22, no. 1 (1985); Lucie Cheng Hirita, "Free, Indentured, Enslaved: Chinese Prostitutes in Nineteenth Century America," *Signs* 5, no. 1 (1979): 3–29.

17. Karen Leonard, *Making Ethnic Choices* (Philadelphia: Temple University Press, 1992); and Nayan Shah, "The Race of Sodomy: Asian Men, White Boys, and the Politics of Sex in California and British Columbia 1910–1928" (manuscript, Columbia University, 2000).

18. James Millette, "The Wage Problem in Trinidad and Tobago, 1838–1938," in *The Colonial Caribbean in Transition,* ed. Bridget Brereton and Kevin A. Yelvington (Mona, Jamaica: The Press University of the West Indies, 1999), 63; Bill Freund, *Insiders and Outsiders. The Indian Working Class of Durban, 1910–1990* (Pietermaritzburg: University of Natal Press, 1995), 5; Look-Lai, *Indentured Labor,* 12; and Alicja Muszynski, "Race and Gender: Structural Determinants in the Formation of British Columbia's Salmon Cannery Labour Force," *Canadian Journal of Sociology* 13, nos. 1–2 (1988):103–20.

19. Robert J. Moore, "Colonial Images of Blacks and Indians in Nineteenth Century Guyana," in Brereton and Yelvington, eds., *The Colonial Caribbean,* 149;

and D. H. Heydenrych, "Indian Railway Labour in Natal, 1876–1895: The Biggest Indian Work Force in the Colony," *Historia* 31, no. 3 (1986): 11–20.

20. Takaki, *Iron Cages*, 219.

21. Ron Takaki, *Strangers from a Different Shore: A History of Asian Americans* (Boston: Little, Brown, 1989), 94.

22. Robert Lee, *Orientals: Asian Americans in Popular Culture* (Philadelphia: Temple University Press, 1999).

23. Alexander Saxton, *The Indispensable Enemy: Labor and the Anti-Chinese Movement in California* (Berkeley: University of California Press, 1971), 273.

24. Samuel Gompers and Herman Gutstadt, *Meat vs. Rice. American Manhood Against Asiatic Coolieism. Which Shall Survive?* (San Francisco: Asiatic Exclusion League, 1908), 14.

25. W. E. B. Du Bois, *Black Reconstruction in America, 1860–1880* (New York: Athenaeum, 1992), 607.

26. Takaki, *Iron Cages*, 219. Lee, *Orientals*, 55.

27. Look-Lai, *Indentured Labor*, 95.

28. Takaki, *Iron Cages*, 121.

29. Moore, "Colonial Images," and Bridget Brereton, "The Foundations of Prejudice: Indians and Africans in Nineteenth Century Trinidad," *Caribbean Issues* 1., no. (1974):15–28.

30. Walter Rodney, *A History of the Guyanese Working People, 1881–1905* (Baltimore: Johns Hopkins University Press, 1981), 180–81. In various Afro-Jamaican folk faiths, there is the figure of the *duppy*, ("ghost") which the obeah men, the healers, use to "set upon" people and do harm to them; the most popular *duppies* were Baby, Indian, and Chinese, indications of the reverence and contempt with which the Indians and Chinese were held by the Afro-Jamaicans. Barry Chevannes, *Rastafari: Roots and Ideology* (Syracuse: Syracuse University Press, 1994), 25.

31. Mahabir, *The Still Cry*, 52.

32. Look-Lai, *Indentured Labor*, 112–13 and 165.

33. Takaki, *Strangers*, 86.

34. Look-Lai, *Indentured Labor*, 180.

35. For the complex sexual history of the Indians in the plantation colonies, see Madhavi Kale, "Projecting Identities: Empire and Indentured Labor Migration from India to Trinidad and British Guiana, 1836–1885," in *Nation and Migration*, ed. Peter van der Veer (Philadelphia: University of Pennsylvania Press, 1995); Brij V. Lal, "Veil of Dishonour: Sexual Jealousy and Suicides on Fiji Plantations," *Journal of Pacific History* 20 (1985): 135–55; Jo Beall, "Women Under Indentured Labour in Colonial Natal, 1860–1911," in *Women and Gender in Southern Africa to 1945*, ed. C. Walker (Cape Town: David Philip, 1990); and Rhoda Reddock, "Freedom Denied: Indian Women and Indentureship

in Trinidad and Tobago, 1845–1917," *Economic and Political Weekly*, 26 October 1985, WS85–86.

36. Moore, "Colonial Images," 154–55; Look-Lai, *Indentured Labor*, 139 and 206.

37. Frederick Douglass, "Our Composite Nationality: An Address Delivered in Boston, Massachusetts, on 7 December 1869," in *The Frederick Douglass Papers*, Vol. 4 (New Haven: Yale University Press, 1991), 252 and 254.

38. One should keep in mind the solidarity between Asian and Chicano labor in California in the early 1900s. When a Chicano member of the Oxnard Sugar Beet and Field Laborers Union was killed during a strike, the unity across ethnic lines was immense. One report from 1903 notes:

> There have been labor gatherings and parades during the past week. Dusky skinned Japs and Mexicans march through the streets headed by one or two former minor contractors and beet laborers four abreast and several hundred strong. They are a silent grim band of fellows, most of them young and belonging to the lower class of Japs and Mexicans.

Oxnard Courier, 7 March 1903.

39. This was not just in the Caribbean, but also in South Africa, as in "Festival of Mohurrum. A Moribund Ceremony," *Natal Advertiser*, 21 December 1912.

40. Basdeo Mangru, "Tadjah in British Guiana: Manipulation or Protest?" in *Indenture and Abolition* (Toronto: TSAR, 1993), 55.

41. Ibid., 53.

42. For a superb analysis of the politics of Carnival, see Ana Maria Alonso, "Men in 'Rags' and the Devil on the Throne: A Study of Protest and Inversion in the Carnival of Post-Emancipation Trinidad," *Plantation Society in the Americas* 3, no. 1 (1990): 73–120.

43. Mangru, "Tadjah," 54.

44. Ibid., 53.

45. My analysis is in the debt of Prabhu Prasad Mohapatra's landmark but as yet unpublished work, notably his paper "The Hosay Massacre of 1884: Class and Community Among Indian Labour in Trinidad."

46. Karl Marx, "On the Question of Free Trade," *The Poverty of Philosophy* (Moscow: Progress Publishers, 1955), 193–94.

47. R. W. Beachey, *The British West Indies Sugar Industry in the Late 9th Century* (Oxford: Basil Blackwell, 1957), 123; and Kusha Haraksingh, "Control and Resistance Among Overseas Indian Workers: A Study of Labor on the Sugar Plantations of Trinidad, 1875–1917," *Journal of Caribbean History* 14 (1981): 1–17.

48. K. O. Laurence, "Indians as Permanent Settlers in Trinidad Before 1900," in La Guerre, *Calcutta to Caroni*, 106–7.

49. Brinsley Samroo, "Politics and Afro-Indian Relations in Trinidad," in La Guerre, *Calcutta to Caroni*, 80.

50. Kelvin Singh, *Bloodstained Tombs: The Mohurrum Massacre, 1884* (London: Macmillan Caribbean, 1988); Kim Johnson, "1884: The Indians Didn't Believe

Police Warnings," *Trinidad Express,* 12 September 1999; Kale, "Projecting Identities," 83–86.

51. Kale, "Projecting Identities," 85.

52. Steven Vertovec, " 'Official' and 'Popular' Hinduism in Diaspora: Historical and Contemporary Trends in Surinam, Trinidad and Guyana," *Contributions to Indian Sociology* 28, no. 1 (1994): 136–37. Much the same was encouraged in South Africa, where, during the decisive 1912–13 struggle, Swami Shankeranand visited Natal, where he felt he "never had occasion to realise that he was in a land which is hostile to Asiatics," to generate enthusiasm for Hinduism over class antagonism. "The Swami," *Natal Advertiser,* 31 December 1912; "Young Men's Vedic Society. Inaugural Ceremony," *Natal Advertiser,* 30 November 1912; "Dipavali Festival," *Natal Advertiser,* 20 October 1912.

53. In the 1950s, Muhammed Rafeeq felt that Muslims in Trinidad "maintained the cardinal doctrines with unadulterated purity." This illusion was only partly true due to the influx of clerics in the late nineteenth century. Muhammed Rafeeq, "History of Islam and Muslims in Trinidad," *The Islamic Review* (September 1954): 22; and Mary Arnett, "Trinidad Muslim League," *Muslim World* 48 (January 1958): 52–62.

54. Clem Seecharan, *India and the Shaping of the Indo-Guyanese Imagination, 1890s–1920s* (Leeds: Peepal Tree, 1993).

55. Mangru, "Tadjah," 49.

56. Ajai Mansingh and Laxmi Mansingh, "Hosay and Its Creolization," *Caribbean Quarterly* 41, no. 1 (1995): 25–39.

57. Mahabir, *The Still Cry,* 135.

58. Gustav Thaiss, "Contested Meanings and the Politics of Authenticity," in *Islam, Globalization and Postmodernity,* ed. Akbar Ahmed and Hastings Donnan (London: Routledge, 1994), 60.

59. Look-Lai, *Indentured Labor,* 209–10.

60. Aisha Khan, "What Is 'a Spanish'? Ambiguity and 'Mixed' Ethnicity in Trinidad," in *Trinidad Ethnicity* ed. Melvin A. Yelvington (Knoxville: University of Tennessee Press, 1993), 190.

61. Shalini Puri, "Race, Rape and Representation: Indo-Caribbean Women and Cultural Nationalism," *Cultural Critique* 36 (spring 1997): 132.

62. Kelvin Singh, *Race and Class Struggles in a Colonial State, Trinidad 1917–1945* (Mona, Jamaica: The Press University of the West Indies, 1994), 65.

63. Etienne Balibar, *The Philosophy of Marx* (London: Verso, 1995), 97–100.

64. Brinsley Samaroo, "The Trinidad Workingmen's Association and the Origins of Popular Protest in a Crown Colony," *Social and Economic Studies* 21, no. 2 (June 1972): 207; and Marianne D. Ramesar, "Recurrent Issues Concerning Indian Immigrants to Trinidad," in La Guerre, *Calcutta to Caroni,* 139.

65. Jacqueline Jenkinson, "The 1919 Race Riots in Britain," in *Under the Imperial Carpet: Essays in Black history, 1780–1950* (Crawley: Rabbit Press, 1986), 182–

207; Ron Ramdin, *Reimagining Britain. 500 Years of Black and Asian History* (London: Pluto, 1990), 119–21.

66. Singh, *Race and Class*, 31.

67. Rhoda E. Reddock, *Women, Labour and Politics in Trinidad and Tobago* (London: Zed, 1994), 122.

68. Samroo, "The Trinidad Workingmen's Association," 213; Tony Martin, *Marcus Garvey, Hero* (Dover: The Majority Press, 1983), 52; Sahadeo Basdeo, "Indian Participation in Labour Politics in Trinidad, 1919–1939," *Journal of Indian History* 60 (1982): 179–98.

69. Singh, *Race and Class*, 11.

70. Reddock, *Women*, 129–33 and Singh, *Race and Class*, 150. What is so significant here is that it was the white orthodoxy that interrupted liberal values and it is the East Indians (otherwise stereotyped as traditional) who stood for the freedom of women and men to chose their marital destiny.

71. Singh, *Race and Class*, 185; and Samaroo, "Politics," 87–89.

72. Samaroo, "Politics," 84.

73. Reddock, *Women*, 146.

74. Stephen Davis, *Bob Marley: Conquering Lion of Reggae* (London: Plexus, 1988), 109–10.

75. Mahabir, *The Still Cry*, 76.

76. Ajai Mansingh and Laxmi Mansingh, "Hindu Influences on Rastafarianism," in *Caribbean Quarterly Monographs: Rastafari*, ed. Rex Nettleford (Kingston: Caribbean Quarterly, and Mona: The Press University of the West Indies, 1985), 96–115; Ajai Mansingh, "Rasta-Indian Connection," *Daily Gleaner*, 8 August 1982; and "Rastafarianism: The Indian Connection," *Daily Gleaner*, 18 July 1982.

77. We are told that there are "serious errors" in their work (Clinton Hutton and Nathaniel S. Murrell, "Rasta's Psychology of Blackness, Resistance and Somebodiness," in *Chanting Down Babylon: The Rastafari Reader*, ed. N. S. Murrell, W. D. Spencer, and A. A. McFarlane [Philadelphia: Temple University Press, 1998], 46), but when we observe the sources that challenge these errors, things are not so clear. For instance, Hutton and Murrell turn us to Savishinsky who is less dogmatic. Drawing from others, he argues that the roots of Jamaican ganja use "are just as likely to be found in Africa as in India." Neil J. Savishinsky, "African Dimensions of the Jamaican Rastafarian Movement," in Murrell, Spencer, and McFarlane, *Chanting Down Babylon*, 130–31.

78. Rupert Lewis, "Marcus Garvey and the Early Rastafarians: Continuity and Discontinuity," in Murrell, Spencer, and McFarlane, *Chanting Down Babylon*, 148.

79. Mansingh and Mansingh, "Hindu Influences," 100; Rhoda Reddock, *Women*, 76–91; Verene A. Shepherd, *Transients to Settlers: The Experience of Indians in Jamaica, 1845–1950* (Leeds: Peepal Tree, 1994).

80. Tej Bhatia, "Trinidad Hindi: Its Genesis and Generational Profile," in *Lan-*

guage Transplanted: The Development of Overseas Hindi, ed. R. K. Barz and J. Siegel (Wiesbaden: Otto Harrassowitz, 1988), 191.

81. Derek Blackheartman Bishton, *A Journey into the Rasta* (London: Chatto & Windus, 1986), 106.

82. Mansingh and Mansingh, "Hindu Influences," 98.

83. It does not take a Ph.D. to see the commonalities: Benjamin Zephariah is a Jamaican Rasta whose look "repeatedly gets him cries of 'Sadhu, Sadhu,' when he walks the streets of India." Namrita Gokhale, "Comic Is Literary, Too," *Times of India*, 1 March 2000.

84. Ibid., 103.

85. Horace Campbell, *Rasta and Resistance: From Marcus Garvey to Walter Rodney* (Trenton: Africa World Press, 1987), 42. The claim is important to historians like Campbell because it demonstrates the continuity of African traditions. Ironically, the Mau Mau themselves may simply have adopted the custom as part of a vow not to cut their hair until Kenya was free from the British. Savishinsky, "African Dimensions," 143. Chevannes first felt that the custom came from the Mau Mau in the 1950s, but he later claimed that perhaps two groups, the Youth Black Faith and the Higes Knots, adopted the dreads in the 1940s to emulate an African custom. Barry Chevannes, *Rastafari: Roots and Ideology* (Syracuse: Syracuse University Press, 1994), x–xi. This is a knotty problem. Over time dreads came to represent a critique of the "clean-cut" Babylonian system and the locks of the lion, the Lion of Judah, Haile Selassie. Peter Clarke, *Black Paradise: The Rastafarian Movement* (San Bernardino: Borgo Press, 1986), 90.

86. Savishinsky, "African Dimensions," 131–133; Kenneth Bilby, "The Holy Herb: Notes on the Background of Cannabis in Jamaica," in *Rastafari*, ed. Rex Nettleford (Kingston: The Press University of the West Indies, 1985), 90.

87. Raymond Prince, Rochelle Greenfield, and John Marriott, "Cannabis or Alcohol? Observations on Their Use in Jamaica," *Bulletin of Narcotics* 1, no. 1 (1972): 1–9; J. Schaeffer, "The Significance of Marihuana in a Small Agricultural Community in Jamaica," in *Cannabis and Culture*, ed. V. Rubin (London: Mouton, 1975). This was so in Trinidad as well, see J. C. Jha, "The Indian Heritage in Trinidad," in La Guerre, *Calcutta to Caroni*, 11, as in Guyana both among the East Indians and the Chinese, see Brian L. Moore, "Leisure and Society in Postemancipation Guyana," in Brereton and Yelvington, *The Colonial Caribbean in Transition*, 121–24.

88. Mahabir, *The Still Cry*, 58.

89. Chevannes, *Rastafari*, 153.

90. William F. Lewis, *Soul Rebels. The Rastafari* (Prospect Heights: Waveland, 1993), 21–22 and 53.

91. Hélène Lee, *Le Premier Rasta* (Paris: Flammarion, 1999), 45–48, and elsewhere for the first comprehensive history of Howell's role at the start of Rastafarianism. For an account of the links between Garvey and Howell, see Robert Hill, "Dread History: Leonard P. Howell and Millenarian Visions in Early Rastafarian Religions in Jamaica," *Yard Roots* 1, no. 4 (1982): 12–16.

92. I am using the fourth edition, which is entitled *The Great Book of Magical Art, Hindu Magic and East Indian Occultism, and The Book of the Secret Hindu, Ceremonial, and Talismanic Magic* (Chicago: The de Laurence Company, 1915), 372.

93. William de Laurence, *The Great Book*, 594–628. Dream Books drew from the Theosophist traditions, as well as from the general Orientalist fascination with gypsies and fortune tellers. *Gipsy Witches Dream Book and Fortune Teller* (New York: Dick & Fitzgerald, 1890) and C. B. Case, *Oriental Dream Book, with interpretations of all dreams as vouched for by the Orientals, Gypsies, witches, Egyptians, augurs, astrologers, magi, fortune-tellers, sooth-sayers, prophets, seers and wise men of ancient and modern times* (Chicago: Shrewesbury, 1916).

94. Roy Ottley, *"New World A-Coming." Inside Black America* (Cleveland: The World Publishing Company, 1945). 55.

95. Ibid., 86–87.

96. Max Stein, *Lucky Numbers Policy Player's Dream Book* (Chicago, n.p., 1928) and *The Genuine Afro Dream Book* (Wilmington, n.p., 1941).

97. Kelvin A. Yelvington, "The War in Ethiopia and Trinidad, 1935–1936," in Brereton and Yelvington, *The Colonial Caribbean in Transition*, 189–225.

98. The occult obsession with rules and exclusions comes out nicely in Howell's diatribe against those who are "guilty of obeah," "obeah dogs," "fortune teller witch and old hige," "ghost, witch, lizards," "John Crows," and "Rum Bottles." G. G. Maragh, *The Promise Key* (Clarendon, Jamaica: Black International Iyahbinghi Press, 1991), 23. Maragh's book is also reprinted with a rather laborious commentary in Murrell, Spencer, and McFarlane, *Chanting Down Babylon*, 361–89.

99. The latter speculation is from Madhukar Shah cited in Murrell, Spencer, and McFarlane, *Chanting Down Babylon*, 386–87. Lee suggests that Howell was taken in by a Mr. Laloo en route back to Jamaica from Harlem, but she is not able to offer more on him. Lee, *Le Premier Rasta*, 124.

100. Mansingh and Mansingh, "Hindu Influences," 105.

101. Howard Johnson, "The Anti-Chinese Riots in Jamaica," *Caribbean Quarterly* 28, no. 3 (1982): 19–32. The situation is similar in Trinidad, for which see Howard Johnson, "The Chinese in Trinidad in the Late Nineteenth Century," *Ethnic and Racial Studies* 10, no. 1 (January 1987): 82–95.

102. These classics are collected on *Ska's the Limit, 1959–1964* (New York: Island Records, 1997); for more on Leslie Kong, see "King Kong," *Giant Robot* 17 (2000): 49. The second guitarist of the Vagabonds, Phil Chen, offers his wonderful tale of being Chinese Jamaican in the world of ska. See Phil Chen, "Copacetic Man," *Giant Robot* 17 (2000): 44–49.

103. A good introduction to reggae can be found in Kevin O'Brien Chang and Wayne Chen, *Reggae Routes: The Story of Jamaican Music* (Philadelphia: Temple University Press, 1998). For a provocative essay on creolization (but one that argues that it happens least in Jamaica), see Christine Ho, "'Hold the

Chow Mein, Gimme Soca': Creolization of the Chinese in Guyana, Trinidad and Jamaica," *Amerasia Journal* 15, no. 2 (1989): 3–25.

104. In 1930, for instance, Garvey's *Blackman* praised the "progressive nature of Trinidad's Indians and wished them well," but there was no sense that the UNIA did not fully welcome East Indians (who were at the nether reaches of West Indian society). Martin, *Marcus Garvey,* 86. On Gandhi, see Brian M. Du Toit, "The Mahatma Gandhi and South Africa," *The Journal of Modern African Studies* 34, no. 4 (1996): 653–54.

105. Singh, *Race and Class,* 47, and for the farmers' unity, see page 78. The Garveyist Howard Bishop said much the same thing on behalf of the TWA in 1926, quoted on page 132.

106. Prashad, *Karma of Brown Folk,* 173.

107. Lee, *Le Premier Rasta,* 127.

108. Basdeo Mangru, "The Rose Hall Sugar Workers' Strike of 1913: The Beginning of the End of Indian Indentureship," *Indenture and Abolition,* 81–97.

109. *Indian Opinion,* 2 September 1905. The most comprehensive account of Dube's life is by Manning Marable, "African Nationalist: The Life of John Langalibalele Dube" (Ph.D. diss., University of Maryland, 1976). An account of the Gandhi-Dube relationship is given in "Mahatma Gandhi and John Dube," *Hindustan Times,* 26 January 1992.

110. M. K. Gandhi, *An Autobiography. The Story of My Experiments with Truth* (Boston: Beacon Press, 1957), 313–18.

111. *Young India,* 20 April 1921; M. K. Gandhi *Collected Works,* vol. 20 (New Delhi: Publications Division, 1958), 15.

112. Maureen Swan, "The 1913 Natal Indian Strike," *Journal of Southern African Studies* 10, no. 2 (April 1984): 256; Jo Beall and M. D. North-Coombes, "The 1913 Disturbances in Natal: The Social and Economic Background to 'Passive Resistance,'" *Journal of Natal and Zulu History* 6 (1983): 48–81.

113. In the *Natal Advertiser:* "The Indian Strike," 23 October 1913, "Fight with Natives. Pitched Battle in a Plantation," 11 November 1913; "The Indian Revolt: Serious Developments," 14 November 1913; and "Contumacious Natives: Evil Example of Indians," 20 November 1913.

114. "White Man's Rule. Effect on the Coloured Races. Speech by Dr. Abdurahman," *Natal Advertiser,* 30 September 1913. Abdurahman offered his support "in every possible way" to the passive resistance in October. "Rand Hindus Meet. Sympathy with the Strikers," *Natal Advertiser,* 30 October 1913.

115. Anil Sookdeo, "The Transformation of Ethnic Identities: The Case of 'Coloured' and Indian Africans," *Journal of Ethnic Studies* 15, no. 4 (1988): 69–83.

116. "Interview to the Reverend S. S. Tema, 1 January 1939," *Harijan* (18 February 1939); M. K. Gandhi, *Collected Works,* vol. 20 (New Delhi: Publications Division, 1958), 68: 272–74.

117. Sanjay Sharma, John Hutnyk, and Ashwani Sharma, "Introduction," in *Dis-Orienting Rhythms. The Politics of the New Asian Dance Music,* ed. Sanjay Sharma, John Hutnyk, and Ashwani Sharma (London: Zed Books, 1996), 1.

Chapter 4: The Merchant Is Always a Stranger

1. Malcolm X, "Black Man's History," in *The End of White World Supremacy*, ed. Benjamin Goodman (New York: Merlin House and Monthly Review Press, 1971), 35.

2. W. E. B. Du Bois, *The Black North in 1901. A Social Study* (New York: Arno Press, 1969), 8–9.

3. Ibid., 10.

4. Kevin Gaines, *Uplifting the Race: Black Leadership, Politics and Culture in the Twentieth Century* (Chapel Hill: University of North Carolina Press, 1996), 95–96.

5. Manning Marable, *How Capitalism Underdeveloped Black America* (Boston: South End Press, 1983), 146.

6. Lewis R. Gordon, *Her Majesty's Other Children. Sketches of Racism from a Neocolonial Age* (Lanham: Rowan & Littlefield, 1997), 117.

7. Jeffrey Melnick, *A Right to Sing the Blues: African Americans, Jews and American Popular Song* (Cambridge: Harvard University Press, 1999), 9–10.

8. Seth M. Scheiner, *Negro Mecca: A History of the Negro in New York City, 1865–1920* (New York: New York University Press, 1965), 131–33.

9. Roy Ottley, *"New World A-Coming." Inside Black America* (Cleveland: The World Publishing Company, 1945), 123.

10. James Baldwin, "Negroes Are Anti-Semitic Because They're Anti-White," in *Black Anti-Semitism and Jewish Racism*, ed. Nat Hentoff (New York: Schocken Books, 1970), 9. This is made clear in an anecdotal way by Harold Cruse, "My Jewish Problem and Theirs," in *Black Anti-Semitism*, ed., as in Claude Brown's memories of the garment trade, where he notes that older blacks who worked for a Mr. Goldberg "didn't know Goldberg from Massa Charlie; to them, Goldberg was Massa Charlie." Claude Brown, *Manchild in the Promised Land* (New York: New American Library, 1965), 298. Central to my story here is Karen Brodkin's *How Jews Became White Folks and What That Says About Race in America* (New Brunswick: Rutgers University Press, 1994).

11. Cheryl Greenberg's ongoing book project on blacks and Jews; Howard M. Brotz, *The Black Jews of Harlem: Negro Nationalism and the Dilemmas of Negro Leadership* (New York: Schocken Books, 1970); Melnick, *A Right to Sing the Blues;* Michael Lerner and Cornell West, *Jews and Blacks: A Dialogue on Race, Religion, and Culture in America* (New York: Plume, 1995); E. Kyle Minor, "That's Right, It's Afro-Semitic," *New York Times,* 4 February 2001, sec. 14, 5. One should not forget the insight of Hasia Diner that the American Jewish community's antiracism contributed toward their assimilation (a reversal of Toni Morrison's idea that racism is the easiest way to gain acceptance for migrants). "The involvement with blacks and the keen interest displayed in their plight fulfilled the needs of a group seeking to complete the process of adaptation." Hasia Diner, *In the Almost Promised Land: American Jews and Blacks, 1915–1935* (Baltimore: Johns Hopkins University Press, 1995), 236.

12. Scheiner, *Negro Mecca,* 71.

13. Winston McDowell, "Race and Ethnicity During the Harlem Jobs Campaign, 1932–1935," *Journal of Negro History* 69, nos. 3–4 (1984): 134–46; Cheryl Greenberg, "The Politics of Disorder: Reexaminging Harlem's Riots of 1935 and 1943," *Journal of Urban History* 18, no. 4 (1992): 395–441.

14. Nannie H. Burroughs, "The Causes of the Harlem Riot [13 April 1935]," in *Black Women in White America. A Documentary History,* ed. Gerda Lerner (New York: Vintage, 1973), 408–10.

15. Ottley, *"New World A-Coming,"* 116–21.

16. W. E. B. Du Bois, *The Philadelphia Negro. A Social Study* (New York: Schocken Books, 1967), 123.

17. Scheiner, *Negro Mecca,* 80.

18. Ottley, *"New World A-Coming,"* 125.

19. Mark Naison, *Communists in Harlem During the Depression* (Urbana: University of Illinois Press, 1983), 100–101.

20. Abram L. Harris, *The Negro as Capitalist. A Study of Banking and Business Among America's Negroes* (Philadelphia: American Academy of Political and Social Science, 1936), 182–83. E. Franklin Frazer, *Black Bourgeoisie: The Rise of the New Middle Class* (New York: The Free Press, 1957), 166–67.

21. Mark Solomon, *The Cry Was Unity: Communists and African Americans, 1917–1936* (Jackson: University Press of Mississippi, 1998), 260–61.

22. Georg Simmel, "The Stranger," in *The Sociology of Georg Simmel,* ed. Kurt H. Wolff (New York: The Free Press, 1964), 403. Robert E. Park offers a U.S. version of Simmel's theory of the stranger in "The Nature of Race Relations" and "Human Migration and the Marginal Man," both collected in Park, *Race and Culture* (Glencoe, Ill.: The Free Press, 1950), 81–116 and 345–56.

23. Edna Bonacich, "A Theory of Middleman Minorities," *American Sociological Review* 38 (1973): 583. For a useful critique, see David O'Brien and Stephen S. Fugita, "Middleman Minority Concept: its explanatory value in the case of the Japanese in California Agriculture," *Pacific Sociological Review* 25 (1982): 185–204.

24. Robert Gregory, *India and East Africa: A History of Race Relations Within the British Empire, 1890–1939* (Oxford: Clarendon Press, 1971), 96.

25. The parallel is with the serfs in Russia who rebelled in the name of the tsar, or of the peasants in India who burned the account books of the moneylenders, often in the name of the British monarch. Daniel Field, *Rebels in the Name of the Tsar* (Boston: Houghton Mifflin, 1976); and Ranajit Guha, *Elementary Aspects of Peasant Insurgency* (New Delhi: Oxford University Press, 1983).

26. Eliot Fremont-Smith, "An Eloquent Testament," *New York Times,* 5 November 1965, 35.

27. Gordon Parks, "The Violent End of a Man Called Malcolm X," *Life,* 5 March 1965, 28–30.

28. Diane C. Fujino, "To Serve the Movement: The Revolutionary Practice of

Yuri Kochiyama," in *Legacy to Liberation: Politics and Culture of Revolutionary Asian Pacific America,* ed. Fred Ho et al. (San Francisco: AK Press, 2000), 257–66. Diane Fujino, one of the editors of *Legacy to Liberation,* is currently writing a biography of Kochiyama. Also see Norimitsu Onishi, "Harlem's Japanese Sister. Immigrants' Daughter Who Embraced Malcolm X Keeps a Radical Flame Alive," *New York Times,* 22 September 1996.

29. Joe Wood, "Malcolm X and the New Blackness," in *Malcolm X: In Our Own Image,* ed. Joe Wood (New York: St. Martin's Press, 1992), 3.

30. Michael Eric Dyson, *Making Malcolm. The Myth and Meaning of Malcolm X* (New York: Oxford University Press, 1995), 85–88; and Adolph Reed Jr., "The Allure of Malcolm X and the Changing Character of Black Politics," in Wood, *Malcolm X,* 207–10.

31. Wood, "Malcolm X," 8.

32. G. Breitman, ed., *Malcolm X Speaks* (New York: Grove Press, 1990), 217.

33. Jane I. Smith, *Islam in America* (New York: Columbia University Press, 1999), 137.

34. Ahmed Kamal, "Food, Peasants and Politics in East Bengal, 1947–54," *Journal of the Asiatic Society of Bangladesh* 36, no. 1 (1991): 27–53. For a contemporary ethnography of migration from Bangladesh (to the Persian gulf), see Katy Gardner, *Global Migrants, Local Lives: Travel and Transformation in Rural Bangladesh* (Oxford: Clarendon, 1995).

35. Alaudin has conducted extensive interviews with the old-timers, and the results of his journey will soon be made into a documentary (with Vivek Renjan Bald) provisionally entitled "East Harlem, East Bengal." The tradition continues, with a chain of Chinese Muslim halal restaurants (Jane H. Lii, "Where's the Pork? Not Here," *New York Times,* 7 September 1997, sec. 13, 4) as well as west Asian grocery and butcher shops (Deena Yellin, "New Stores Helping Muslims Adhere to their Dietary Laws," *The Record* [Bergen County, NJ] 17 March 1998, B1).

36. Louis A. DeCaro Jr., *On the Side of My People: A Religious Life of Malcolm X* (New York: New York University Press, 1996), 151; Karl Evanzz, *The Messenger: The Rise and Fall of Elijah Muhammed* (New York: Pantheon, 1999), 183. This was not the only piece of Pakistan in the lives of the Nation and Malcolm X. Nation members had to buy their Pakistani produced *Qurans* from a Pakistani importer in Newark, N.J.

37. Richard Brent Turner, *Islam in the African American Experience* (Bloomington: Indiana University Press, 1997), 92.

38. Vijay Prashad, *Karma of Brown Folk* (Minneapolis: University of Minnesota Press), 27–34.

39. Turner, *Islam,* 95.

40. Ibid., 93.

41. Ibid., 110.

42. Smith, *Islam,* 74.

43. Turner, *Islam*, 122–23.

44. Ibid., 129.

45. Ibid., 11–46; Amir Nashid Ali Muhammad, *Muslims in America* (Beltsville: Amana, 1998), xiii (sets the number at 20 percent); for a useful overview of the several new books on African Muslims in the antebellum U.S., see Moustafa Bayoumi, "Moorish Science," *Transition* 80 (2000): 100–119.

46. It is hard to parse this rather bizarre argument. For more details, see Claude Andrew Clegg III, *An Original Man: The Life and Times of Elijah Muhammad* (New York: St. Martin's Press, 1997), 43–49.

47. Evanzz, *The Messenger,* 67–69.

48. Ibid., 400–403.

49. Turner, *Islam*, 112–13.

50. The bridge between the more institutionalized forms of Christianity and the Nation of Islam, in this regard, would be figures such as Father Divine, who claimed that he was the "reincarnated God" as he stood before his large following in the Harlem of the 1930s and 1940s.

51. Ottley, *"New World A-Coming,"* 56–57.

52. Jan Carew, *Ghosts in Our Blood* (Chicago: Lawrence Hill, 1994), 118 and 124.

53. And there are, of course, others. I've ignored the entire world of jazz, where not only the Ahmadiyyas, but also other strands of Islam had a marked impact. Moustafa Bayoumi's East of the Sun (West of the Moon): Islam, the Ahmadis and African America (talk at the Blacks and Asians: Revisiting Racial Formations conference at Columbia University, New York, 10 November 2000) offers a unique view of John Coltrane and the Ahmadiyya movement (notably in the tune "A Love Supreme," or is it "Allah Supreme"—go listen to it again!). The Schomburg Museum has flyers from the 1960s and 1970s advertising cultural bazaars organized by the Mosque of Islamic Brotherhood. At one such event on August 28, 1971, the Afro-American Arts and Cultural Center played host to Alice Coltrane, Joe Lee Wilson, Askia Muhammad Touré, Sonia Sanchez, and Jalil Abdul-Azim. The link between Islam and jazz is deep and needs to be plumbed.

54. Jeff Chang, "Race, Class, Conflict and Empowerment: On Ice Cube's Black Korea," *Amerasia Journal* 19, no. 2 (1993): 87–107. It is important to recognize that Ice Cube did not speak for either the black community or for rappers. Chuck D of Public Enemy has been a fierce opponent of malt liquor, whether in his lawsuit against McKenzie River in 1991 or else his song "1 Million Bottlebags" ("What is Colt 45, another gun to the brain . . . "). For a response to Ice Cube, check out Skankin' Pickle's "Ice Cube, Korea Wants a Word with You," on *Skankin' Pickle Fever* (Dill Records, 1997).

55. Lynell George, *No Crystal Stair. African-Americans in the City of Angels* (London: Verso, 1992), 84.

56. Bruce Cumings, *Korea's Place in the Sun: A Modern History* (New York: W. W. Norton, 1997), 287.

57. Ibid., 296.

58. Harry Raymond, "Lenox Ave. Tells Wall St.: Let the Koreans Alone," *Daily Worker*, 5 July 1950; "'Hands Off Korea'—Robeson, Davis Tell Rally," *Daily Worker*, 6 July 1950; "Korea Hit by KKK Terror," *Daily Worker*, 9 July 1950.

59. "Negro Troops in Korea," *Daily Worker*, 16 July 1950.

60. William T. Bowers, William M. Hammond, and George L. MacGarrigle, *Black Soldier/White Army. The 24th Infantry Regiment in Korea* (Washington, DC: Center of Military History, 1996), 140.

61. "NAACP Finds Bias Among American Units in Korea," *The Jewish Times*, 8 March 1951; Thurgood Marshall, "Summary Justice: The GIs in Korea," *The Crisis* (May 1951): 297–355; Bowers, *Black Soldier*, 186–88.

62. Cumings, *Korea's Place in the Sun*, 304.

63. For a good critique, see John Lie, *Han Unbound: The Political Economy of South Korea* (Stanford: Stanford University Press, 1998). Incidentally, one of the *chaebols* is Hyundai, and Rodney King, the spark that lit the Los Angeles praire fire of 1992, was driving one of their cars before he was beaten by the police.

64. Cumings, *Korea's Place in the Sun*, 443.

65. Gerald Horne, *Fire This Time. The Watts Uprising and the 1960s* (Charlottesville: University Press of Virginia, 1995), 311.

66. Ibid., 109–10.

67. The two best introductions, from different standpoints, are Nancy Abelmann and John Lie, *Blue Dreams: Korean Americans and the Los Angeles Riot* (Cambridge: Harvard University Press, 1995); and Pyong Gap Min, *Caught in the Middle: Korean Communities in New York and Los Angeles* (Berkeley: University of California Press, 1996).

68. On the Jews, see Wendy Elliott, "The Jews of Boyle Heights, 1900–1950: The Melting Pot of Los Angeles," *Southern California Quarterly* 78, no. 1 (1996): 1–10; and Deborah Dash Moore, *To the Golden Cities: Pursuing the American Jewish Dream in Miami and LA* (New York: Free Press, 1994). On the Italians, see Gloria Ricci Lothrop, "The Italians of Los Angeles," *Californians* 5, no. 3 (1987): 28–43.

69. Edward T. Chang, "Jewish and Korean Merchants in African American Neighborhoods: A Comparative Perspective," *Amerasia Journal* 19, no. 2 (1993): 10.

70. I can only indicate the anguish in the aftermath of the riot by pointing to two texts, one an essay by Elaine Kim, "Home Is Where the Han Is," in *Reading Rodney King: Reading Urban Uprising*, ed. Robert Cooding Williams (New York: Routledge, 1993): 215–35, and the other is a book of interviews edited by Elaine Kim and Eui-Young Yu, *East to America: Korean American Life Stories* (New York: The New Press, 1997). Among African Americans the anger was no less profound. For one example just as the flames of L. A. began to die down, see Khalif Khalifah, ed., *Rodney King and the LA Rebellion: Analysis*

and Commentary by 13 Independent Black Writers, (Los Angeles: Khalifah Book Sellers, 1992).

71. Eliot G. Means, *Residential Orientals on the American Pacific Coast* (New York: Institute of Pacific Relations, 1927), 346–47.

72. Horne, *Fire This Time*, 221.

73. Sonora McKeller, "Watts—Little Rome," in *From the Ashes. Voices of Watts*, ed. Budd Schulberg (New York: Meridian Books, 1969), 213.

74. Maya Angelou, *I Know Why the Caged Bird Sings* (New York: Random House, 1969), 205–6.

75. Chang, "Jewish and Korean Merchants," 10; but also Ella Stewart, "Communication Between African Americans and Korean Americans: Before and After the Los Angeles Riots," *Amerasia Journal* 19, no. 2 (1993): 23–53.

76. George, *No Crystal Stair*, 78.

77. Abelmann and Lie, *Blue Dreams*, 149–62.

78. Min, *Caught in the Middle*, 135–39.

79. George, *No Crystal Stair*, 83.

80. Abelmann and Lie, *Blue Dreams*, 97–98.

81. Kyeyoung Park, "The Morality of a Commodity: A Case Study of 'Rebuilding LA without Liquor Stores,'" *Amerasia Journal* 21, no. 3 (winter 1995–96): 7–8.

82. Abelman and Lie, *Blue Dreams*, 143–47; and Cumings, *Korea's Place in the Sun*, 435–36 and 449.

83. Abelman and Lie, *Blue Dreams*, 33; and Min, *Caught in the Middle*, 3 and 28.

84. Abelman and Lie, *Blue Dreams*, 38.

85. "Voices from South Central," *Against the Current* 7, no. 3 (July–August 1992): 8.

86. Keith Bradsher, "Korean American Exodus Continues in Los Angeles," *New York Times*, 6 January 1997, A15.

87. Quintard Taylor, *The Forging of a Black Community: Seattle's Central District Through the Civil Rights Era* (Seattle: University of Washington Press, 1994), 74.

88. Angelou, *I Know Why*, 206.

89. John Okada, *No-No Boy* (Seattle: University of Washington Press, 1976), 5.

90. Taylor, *The Forging*, 174–75.

91. Horne, *Fire This Time*, 224; but also the excellent work of Scott Tadao Kurashige, "Transforming Los Angeles: Black and Japanese American Struggles for Racial Equality in the 20th Century" (Ph.D. diss., University of California, Los Angeles, 2000).

92. Peter Y. Hong, "Another King of Holiday Bowl Tradition," *Los Angeles Times*, 2 January 1996, B8.

93. Don Terry, "Last Rites for a Cherished 'Landmark of Diversity,'" *New York Times,* 8 May 2000.

94. Scott Kurashige, "Holiday Bowl vs. the Wrecking Ball," *The Rafu Shimpo* (22 June 2000): 1.

95. Ottley, *"New World A-Coming,"* 330.

96. "Philly Cheese Steak (skit)," Eve-Ruff Ryder's First Lady, *Let There Be* (Los Angeles: Ruff Ryder/Interscope Records, 1999).

97. Work on immigrant merchants shows us that they often prefer to hire other immigrants—for a variety of reasons, including that immigrants work hard on account of their deep desire to make "it." Chang, "Jewish and Korean Merchants," 13; Kim Dae Young, "Beyond Co-Ethnic Solidarity: Mexican and Ecuadorian Employment in Korean-Owned Businesses in New York City," *Ethnic and Racial Studies* 22, no. 3 (1999): 581–605; Judith Goode and Jo Anne Schneider, *Reshaping Ethnic and Racial Relations in Philadelphia* (Philadelphia: Temple University Press, 1994), 158.

98. Jay MacLeod, *Ain't No Makin' It: Aspirations and Attainment in a Low-Income Neighborhood* (Boulder: Westview, 1995).

99. Mike Davis, *Magical Urbanism. Latinos Reinvent the US Big City* (London: Verso, 2000), 52–55.

100. Monica Rhor, "High Demand for Halal Foods in Philly," *AP State and Local Wire* (28 July 1999).

101. L. L. Berry, *A Century of Missions of the African Methodist Episcopal Church, 1840–1940* (New York: Gutenberg Print, 1942), 54.

102. Ibid., 257.

103. Daniel A. Payne, *History of the African Methodist Episcopal Church* (Nashville: African Methodist Episcopal Sunday School Union, 1891), 322.

104. Berry, *A Century,* 52–53.

105. Albert Memmi, *Racism* (Minneapolis: University of Minnesota Press, 2000), 108–9; Etienne Balibar, "Racism and Crisis," *Race, Nation, Class* (London: Verso, 1991), 220–26.

106. I tell this story at length in "The Sickness of Xenophobia" (Madison: Progressive Media Project, May 3, 2000); the article was carried by about twenty major newspapers.

107. Ottley, *"New World A-Coming,"* 53.

108. Horne, *Fire This Time,* 111.

109. "Bronx Crowds Angry but Calm After Verdict," *Washington Post,* 25 February 2000.

110. Malcolm X and Alex Haley, *The Autobiography of Malcolm X* (New York: Grove Press, 1966), 114.

Chapter 5: Kung Fusion

1. The quote is from dead prez, "Police State," *Let's Get Free* (New York: Loud Records, 2000).

2. Hsin Hsin, "Bruce's Opinion on Kung Fu, Movies, Love and Life," in *Words of the Dragon. Interviews, 1958–1973*, ed. John Little (Boston: Charles E. Tuttle, 1997), 119.

3. Ibid., 128.

4. Robert Lee, *Orientals: Asian Americans in Popular Culture* (Philadelphia: Temple University Press, 1999), 35–36.

5. Bruce Lee was very aware of this, as in his 1966 letter to William Dozier, executive producer of the series (reproduced in Little, *Words of the Dragon*, 76–77).

6. Bruce Thomas, *Bruce Lee. Fighting Spirit* (Berkeley: Frog, 1994), 143. This is a frequent theme in Bruce Lee's interviews, as in his 1966 statement to the *Washington Post* on *The Green Hornet*. "It sounded like typical houseboy stuff," Lee told the *Post*, and he told his producer that "if you sign me up with all that pigtail and hopping around jazz, forget it," Little, *Words of the Dragon*, 60. In 1970, Bruce Lee announced that "it's about time we had an Oriental hero. Never mind some guy bouncing around the country in a pigtail or something. I have to be a real human being. No cook. No laundryman," Little, *Words of the Dragon*, 98. This is not to say that cooks and laundrymen are not "real human beings," but that the stereotype itself effaced the real cooks and real laundrymen.

7. Thomas, *Bruce Lee*, 78–79.

8. "Kung Fu: A Sweet Poison," *Getting Together* (October 22–November 4, 1972): 4.

9. Jim Kelly with David W. Clary, "Whatever Happened to Jim Kelly?" *Black Belt Magazine*, May 1992.

10. dead prez, "Psychology," *Let's Get Free*.

11. Toshio Whelchel, *From Pearl Harbor to Saigon. Japanese American Soldiers and the Vietnam War* (London: Verso, 1999), 104.

12. Ibid., 46.

13. In 1966 of U.S. troop casualties, black soldiers made up 22 percent even though they made up only 11 percent of the force. Daniel Patrick Moynihan's racist report on the black family was written in the service of mobilization for the war. "Given the strains of disorganized and matrifocal family life in which so many Negro youth come of age," wrote Moynihan in 1964, "the armed forces are a dramatic and desperately needed change; a world away from women, a world run by strong men and unquestioned authority." Christian G. Appy, *Working-Class War: American Combat Soldiers and Vietnam* (Chapel Hill: University of North Carolina Press, 1993), 31.

14. Jon Shirota, "I'm Not a Militant: Equal Opportunity Sensei," *Black Belt Magazine*, January 1973.

15. Mike Marqusee, *Redemption Song. Muhammad Ali and the Spirit of the Sixties* (London: Verso, 1999), 162.

16. "The Fort Hood Three," pamphlet from 1966 collected in *Hightlights of a Fighting History. 60 Years of the Communist Party USA* (New York: International Publishers, 1979), 374–75.

17. In 1965, during the Watts rebellion, Minister John Shabazz compared the Vietnam War with Watts as he went after King for his ambivalence on both counts. He argued against the "black man being an Asiatic, fighting an Asiatic war." Gerald Horne, *Fire This Time*, 144.

18. Martin Luther King Jr., "A Time to Break Silence," in *The Essential Writings and Speeches of Martin Luther King, Jr.*, ed. James M. Washington (San Francisco: Harper, 1986), 233–34.

19. Peter Matthiessen, *Sal Si Puedes [Escape if you can]: Cesar Chavez and the New American Revolution* (Berkeley: University of California Press, 2000), 22.

20. Alice Echols, *Daring to be Bad: Radical Feminism in America, 1967–1975* (Minneapolis: University of Minnesota Press, 1990), 54.

21. Connie Matthews, "The Struggle Is a World Struggle," *The Black Panthers Speak,* ed. Philip S. Foner (New York: De Capo, 1995), 158.

22. In late 1974, *The Man with the Golden Gun* tore through the world's cinema halls, making $13 million despite its rather slipshod production and strained plot. Set in Asia, the film pits British agent James Bond against international scoundrel Scaramanga in a battle of titans. In the midst of the movie, Bond is imprisoned at a Bangkok kung fu school where he takes on all the students and teachers by himself. Bond makes his escape with a furloughed Texan policeman (J. W. Pepper) who yells at the martial arts aficionados who try to catch Bond: "Now if you pointy heads would get out of them p-jamas, you wouldn't be late for work." Ian Fleming's 1965 book of the same name (with a similar plot) is not set in Asia, but in the Caribbean. Bond, in 1965, was to take on the Cuban Revolution, while Bond, in 1974, was to be imperialism's adversary against Vietnam. Perhaps this what the lawman meant by "pointy heads," a reference to the hats worn by the Vietnamese peasantry.

23. Robert Brenner, "The Economics of Global Turbulence," *New Left Review* 229 (May/June 1998); and Peter Gowan, *The Global Gamble. Washington's Faustian Bid for World Dominance* (London: Verso, 1999).

24. Walden Bello, *Dark Victory. The United States, Structural Adjustment and Global Poverty* (Penang: Third World Network, 1994).

25. Fred Halliday, *The Making of the Second Cold War* (London: Verso, 1983), 86–92.

26. Koushik Banerjea, "Ni-Ten-Ichi-Ryu: Enter the World of the Smart Stepper," in *Travel Worlds: Journals in Contemporary Cultural Politics,* ed. Raminder Kaur and John Hutnyk (London: Zed Press, 1999), 22; and May Joseph, *Nomadic Identities: The Performance of Citizenship* (Minneapolis: University of Minnesota Press, 1999), 54.

27. Little, *Words of the Dragon,* 70.

28. Bruce Lee, *The Tao of Gung Fu* (Boston: Charles E. Tuttle, 1997), 166; and Thomas, *Bruce Lee*, 64.

29. Lee, *The Tao*, 176–77.

30. Ibid., 179–80.

31. Little, *Words of the Dragon*, 120.

32. Shirota, "I'm Not a Militant."

33. Ibid.

34. Flyers for such tournaments are collected at the Schomburg Research Center in Black Culture.

35. John Corcoran and Emil Farkas, *The Original Martial Arts Encyclopedia* (Los Angeles: Pro-Action, 1993), 309.

36. To reach Moses Powell, call 212–673–0899 or else visit him on the Web at http://espytv.com/sanuces.html.

37. To reach Tayari Casel, send an E-mail message to TwoNaRow<ca>ix.netcom.com.

38. Where the BKF and the martial artists of the 1970s seem to have changed is that their critique of imperialism has been lost in the service of a 1990s new age drive to help "a person to gain inner peace and maintain focus." For more information on BKF, go to://www.bkf-international.com.

39. Little, *Words of the Dragon*, 136, and 88–90. Bruce Lee's views found reflection in his movies. In *Enter the Dragon,* he brought in Angela Mao Ying to play his brave and noble kung fu warrior sister. When she is cornered by a gang, she kills herself in a suicide, an act that is at odds with the bravery displayed by Angela Mao Ying's characters in *Hap Ki Do* (1970) and *Lady Whirlwind* (1971).

40. Echols, *Daring to Be Bad*, 64. Martha McCaughey, *Real Knockouts: The Physical Feminism of Women's Self-Defense* (New York: New York University Press, 1997).

41. Cedric Robinson argues that the 1970s black cinema took the image of the Communist feminist Angela Davis and reduced it to the ultra-sexual body of Pam Grier. Grier was not so one-dimensional, for her roles transformed the image of the black woman from the servile mammy (as with Hattie Mc-Daniel in the 1939 *Gone with the Wind*) and from the tragically lifeless (as with Lena Horne in the 1943 *Stormy Weather*) to the tough and streetwise Cleopatra Jones and Foxy Brown. But, yes, Robinson is right that the black woman was, in Grier especially, the epitome of uncontrolled sexuality ("she's black and she's stacked," as in *Coffy*), this despite the story line about the rebellious ghetto. The world of black kung fu did not go along the grain of Shaft and Coffy. Tamara Dobson in *Cleopatra Jones* (1973) acts as a secret agent who can kick ass and look good while doing it. Cleo does not flail around or resort to a gun, but she reserves her energy to trounce her enemy with kung fu skill. Cedric J. Robinson, "Blaxploitation and the Misrepresentation of Liberation," *Race & Class* 40, no. 1 (July–September 1998): 1–12.

42. Thomas, *Bruce Lee*, 276.

43. David Walker, "Jim Kelly and Me," *Giant Robot* 11 (summer 1998); www.gi-antrobot.com/issues/issrell/kelly/index.html.

44. Donald Bougle misses all this when he writes, in passing, of the "stolid and wooden Jim Kelly." *Toms, Coons, Mulattoes, Mammies and Bucks: An Interpretive History of Blacks in American Films* (New York: Continuum, 1989), 245.

45. *Black Belt Jones,* 1974, produced by Warner Bros. and the Shaw brothers.

46. While Yvonne Tasker makes several good points in her section on black action films, she misses the contradictions in the films with her suggestion that Gloria Hendry's role as Sidney has "a certain novelty value." Yvonne Tasker, *Spectacular Bodies. Gender, Genre and the Action Cinema* (London: Comedia/Routledge, 1993), 21–26.

47. Stokely Carmichael and Charles V. Hamilton, *Black Power: The Politics of Liberation* (New York: Random House, 1967), 44. My analysis parallels that of Jeffrey Ogbar, "Yellow Power: The Formation of Asian American Nationalism in the Age of Black Power, 1966–1975" (talk at the Blacks and Asians: Revisiting Racial Formations conference at Columbia University, November 10, 2000).

48. Carmichael and Hamilton, *Black Power,* 77–81.

49. On the Brown Berets, Carlos Muñoz Jr., *Youth, Identity, Power. The Chicano Movement* (London: Verso, 1989), 85–86; and Tony Castro, *Chicano Power: The Emergence of Mexican America* (New York: Dutton, 1974), 134–36. On the American Indian movement, Paul Chaat Smith and Robert Allen Warrior, *Like a Hurricane: The Indian Movement from Alcatraz to Wounded Knee* (New York: The New Press, 1996), 127–48.

50. Ron Jacobs, *The Way the Wind Blew. A History of the Weather Underground* (London: Verso, 1997), 13.

51. Echols, *Daring to Be Bad,* 44.

52. For the full extent of the relationship, see Robin D. G. Kelley and Betsy Esch, "Black Like Mao: Red China and Black Revolution," *Souls* 1, no. 4 (fall 1999): 6–41.

53. Mao Ze-dong, "The United Front in Cultural Work," *Selected Works,* vol. 3 (Peking: Foreign Languages Press, 1965), 236.

54. Rod Bush, *We Are Not What We Seem: Black Nationalism and Class Struggle in the American Century* (New York: New York University Press, 1999), 211; and Komozi Woodard, *A Nation Within a Nation. Amiri Baraka (LeRoi Jones) and Black Power Politics* (Chapel Hill: University of North Carolina Press, 1999), 74.

55. "Young Lords Party Will Visit Chinatown," *Getting Together* 2, no. 8 (November 1971): 4; "YLP Leader Convicted," *Getting Together* (3–17 March 1972): 3; "Young Lords Step Forward," *Getting Together* (5–19 August 1972): 3; Palante, "Letter from Prison," *Getting Together* (2–15 September 1972): 7.

56. Marlene Tanioka and Aileen Yamaguchi, "Asians Make Waves," *Gidra* (March 1970): 6–7.

57. There is a PLO statement in *West River Times, East River Echo* 1, no. 1 (August 1975): 2; Stokely Carmichael's speech of August 31, 1968, is available in the Social Protest Project, Bancroft Library, University of California, Berkeley; at the Bancroft, as well, there is a collection of Black Panther telegrams to the Iranian consulate, flyers for a July 16, 1970, rally in support of the "Iranian 41," and a statement from the BPP; finally, "Ethiopian Students Speak Out," *Wei Min* 3, no. 9 (September 1974): 8.

58. "Bobby (DeAnna Lee interviews Bobby Seale in San Francisco County Jail)," *Gidra* (June–July 1970): 14.

59. Amy Uyematsu, "The Emergence of Yellow Power," *Gidra* (October 1969): 10.

60. "Moritsugu 'Mo' Nishida interviewed by Fred Ho," in *Legacy to Liberation: Politics and Culture of Revolutionary Asian Pacific America,* ed. Fred Ho et al. (San Francisco: AK Press, 2000), 300; and Eric Nakamura, "Hardcore Asian American," *Giant Robot* 10 (spring 1998): 74–75.

61. Bobby Seale, *Seize the Time* (Baltimore: Black Classic Press, 1991), 72.

62. *Giant Robot* magazine's no. 10 issue in spring 1998 carried a series of interviews with these men done by Martin Wong: "A Gang of Four," 70–71 [Aoki]; "Yellow Panther: By Any Means," 66–69 [Lee]; "Panther and Beyond," 76–78 [Kurose].

63. Ho, *Legacy to Liberation,* 330–31.

64. Alex Hing acknowledged to Fred Ho (*Legacy to Liberation,* 284 and 290), as well as in an interview with me, that "women were the backup and did most of the work," but at the same time they did not get leadership positions until the Red Guard merged with I Wor Kuen in 1971, when most of the leadership was female. In 1970 Frances Beale of SNCC wrote that although the black militant man rejected white cultural values, "when it comes to women he seems to take his guidelines from the pages of *Ladies' Home Journal.*" Echols, *Daring to Be Bad,* 107. There is much to what Beale says of the Red Guard and other nationalist formations, but it should also be pointed out that the Red Guard and the I Wor Kuen worked with the contradictions of sexism, unlike other groups that tried to deny the role of feminism within the struggle. For an introduction, see Miya Iwataki, "The Asian Women's Movement: A Retrospective," *East Wind* 2, no. 1 (spring/summer 1983): 35–41.

65. The membership in the Red Guard Party was not restricted to Chinese Americans, as illustrated by the presence of Japanese Americans such as Stan Kadani and Neil Gotanda.

66. The Hardcore, according to Mo Nishida "openly identified ourselves with the Panthers." Ho, *Legacy to Liberation,* 301.

67. The Asian American Community Action Research Program is well covered by Marge Taniwaki, and its polycultural heritage may be seen in the Chicano antipoverty movement (of Corky Gonzalez and others) alongside the veterans of the internment camps from the 1940s. Ibid., 65–73.

68. Most of my information comes from the *Red Guard Community News,* 1969 onward, and an interview with Alex Hing as well as Steve Louie.

69. Laura Ho, "Red Guard Party," *Gidra* (May 1969): 4.

70. Duane Kubo and Russell Kubota, "Alex Hing at UCLA," *Gidra* (June–July 1970): 2.

71. "Over 300 at Meeting on Situation at State College," *Nichi Bei Times*, 8 December 1968, 4; and H. M. Imazeki, "Local Open Forum Views Dr. Hayakawa as 'Puppet,'" *Hokubei Mainichi*, 9 December 1968.

72. *Black Panthers Speak*, 124–27.

73. The frustration with quietism traversed the political and class spectrum, as in the 1972 words of W. K. Wong (advisor to the Six Companies in San Francisco's Chinatown) that "if you're politically strong, like the blacks or the Mexicans, you can go up and demand this and that. Chinatown has never really demanded anything because, up to now, there just aren't enough of us with political muscles." Victor G. Nee and Brett de Bary Nee, *Longtime Californ': A Documentary Study of an American Chinatown* (Stanford: Stanford University Press, 1986), 247. This is not to minimize the role of the Chinese American Left, documented by Him Mark Lai, "To Bring Forth a New China, To Build a Better America: The Chinese Marxist Left in America to the 1960s," in *Chinese America. History and Perspectives* (San Francisco: Chinese Historical Society, 1992), 3–82.

74. "People of the World Unite! Interview with Alex Hing and Pat Sumi," *Gidra* (October 1970); Alex Hing's two "Dear Comrades" letters in *Gidra* (August 1970): 17 and (October 1970): 6; "Glad They're Back," *Gidra* (October 1970): 4.

75. Junot Díaz deserves all credit for this formulation.

76. Van Troi Pang, "To Commemorate My Grandfather," in *Moving the Image: Independent Asian PacificAmerican Media Arts*, ed. Russell Leong (Los Angeles: UCLA Asian American Studies Center, 1991), 44. When Alex Hing was asked many years later what he thought of Bruce Lee, he had this to offer: "When he was alive, I was very critical of him because he played Kato. Being an ultra-leftist, I felt, 'Oh here's Bruce Lee playing the servile role and fighting for this white guy. We've got to get off of that.' It wasn't till he passed away until I began to appreciate his contributions. He played a major role in having a more positive view of Asians out there. To be that good of a martial artist, you've got to put in a lot of work. Maybe it's easier to say let's break out of that and do something easier! If we had a home-grown Jet Li from the U.S., we'd all be flocking. We wouldn't put that down." Martin Wong, "Red Star in America," *Giant Robot* 10 (spring 1998): 81. Of course, Bruce Lee *was* home-grown, or at least, if we reassess the idea of "home" in this century!

77. Thomas, *Bruce Lee*, 146.

78. David Hillard and Lewis Cole, *This Side of Glory* (Boston: Little, Brown, 1993), 247.

79. Timothy B. Tyson, *Radio Free Dixie. Robert F. Williams and the Roots of Black Power* (Chapel Hill: University of North Carolina Press, 1999), 295; Mary Kochiyama, "Robert Williams," *Asian American Political Alliance Newspaper* 2, no. 1 (November 1969): 2. Ho's early journalism for *La Correspondance Internationale* is on antiblack racism in the United States, such as "Lynching"

(no. 59, 1924) and "Ku Klux Klan" (no. 74, 1924). These pieces formed part of a pamphlet that Ho published in Moscow on the question of African American oppression. They are collected in Bernard Fall, ed., *Ho Chi Minh on Revolution* (New York: Signet, 1967), 51–58. There is a Japanese biography of Robert Williams by Yoriko Nakajima, written in the late 1960s.

80. Marika Sherwood, *Kwame Nkrumah: The years abroad, 1935–1947* (Legon, Ghana: Freedom Publications, 1996).

81. V. I. Lenin, "Inflammable Material in World Politics," *Proletary* 33 (July 23 or August 5, 1908); V. I. Lenin, *Collected Works,* vol. 15 (Moscow: Progress Publishers, 1963), 182–88.

82. Pierre Queuille, *Histoire de l'Afro-Asiatime jusqu'à Bandoung. La naissance du tiers-monde* (Paris: Payot, 1965), 50–56. Much of the Afro-Asian political trajectory drew from the Pan-Asianism of the 1920s (Association of Greater Asia, founded in 1924, and the conference on Asian peoples in Nagasaki in 1926) and the Pan-Africanism of an earlier period (the four congresses from 1919–27, and then the 1945 Congress in Manchester).

83. Cedric Robinson, *Black Marxism: The Making of the Black Radical Tradition* (Chapel Hill: University of North Carolina Press, 2000) and the ongoing project by Aijaz Ahmed for Leftword Books in New Delhi on Asian Marxists.

84. Aimé Cesaire, *Letter to Maurice Thorez* (Paris: Éditions Présence Africaine, 1957), 12. Down the page, Cesaire writes, "But it would also interest me, and still more so, to see the African brand of communism blossom forth and flourish. In all likelihood, it would offer us variants—useful, valuable, original variants, and the wisdom in us that is our age-old heritage would, I am certain, shade or complete a good many of the doctrine's points." Cesaire could not entirely cut himself off from the appeal of the Left to people of color. In 1952 a Morehouse professor wrote to Martin Luther King Jr. that "I think there can be no doubt about it that the appeal of Communism to the Eastern nations today can be traceable to a large degree to the Soviet attitude toward race." Taylor Branch, *Parting The Waters: America in the King Years, 1954–1962* (New York: Touchstone, 1988), 210. When Reverend C. T. Vivian was in Moscow in the 1950s he stayed with a group of Africans. They spent an evening being very critical of Moscow, and C. T. felt this had to do with their good feelings for the United States. He was wrong. Late that night he realized that "the Africans did not agree entirely with the Soviets, but they could see no way to deal with Jim Crow U.S.A. They were willing to compromise on their politics, but they were not going to compromise on their dignity." Lecture at Trinity College, January 16, 2001.

85. Stuart Schram, ed., *Political Thought of Mao Tse-tung* (New York: Praeger, 1972), 412.

86. The Taiwanese government at this time adopted a more racialized notion of the people. In March 1957, for instance, the Taiwan government approved the formal establishment of the Yellow Emperor religion, a sect with grave racial undertones. In 1976, one of the teachers of the sect introduced martial arts, but his was not to be the barefoot arts of the people, since he founded his art on the ecstasy of *qigong*. Bruce Lee would have found this distasteful, and so did the racialist leader of the sect, Wang Hansheng, who ordered the Martial

Way disbanded. Christian Joachim, "Flowers, fruit and incense only: Elite versus popular in Taiwan's religion of the Yellow Emperor," *Modern China* 16, no. 1 (January 1990): 3–38.

87. Jawaharlal Nehru, "India and Africa," *Selected Works of Jawaharlal Nehru,* vol. 1 (New Delhi: Oxford University Press, 1984), 453–53, and 506.

88. Hari Sharan Chhabra, "India's Africa Policy," *India Quarterly* 41, no. 1 (1985): 68–73; but for a contrary view, see Anirudha Gupta, "A Note on Indian Attitudes to Africa," *African Affairs* 69, no. 275 (1970): 170–78.

89. Immanuel Wallerstein, *Africa: The Politics of Independence* (New York: Vintage, 1961), 146.

90. Alan Hutchison, *China's African Revolution* (London: Hutchinson, 1975), 56; and Udo Weiss, "China's Aid to and Trade with the Developing Countries of the Third World," *Asia Quarterly* 3 (1974): 203–314 and 4 (1974): 263–309. There was tremendous depth to these exchanges, for, as Baker shows us, the Chinese low-cost, low-technology agricultural systems increased yields in Senegal. Kathleen Baker, "The Chinese Agricultural Model in West Africa: The Case of Market Gardening in the Region du Cap Vert, Senegal," *Pacific Viewpoint* 26, no. 2 (1985): 401–4. Emmanuel John Hevi's two books, one a memoir of his time in China (*An African in China* [New York: Praeger, 1963]) and the other an assessment of Chinese assistance in Africa (*The Dragon's Embrace: The Chinese Communists and Africa* [Washington: Praeger, 1966]), are good illustrations of cold war scholarship. Hevi captures the attempt by the Chinese to move away from xenophobia, but he misses the heart of the PRC's experiments with Third World solidarity.

91. Julius K. Nyerere, "Tanzania's Long March Is Economic (4 June 1965)," in *Freedom and Socialism. Uhuru na Ujamaa; A Selection from Writings and Speeches,* ed. Julius K. Nyerere (Dar es Salaam: Oxford University Press, 1968), 33–34.

92. Hutchison, *China's African Revolution,* 50.

93. Kwame Nkrumah, *I Speak of Freedom: A Statement of African Ideology* (New York: Praeger, 1961), 155. And besides, places like India and Tanzania used their place as part of the Third World strategically to garner resources from the other two worlds (which often included China). The Chinese helped the Tanzanians build the Tanzam Railroad, but the United States assisted the Tanzanians to build the Dar es Salaam–Tunduma road. As President Nyerere put it, Tanzania wanted to "compare the advantages of different offers before turning any of them down." Julius K. Nyerere, *Freedom and Socialism,* 203.

94. From Asia: Afghanistan, Burma, Cambodia, Ceylon, China, India, Indonesia, Iran, Iraq, Japan, Jordan, Laos, Lebanon, Nepal, Pakistan, the Philippines, Saudi Arabia, Syria, Thailand, Turkey, North Vietnam, South Vietnam, and Yemen. From Africa: Egypt, Ethiopia, the Gold Coast, Liberia, Libya, and the Sudan.

95. "Speech by President Soekarno at the Opening of the Asian-African Conference, April 18, 1955," in *The Asian-African Conference. Bandung, Indonesia, April 1955,* ed. G. M. Kahin (Ithaca: Cornell University Press, 1956), 43. On neocolonialism, Sukarno said that "colonialism has also its modern dress, in

the form of economic control, intellectual control, actual physical control by a small but alien community within the nation. It is a skillful and determined enemy, and it appears in many guises. It does not give up its loot easily" (44).

96. David Kimche, *The Afro-Asian Movement* (New Brunswick: Transaction Books, 1973).

97. Kahin, *The Asian-African Conference,* 75.

98. The most comprehensive account of the destruction of solidarity is Penny M. Von Eschen, *Race Against Empire: Black Americans and Anticolonialism, 1937–1957* (Ithaca: Cornell University Press, 1997). Du Bois and the CPUSA attempted to keep the tradition alive, but their minority view was not to hold the day: "Negro Press in U.S. Hails Bandung Meet," *Daily Worker,* 5 May 1955; "Bandung and the World Today," (discussion held on December 5, 1955, at the YMCA auditorium in Harlem); "Robeson and DuBois at Rally Tomorrow," *Daily Worker,* 29 April 1957; Abner Berry, "They're Great in a Crisis," *Daily Worker,* 16 June 1955; "Newsman at Bandung Says Asia 'Knew All About U.S. Negroes,'" *Daily Worker,* 8 June 1955.

99. In 1946, U.S. Secretary of State James Byrnes protested Soviet election policy in the Balkans. The Soviet foreign ministry replied that "the Negroes of Mr. Byrnes' own state of South Carolina were denied the same right." Frances Stonor Saunders, *The Cultural Cold War: The CIA and the World of Arts and Letters* (New York: The New Press, 1999), 291.

100. "Interview with Adam Clayton Powell, Jr.: Red China Exposed: Not dominant in Asia," *U.S. News & World Report,* 29 April 1955; "Capitol Stuff," New York *Daily News,* 6 May 1955; "Interview with Max Yergan: Why There's No Colored Bloc," *U.S. News & World Report,* 3 June 1955; Abner Berry, "Foreign Policy for Patriotic Negroes," *Daily Worker,* 29 May 1955; Richard Wright, *The Color Curtain: A Report on the Bandung Conference* (Cleveland: The World Publishing House, 1956), 177–78. This response is also there from the National Urban League, but it did adjudge the conference important enough to warrant a pamphlet: Louis Lautier, *Bandung. A Common Ground* (Washington, DC: National Urban League, 1955).

101. Wright, *Color Curtain,* 140 and 157. For more on the book, see Herbert Aptheker, "Richard Wright Gives Views on Bandung," *Daily Worker,* 26 April 1955; Tillman Durdin, "Richard Wright Examines the Meaning of Bandung," *New York Times* 18 March 1956.

102. George Plimpton, *Shadow Box* (New York: Berkeley Publishing, 1977), says that the line comes from Ali's friend Bundini.

103. Marqusee, *Redemption Song,* 267–79.

104. Thomas, *Bruce Lee,* 97.

105. Ibid., 278.

106. Nadya Labi, "Tae-Bo or Not Tae-Bo?" *Time,* 15 March 1999, 77. What is forgotten now is that Billy Blanks was a leading karateka. In November 1980 he won silver (open weight) and bronze (80 kg division) medals in Spain at the Fifth WUKO championships.

107. Kilinidi Iyi, "African Roots in Asian Martial Arts," *African Presence in Early Asia*, ed. Ivan Van Sertima and Runoko Rashidi (New Brunswick: Transaction Books, 1985) 142.

108. J. Lowell Lewis, *Ring of Liberation: Deceptive Discourse in Brazilian Capoeira* (Chicago: University of Chicago Press, 1992). Capoeira also resembles other American self-defense forms such as the Cuban *maní,* the Venezuelan *broma,* and the Martinican *ladjá.*

109. Phillip Zarrilli, *When the Body Becomes All Eyes: Paradigms, Discourses, and Practices of Power in Kalanppayattu* (New York: Oxford University Press, 1998).

110. Shifu Nagaboshi Tomio (Terence Dukes), *The Bodhisattva Warriors* (York Beach, ME: Samuel Weiser, 1994), 342–43.

111. Another story that is often left out of the mix is that of Kali, the martial arts traditions of the Filipinos. Legend has it that the art came to the archipelago in the late thirteenth century from Borneo. Their sword was called the *kali,* but there is also a suggestion that this itself came from Bengal, where the goddess Kali carries a sword in her hand. In numerous African languages the word Kali refers to fierceness.

112. Wayne Chandler, "The Jewel in the Lotus: The Ethiopian Presence in the Indus Valley Civilization," and Graham W. Irwin, "African Bondage in Asian Lands," *African Presence.* We get some of this from hip-hop artist Nas, who raps that he is "like the Afrocentric Asian, half man, half amazin," and that he exhales "the yellow smoke of Buddha through righteous steps," the mix of Nation of Islam and the Afrocentric claim on Buddha. This is on his "Ain't Hard to Tell" track from *Illmatic,* 1994.

113. Kamau Ryu, System of Self-Defense, www.kamauryu.com/intro.html.

114. W. E. B. Du Bois, "Egypt and India," *The Crisis* 18, no. 2 (June 1919): 62.

115. W. E. B. Du Bois, *Dark Princess* (Jackson: Banner Books, 1995), 249 and 311.

116. Tre' Boogie, "The Arsonists: The Art of Jeet Kune Flow," *The Iron Fist Magazine,* 30 December 1999.

DotComrades

My editor, Tisha Hooks, bears responsibility for this book. She met me one afternoon in Philadelphia and we talked in general about an account of Afro-Asian traffic. This conversation led to a manuscript, which she edited with a keen eye, and then to this book. I wouldn't have expected to do this book so fast if not for her insights and enthusiasm. The theoretical idea behind the book, polyculturalism, came from my comrade and friend Robin D. G. Kelley. Robin has so many scintillating ideas that I was happy to steal this and run with it. I've had two great activists on my mind as I conceptualized the project, and red salute to both of them: Yuri Kochiyama and Grace Lee Boggs. They allow us to envision a revolutionary Afro-Asian praxis.

A host of friends who work on the same theme offered their generous commentary and, sometimes, warned me when I went too far with my own unobstructed optimism. Sudhir Venkatesh, with whom I organized a conference on the general theme at Columbia University in November 2000, read most of the book (and for that conference, Gary Okihiro and Manning Marable helped us out with their generosity). Junot Díaz, always brilliant, read the stuff on Bruce Lee, and forced me to rethink many of my principal propositions. Other interlocutors, sharp thinkers all, include: Koushik Banerjea, Moustafa Bayoumi, Chetan Bhatt, Jeff Chang, Madhav Chari, Karen Chow, Kenneth Cooper, Naresh Fernandes, Lewis Gordon, Cheryl Greenberg, Gerald Horne, Mir Ali Hussain, John Hutnyk, Raminder Kaur, Amitava Kumar, Scott Kurashige, Sunaina Maira, Leyla Mei, Prabhu Prasad Mohapatra, C. M. Naim, Beth Notar, Jeffry Ogbar, Gautam Premnath, Shyamala Raman, Kasturi Ray, Mir Ali Raza, Barbara Sicherman, Alaudin Ullah, Linta Varghese, Phiroze Vasunia, Reetika Vazirani, Kamala Visweswaran, Maurice Wade, Oliver Wang, Daniel L. Widener, Duncan Ryuken Williams, and Johnny Williams. Thanks to my teacher Sid Lemelle, who introduced me to the revolutionary world of southern and southeastern Africa. Alex Hing, Steve Louie, and Renee Tajima-Pena gave me a crash course in the Asian American movement.

Several editors allowed me to test some of these formulations in their pages, notably Russell Leong (*Amerasia Journal*), Judi Byfield and Tiffany Patterson (*African Studies Review*), Khachig Tololyan (*Diaspora*), Nikhil P. Singh and Andrew Jones (*positions*), Bob Wing (*ColorLines*), Mike Albert (*ZNET*), Noorjehan Aziz (*Toronto Review*), Achal Mehra (*Little India*), E.

Evelina Galang and Sunaina Maira (*Screaming Monkeys*), N. Ram (*Frontline*), and Mike Vasquez (*Transition*). Many of my friends in the radio and Internet world indulged me, such as those at Asia Pacific Forum on WBAI (Aniruddha Das, Andy Hsiao, and Sujani Reddy), at KPFA (C. S. Soong), at WWRI (Ron Daniels and the American Urban Radio Network), and the champ of Indo-American Internet, Arthur Pais.

Biju Mathew, who helps me think straight, once said that our kind of work never wins grants. As with everything, he was on target. Thanks to Trinity College for my salary, to the labor movement for the weekend (where all research happens), and to an old feudal hangover, the one-semester sabbatical. I enjoyed the archives at UCLA (the Steve Louie collection), UC Berkeley (the Social Protest collection at the Bancroft), the University of Michigan library, the UMASS-Amherst Du Bois collection, New York Public Library's Schomburg Research Center in Black Culture, and elsewhere. Mary Curry at Trinity's inter-library loan was a constant help. For the images in this book, thanks to Kathleen Helenese-Paul (University of the West Indies at St. Augustine, Trinidad), Linda Seidman (UMASS-Amherst), Bobby Seale, Vikas Kamat, Earl Grant, and (for his help) the ever-brilliant Amitava Kumar. Peace to my brethren of the Asian Dub Foundation and of dead prez for use of their wise lyrics.

Many folks heard versions of this book to help me sharpen and develop the points. I'm in the debt of students and faculty at Brown University (Chas Walker and the YCL, and also Shannah Kurland, Lewis Gordon, Jane Comaroff, and the babies who filled the room with such joy), CUNY Graduate Center (Leyla Mei and the other history graduate students), Goldsmiths College, London (Chetan Bhatt, John Solomos, Parita Mukta, and the Southall Black Sisters, Pragna Patel and Gita Sahgal), Hampshire College (Rudy Malabalan), Harvard University's Institute for Arts and Civic Dialogue (Alisa Solomon and Anna Devere Smith, and also Mark Levin for a spirited dialogue), Northwestern University (Priya Srinivasan and Ji-Yeon Yuh), NYU (Lisa Duggan, Walter Johnson, and Andrew Ross), UC Berkeley (Elaine Kim, Anmol Chaddha, and Loni Ding), UCLA (Sangam, Meg Thornton, and Russell Leong), UCONN (Roger Buckley and Fe Delos Santos), UMASS-Amherst (Sunaina Maira and William Strickland), University of Michigan (Scott Kurashige, Amy Stillman, Geoff Eley, and the ISA crew especially Avani Sheth), Vassar (Ravi Awatramani and Shahin Dastur), and Wesleyan University (Renee Johnson-Thornton, Mayuran Tiruchelvam, Max Mishler, Saj Rahman, and a host of other radical students). Talks organized by the following political organizations helped me hone my views:

Applied Research Center (Bob Wing, Gary Delgado, and Makani Themba-Nixon), Brecht Forum (Sam Anderson, Liz Mestres, Liz Roberts, and Biju Mathew), Center for Third World Organizing (Mark Toney and Julie Quiroz-Martinez), the CPUSA (Sam Webb, Joe Sims, Terrie Albano, and Jarvis Tyner), and the South Asian Journalists' Association (Sreenath Sreenivasan). Sai Madivala and Elisaveta Koriouchkina helped plow through the library and wind me up with some crazy ideas.

I cannot breathe politically without the love and joy of the Youth Solidarity Summer crew (Ash Rao, Amita Swadhin, Biju Mathew, Nidhi Mirani, Prantik Saha, Prerana Reddy, Raju Rajan, Rupal Oza, Sangeeta Kamat, Sharmila Desai, Surabhi Kukke, and V. Balaji). (For more on YSS, go to www.proxsa.org/yss.) And I cannot think of the world of the polycultural Left without my comrades at the Center for Third World Organizing, those on the Board (Leticia Alcantar, Alfredo deAvila, Timothea Howard, Miguel Luna, Martha Matsuoka, Rinku Sen) and those who make the struggle happen (Mark Toney, Julie Quiroz-Martinez, Daniel HoSang, Dana Ginn Paredes, Ed Lee, and Orchid Pussey). (For more on CTWO, see www.ctwo.org.) All praise to Asians for Mumia and South Asians Against Police Brutality and Racism. Red salute to those who hold the line, mainly Brian Steinberg, Joelle Fishman, Libero Della Piana, Tom Connolly, Eda diBaccari, Jack Lucas, Laura Lockwood, Emma Fair, Sudhanva Deshpande, P. Sainath, Mir Ali Raza, and so many others (including Merrilee Milstein, Louise Simmons, Jeff Harmon, Renee White, Edmund Campos, Dario Euraque, Polly Moran, Luis Figueroa, Zaira Rivera, Gustavo Remedi, Maria Bauseros, Michael, and Jo Niemann and four shrimps otherwise known as Claudia, Kata, Martin, and Sebastian). I'm thinking of Syracuse and Naeem, Sorayya, Kamal and Shahid: we talked about some of this while looking at construction sites.

Endless discussions with the Armstrongs and the Prashads, with the Karats, the Roys, and the Boses (making movies, investigating crime, raising wonderful boys). My mother has become my agent in Calcutta; my sister, Leela, talks me up in her book club; and with my brother, Jojo, and nephew, she came to hear me read in Oakland. Margie and Pete are patient with my crazy ideas. My mashis are ever dear to my heart. Cousins, nephews and nieces, scattered, on assignment, beloved—so many cameras in this family. And only one Rosy.

I began to work on this book just when I got news that my father had left us after over a decade of suffering. An autodidact, he taught me to read everything and to make as much sense of complexity as possible. Without those afternoon lectures that captivated my teen years, I doubt that I'd have had the stamina to go about the exercise in this book. Wherever you are, somewhere in the ether, this book is partly to you.

And it is also for two others. Lisa Armstrong, insurgent American, poly-cultural comrade, who heard most of this book and guided me away from the edge of lunacy. As I finished this book, on February 10, 2001, Zalia Maya decided to take her first breath. Named for an abandoned Moorish village in Andalusia, Spain, Zalia, boundless joy to us, emerged with her fist in the air. She still holds it there. Rebel faces of hope, you both.

Credits

Indian Ocean nobleman. Reprinted, by permission, from K. L. Kamat's Timeless Theater Picture Archive.

Mao and Du Bois. Reprinted, by permission, from Special Collections and Archives, W. E. B. Du Bois Library, University of Massachusetts, Amherst.

Coolie lines, nineteenth century. Reprinted, by permission, from the University of the West Indies.

Yuri and Malcolm. Reprinted, by permission, from the National Black Archives.

New Haven courthouse steps. Reprinted, by permission, from Bobby Seale.

Index